This book is for you if:

- you are woman who has suffered domestic abuse - be it physical, financial, emotional and/or mental
- you are person who has been ashamed of your childhood and upbringing
- you are stuck in the pain of incest and you want to break free and spread your wings to fly again
- you have been a victim of your insecurities, low self-esteem and self confidence and in search of that push to get up and start your walk
- you want a good read on resilience, hope, courage and how to get unstuck in your life
- you desire to be encouraged to get up one last time and push through the birth canal of your circumstance
- you want inner growth and personal power
- you are tired of playing small based on your past experiences
- you want to start your purpose walk

WHAT PEOPLE SAY
ABOUT THE BOOK

"Wow! What a life! It is such an intimate account I feel I've known you for twenty years...
I had heart pangs in places throughout your story. I'm sure you've shed a quiet tear
every time you are on the plane leaving Jamaica. Much love."

Matthew Binns

Producer *2fast2furious*

"It is difficult to imagine the levels of determination in the mind of Dr.Ava Eagle Brown
as 'The Mango Girl' recounts a brutal upbringing only the strongest would survive.
Her strength of mind and resilience finally results in success against the longest of odds;
a unique and compelling story."

David Ball, Wales, United Kingdom

Movie Line Producer

"'The Mango Girl' recaptures the vividly brutal youth of Dr Ava Eagle Brown and her
journey to find selfrespect and esteem. The book is littered with the spectrum
of emotions as Ava sets about finding who she is and who she is determined to become;
a must read!"

Diana Mae Fernandez

Design Thinking Business Coach-New York

"It's hard to imagine my mum being abused by her father and held up and abused
at gun point in front of me, her then 3 year old daughter. But I didn't have to imagine it,
I witnessed it. Yet, mum struggled for survival in her native Jamaica reveals a terrifying
tale experienced by a few. Driven by instinct and 'nous', mum overcomes ongoing
spousal abuse by starting a new life against the odds in the UK; a life demanding total
dedication, guts and vision if she is to succeed."

Chardonae Stephenson

Author and Music Student

"It was heartening to hear my student say that he stayed up almost the whole night reading. This followed Ava's book reading session at my University in Jamaica. When I enquired what kept my student up, he said the book by Ava Brown was so riveting that even he, a non-reader, was compelled to read on into the night. This is the nature of the autobiography of my friend whose story of courage, resilience and triumph is an inspiration to many. Ava was not hesitant to be vulnerable as it is clear that her intention is to impact lives and generate change for better. I believe she was successful in this regard and for that I applaud her. God has certainly given Ava "beauty for ashes".

Dr. Garfield Young
University of Technology Jamaica.

ABOUT THE AUTHOR

Dr. Ava Eagle Brown was born and brought up in St. Elizabeth, Jamaica. She trained as a secondary teacher at the Sam Sharpe Teacher's College in Montego Bay, Jamaica, followed later by an MBA in Business Administration from the University of Wales United Kingdom and an MBA from Newport University, Southern California. Ava now holds an honorary doctorate degree which was given now holds an honorary doctorate degree which was given to her for her philanthropy work in women empowerment, homelessness and people transformation.

She lives in London and is the mother of two children, who she calls her life. She is a Transformational Coach, International Motivational Speaker and Author, someone who has a mandate to remind everyone they are possible.

The Mango Girl is an updated version of her first book, Bamboo and Fern, from which she is set to launch a movie campaign. Ava hopes to see this book on the Hollywood stage. She is currently working on part two of *The Mango Girl*, to be called Steel and Stone. She has written and published several books, her original biography; Bamboo and Fern, has sold in more than 45 countries.

Ava's vision is to help other people tap into their full potential by eradicating self-limiting beliefs for them to ultimately live the lives they want, need and desire; essentially a life of abundance.

She was awarded:
- Radio W.O.R.K.S. World Author Awards 2017
- Author of the Year Award
- Powerhouse Woman Award 2017
- Inspirational Role Model Award 2015
- Motivational Woman of 2015 - Black African Women Rock

- Nominated for a BEFFTA Award
- Nominated for London Leadership Peace Award

In addition to her multiple work activities, she is currently championing being an ambassador for Evolve Vulnerable Housing in Croydon, UK where they tackle homelessness on the street and rough sleeping.

Her life has not been an easy one, having gone through numerous storms, namely; domestic violence, child abuse, single parenting, divorce, financial deprivation, marital deception, molestation, and gun violence, to name only a few. And yet she survived and thrived. Ava uses her experiences to help other people and she is on a mission to do that globally, by helping women work through trauma and understand that nothing is impossible. Her motto is the very word impossible, it says 'I'm Possible'. This is the way she has been able to survive.

If you want to become an investor in her movie project, please email her at the addresses below for more information. She can be contacted via:

www.avaeaglebrown.com
www.avabrown.org 447808866870
info@avabrown.org

Dedication

This is dedicated to my mum, Una, and my children, Chardonae Elizabeth and Mikhel Kai, with all my love. You have given me a reason to go on despite the storms. Because of you three, unconditional love is understood by me.

My Mum (Una Beckford). Thank you, Mama, for choosing to bring a child into the world when you were just a child yourself. This could not have been an easy decision, especially when your parents put you out on the streets, so you had to grow up fast. That must have been tough. Until recently, I did not understand your inability to show love emotionally or physically, but I knew you loved us when you sacrificed your last $100 and bought a "tups" of salted fish to ensure we had food to eat. You gave us the most and remained hungry at times, you fussed over us and made us feel like royalty... Mama, I love you.

My daughter, Chardonae Elizabeth (Porkie Pine). Char, as a child, you had to grow up so fast and see some of your mum's struggles. It's my hope that they strengthen you and make you a warrior of a woman but with the heart of an angel. You have been the best daughter I could have asked for and I would not change anything. I am thankful that the challenges have not broken us, but made us a stronger mother and daughter, and most importantly, friends. All my love, Mum xxx

My son, Mikhel Kai (Kai Kai). Mikhel, you came into my life long before this was written, but you are such a sweet son who has added joy daily, whether it is with your smile or just asking for a cuddle. Little did you know that you were adding to my life daily, especially at times when writing, proofreading, or editing *The Mango Girl* was just a difficult thing to do. Those cuddles helped. With all my love, Mum xxx.

Acknowledgements

_____

Auntie Norma Knight, I love you. Thanks for the love through the years and the belief in me. More importantly, thank you for the trip to London that changed the direction of my story.

Jean Marie Thompson, my confidant and friend, thanks for all your support over the years. You gave me the name for my book, without even knowing, in an email you helped me through some of the tough times. You are such a caring soul, someone who took me into her arms despite the risk. Thanks for the late night chats, the running up of your phone bills, and even sending me money when I was stone-broke. Jay, you were my sanctuary. When I needed to off-load, you just sat and took it all in. I always felt better walking away after my sessions with you.

Yvonne Asafu-Adjaye, thanks for being there when I got locked up and could have lost my child to social services. Thanks for standing in the gap for me and being a great friend.

Buju Leonard Brooks, my step-father, the man who fed me when my own father didn't care to. The man who would give me the last piece of meat on his plate and ensured that, regardless of how little, we had food. Thanks for everything.

Uncle Ken Brown, my real daddy, thanks for being my daddy, thanks for showing me how a dad should love his child. You didn't have to, but took it on yourself.

Cheryl Gregory, my love, my friend, my biggest cheerleader and confidant. I am so blessed to have someone like you who has guided me for years and put up with my madness when I got stressed. You are an amazing friend whom I truly love. You have taken so much of my sharp tongue when frustrated, and yet still love me dearly. You are one of my rocks.

Dario Pirjak, the stranger who believed in me and became one of my motivators and my life coach. Your counsel, belief, wisdom, and, most importantly, consistent listening ears are totally appreciated. I admire your zeal for success that's rubbing off on me.

David Ball, the stranger who appeared and totally adopted my kids and called them grandkids, we value you and who you have become on this journey of *The Mango Girl.*

Julie Powell–Robinson, it is good to find you again, my 'bestie'.

Audreia Josephs, my new mum, sister and friend- the day we met was an amazing design by the creator. Thanks for being there as the secret witness. Your additions to this book from a bird's eye view helps to solidify that the later part of my journey wasn't just seen by you; but experienced in parts. We love you for simply being you.

Sonia Poleon, my ride or die chick, girl the times you have held me down, chatted on the phone late at night and even helped with childcare - your friendship and sisterhood - I will cherish always. xx

Angels who gave me wings over the years

The Honourable Ambassador Burchell Whiteman, you gave me my first real chance. May you continue to always be a believer in young people.

Mavis Taylor, Mrs Johnson & Myki Mitchell, my former teachers at St. Elizabeth Technical High School. You guys mothered me and moulded the little ability I possessed at the time.

Mrs Taylor, you fed me when I was hungry, sometimes without even knowing. I thank God for you all, three women who inspired my drive through their belief in me.

I also wish to thank **Chris Day** and **Zara Thatcher** of Filament Publishers for publishing this second edition for me in London in 2017. Also, **Michelle Gent** who edited my revised edition and 'polished the diamond' for you all to enjoy. Your combined help is invaluable.

BONUS

To see pictures of my childhood and get a special video of aspects of my life not included on the book, click this link to claim your special gift today.

http://bit.ly/2rHtMjB

The Mango Girl

DR. AVA EAGLE BROWN

Published by Filament Publishing Ltd
16, Croydon Road, Beddington, Croydon, Surrey CR04PA
Telephone (0)20 8688 2598
www.filamentpublishing.com

The Mango Girl by Dr Ava Eagle Brown
© 2017 Dr Ava Eagle Brown
Second Edition
ISBN: 978-1-912256-07-5

Photography © CantStopFiling
Typesetting © WhiteCraneDesigns
Printed by © Ingramsparks

For more resources or extended permissions, go to:
www.avaeaglebrown.com

"We are scared of the dark, light is comforting as it helps us see shapes and forms. Light helps with recognition and shows what lies ahead of us. We yearn for the comfort of light as it provides silhouettes and form, allowing us to recognise and define what's before us. Are we afraid of the darkness, or is it the truth hiding behind it?"

Table of Contents

DISCLAIMER

I do not remember all of the exact words said in all of the stressful situations I have endured, but I do remember the gist of what was said and I have attempted, to the best of my ability, to recreate the extreme stress and anxiety of those situations.

Follow me on Twitter: @avabrown24

Foreword

———

Dr. Ava Eagle Brown's authentic gathering of her life story is touching, raw, emotional and stimulating. She bravely uncovers shocking truths that stir her readers to challenge their own past fears and obstacles. Ava reminds us that whatever is going on in life right now, whatever the situation, we can learn the lessons that are being offered and grow from them. She encourages us to come through the personal battles as better and not bitter. Thank you Ava for writing Bamboo & Fern, it is a book that will forever remind me to refuse to allow fear to keep me from playing small when it is time to think big and to live each day with purpose and joy.

Darieth Chisolm
Emmy Award Winning TV Host, Author, Speaker,
 & Life Coach
www.DariethChisolm.com

Follow me on Twitter: @avabrown24

Chapter One

THE BIRTH CANAL

"Birth is a special time for any mother; she forgets all her struggles and latches onto the bundle of joy she is gifted with."

*To understand the woman I am today,
you'll have to first learn the story of my beginnings.*

———————

I was born in an old post office in a poor district near George's Valley, Jamaica. My mother, who was only sixteen at the time and far too young to be a mum, was almost as much of a stranger in that district as I was. She had been put out by her parents with 'good riddance' for the trouble she (and I) represented. I've been told that she had chosen that district, which adjoined her own, because that was where she thought my father was from. Of course, she had gone straight to his parents' home, which was one of the community's largest and most impressive, hoping to find shelter. Yet, when she turned up on their doorstep to say that she was

Follow me on Twitter: @avabrown24

pregnant with their son's child, his mother furiously chased my mum away. She answered my mother's request for support and food by mockingly suggesting that she start collecting dirt to make the Milo (a chocolaty drink that all children loved) for her bastard spawn.

Shortly thereafter, the young man who was supposed to be my dad, absconded. In my childish mind, I imagined him as a scared young man, fleeing the massive responsibility that was to come with a child, hoping to live out the rest of his youth in the carefree manner that all young men seem to crave. It was only as an adult, however, that I began to understand the implications of the rumours that had always circulated around me, whispers that my father's parents' response could be based on the fact that he felt I wasn't his child.

Alone and pregnant in that new town, my mother switched her efforts to finding a new boyfriend to be her breadwinner. She quickly found Jack, who was employed at the nearby rice factory, and that was the familial situation into which I was born. Despite Jack making scarcely enough to feed himself, I don't remember my mother ever having a proper job. It was painfully clear to me, even as a young child, that our family was extremely poor. By the time I was seven, the hunger in my belly had already ignited the flame that would propel me out of our one-room house, which was by then bursting at its seams to hold my step-father, mother, and three siblings, as well as myself. Though I had no idea of how I would escape the misery within its walls, I had a fire in my blood that would have burned that little shack down.

Inside the house, a sheet was used to separate us - the adults on one side - and us four children on the other. There was never enough bed space when sleeping four to a bed. And it was not unusual that someone would wet the bed, so we often slept soaked in urine. We awoke each day to the sun and the many daily chores that awaited us. There was taking care of the goats, fetching the water from the only pipe that served our entire community, and carrying it home, collecting wood for the fire, and washing clothes. Sometimes, we even had to cook. Babysitting was something I was expected to do from an early age. We were expected to clean the floor of our room every day using a red dye called 'red oak', which made the concrete floor a deep red, then polish it to a high shine. We weren't allowed to stop until my mother could see her reflection glaring up at her from below.

It always seemed to be my duty to clean our side of the room, but I had to let my frustrations at that unfairness bubble inside of me in silence. If I didn't, a stone, machete, or any solid item within my mum's reach would come hurtling towards me, flung from my mother's strong arm. I must have been born with a streak of rebellion, and my mother who was keenly aware of that, was always ready to squash it out of me. I recall one night when I refused to complete all my chores; my mother showed me who was boss by ensuring I stayed outside for a good few hours in the pitch dark. I had been overly tired from the day when I refused to finish my chores, instead moving my weary feet, along with my siblings, to head inside. But that rebellion had not escaped my mother's attention, and she had already come up with her own plans that were unknown to me - but not for long!

I was at the end of the line filing in the door. When everyone else had made it inside, my mother rapidly slammed the door shut in my face and locked it. She answered my surprised cries by jerking it open again and saying, "You want to come in? Then come in now." Of course, I thought she was serious and I immediately moved into the doorway. Her strong grip, as she grabbed me and gave me a good beating, left me in such shock that I was startled to find myself being pushed right back outside. Hearing the sound of the lock shutting me out was her final punishment.

That was my first taste of my mother's penalty meted out on those who dared to disobey her. The darkness around me seemed darker than ever; my only light was the inconsistent flickering of the Peanie Wallies. The realization that I was alone, left to the elements, filled my heart with a wild fear. All of the ghost stories we were told came rushing back. I could feel every dead person we had ever spoken about floating around me.

I crouched into a tight ball, the night's silence nearly smothering me. It was more than two hours later when my brother opened the door to let me in. That was no heroic or chivalrous effort on my brother's part; my mum had allowed that kindness, I guess that she knew I had learnt my lesson.

My mum told me a story of when she'd taught me another lesson as a child. She stated that I'd refused to hold one of my siblings so she could perform in a concert. She said she got mad and tore off all my clothes as we travelled from the concert venue to our house. She had a very volatile temper and she scarred one of my sisters for life. My sister had gone to the shop on an errand for my mum, but when she didn't come back on time, mum went in search of her. On finding her in a boy's home, she bit flesh from my sister's shoulder, scarring her permanently.

The rule in our house was that as soon children rose out of bed in the morning, they were set to work and then rushed outside. We were forbidden to go back into the house until the sun was setting and we were ready to sleep. If we lingered in the morning, a cloth drenched in cold water would awaken us. However, that was rare, as the bed was normally so full of people that we were either jostled awake or pushed out by the smell and feel of urine. Before we came back in the evenings, we would have to fill up pans with water for the next morning, and wash ourselves. Our house didn't have a bathroom, so everyone bathed outside; boys and girls alike. It wasn't until I started 'feathering' (growing pubic hair) that the adults decided it was time to grant some privacy to that routine, and they built a washroom

Follow me on Twitter: @avabrown24

out of some salvaged corrugated zinc sheets.

On the evenings that my mother cooked dinner, we would all gather around the old makeshift kitchen outside, which stood near where we bathed. After we had collected our dinner, we would each find a somewhat comfortable stone to sit on and eat. There were always dogs around, so our mealtime was filled with as much dog breath as food. As soon as we got our meal, we would try to eat as quickly as possible, with the hope that someone else would 'buss' (be full) so that we could help them finish their meal. There was no TV to watch after dinner, so we stayed outside, sitting on the stones and making jokes with one another or taking turns making up ghost stories. Since we had no electricity, we bottled up the dancing fireflies we called 'Peanie Wallie' to chase the blackness away from around us. Finally, when we were too tired to stay up any longer, we would retreat to the dank and cramped bed. I was always among the last to stay up, simply because I despised the sleeping arrangements.

We each had a sparse wardrobe and the few pieces we had were all hand-me-downs. Each of us had one pair of good shoes, and this was the pair we would wear only to church; school was attended barefooted. There was also only one uniform for each of us, which was the required outfit for primary school attendance, so we had to wash the white blouse every day. We attended the local public school, where our classrooms were always overcrowded. I can remember attending my fourth grade studies alongside more than fifty other pupils crammed into the overcrowded and boisterous room. I'm sure the teachers did their best in these situations, but they always moved the lessons along according to the brightest students' progress, meaning the slower students, like me, were often left behind. Even so, I did my best to keep up. We walked to school like every other child in the district; it was only the ones who went to school outside of our area that were driven. For us, lunch usually consisted of a fried egg and bread, which had been placed in a brown paper bag along with our drink; a mixture of sugar, water, and lime. Unfortunately, by the time lunchtime rolled around at mid-day, the egg would have begun to smell really unpleasant. Sometimes, I would hide my lunch in the bushes near the school and use an object to mark its spot so that I could find it at lunchtime. It never occurred to me there may be mongoose or rats in the bushes. If I had known then what I know now about all the vicious, hungry creatures living around us, I would never had done such a thing!

There were times when there was no food in our house to pack for lunch, and I was left with two choices; go without or stay home. I always chose the go-without option, trying instead to ward off the eventual hunger by eating as hefty a breakfast as possible, although that strategy was a challenge and sometimes completely unfeasible. Occasionally, we could come home for a lunch of overnight-roasted dumpling. These dumplings were a traditional, simple food in Jamaica, made from a paste of flour, water, and salt that has been rolled into a spherical shape and then fried or boiled. The ones we ate had been boiled and then left overnight and cooked on a coal fire; the end result was a roasted dumpling that had absorbed most of the charcoal it had been cooked on. My mother would serve these roasted dumplings with mint tea. We would rush through the meal, drink some water, and run back to school so that we wouldn't miss the afternoon classes.

The truth be told, by the time I reached the school, I was already hungry again. That was a little life lesson that no matter how much effort I put in, very little of my hunger for a better life would be satisfied while I remained reliant on someone else. At the end of each school day, we would rush home, not because we were excited to play evening games with one another, but because we had a pile of chores waiting for us. We did, however, entertain ourselves along the walk home, usually by playing

Follow me on Twitter: @avabrown24

cricket or catch with sour oranges. Sometimes, we would steal some precious minutes to play a game called 'stuck', in which two of us would stand at opposite ends, facing each other, with a third in the middle, trying to 'site' (dodge) a ball, or whatever object we could find for throwing, thrown between the first two. We always played these games in the middle of the road, with passing cars blowing their horns and sending us scattering out of their way. Thankfully, none of us were ever hurt!

It was the custom of the children from our school to gather in little groups to walk home together. I yearned to find that perfect group to fit in, but I was always on the periphery of any group that I tried to join. Mostly, I was pushed aside by teasing remarks about how I was always getting good grades at school. That was just the start, though. At times, some of the meaner girls would wait for me and inflict some type of physical torment; it was an easy escape if they were only intending to pull my hair or spit on me, but things got more challenging when, as a gang, they decided to wallop me with their punching fists and kicking feet. After all the times they beat me up, I never tattled. I would just hobble home and pretend to my mother that I'd had a hard fall or something equally as clumsy. I gave these self-deprecating excuses for my dirty uniform because I didn't want her to get into any more quarrels with anyone in the district. These types of raucous spats between neighbours were common, and boy, did I hate them! Since I was not a tattletale, the bullying went on for a few years. It worsened when I reached grade five and I became more serious about my schoolwork.

As kids, we would roam the entire district (village) and no place was out of bounds for us. We would go searching for fruits, like mangoes, and climb any tree that promised a good view, regardless of how tall it might be. I was a tomboy and had no interest for dolls. I was much more interested in all of the energetic things the boys were doing, possibly because my closest sibling in age was a boy and we went almost everywhere together. We would often hang out with his friends, who were mainly boys. We would go fishing and hunting for birds; just about anything that was an outdoor adventure. There were no limits, as long as we stayed out of trouble.

My brother and I had daily outdoor adventures because we had to hunt for food to snack on if we got hungry between meals. That was our only means to quell the hunger pangs. Today, when I see children who are never far away from a filled refrigerator, who go around laden with the latest technological gadgets, I am shocked to consider how humble our lives were. We made most of our own toys from whatever we could find. We used to collect the sour oranges that were unfit to eat, to make wheels for play-trucks. We would gather empty drink cartons to serve as the people in the trucks. By attaching strings to the front of the play trucks, we could pull our 'cars filled with people' up and down the road. We also made a trap called a 'calaban'. It was a rectangular box made from wicker that we had woven from whatever pliable wood we could find and we used it to catch birds. We would prop it upside down on a stick to hold it up and scatter seeds to bait the birds, leading into the trap. We would hide nearby and watch the unsuspecting bird follow the trail, pecking away and steadily walking forward until it was under the calaban. Before it realized what was happening, we would pull the stick out and trap the bird. I'm sorry to say that in most cases, that bird would then become our snack. We would eat it on the spot after quickly roasting it on a wood fire.

When I was around eight years old, I began to become curious about who my father was. I wondered why my surname was different from my siblings; they all shared my stepdad's surname. To make matters worse, I had my mother's surname. This pointed discrepancy made me feel awkward, more so because I didn't understand the reasoning behind it.

Follow me on Twitter: @avabrown24

In my family, there was hardly any verbal communication, and without being told, I knew there were questions I shouldn't ask. It all came to the surface one day. As I was out with my brother and his group of friends playing our regular bird hunting game. One of the boys suddenly asked me if I knew that my dad was the man named Dave who lived only two minutes walking distance from my house. What was he talking about, I wondered. How could a man who lived so close to me, who acted like such a stranger, be my dad? My brother, who was protective of me, was furious with that sort of talk going on and wound up starting a fight with the other boy.

When we went home that evening, I casually mentioned that strange comment to my mum, I was hoping to have her spill the secret as to whether it was true or not. She immediately grew enraged, throwing stones, ashes, pots, pans, and anything else at me. I was completely confused as to what I had done wrong to trigger her outburst, but I learned that I had better kill that curiosity. Afterward, life continued on as usual and the subject never came up again. When I was out and about, however, I would see that man who was supposed to be my father. I dared not approach him and he never showed any special interest in me except to say a regular 'hello' or ask me to run to the local shop; I was treated no differently to the multitude of children who wandered past his house. I always complied with his request without question because we were taught to respect our elders; he always gave a little token for our efforts, so I wasn't about to complain.

At age ten and a half, our family situation changed drastically when my stepdad lost his job at the rice factory. My mother had just recently given birth to two more babies, which meant that I was meant I was expected to acquire a more adult role as a partial breadwinner for the family. It became my responsibility each day to go to a privately-owned property nearby, where there grew an abundance of mango trees. I would pick as many of the mangoes as I could to sell throughout the day. I was anxious about the prospect because that property was where airplanes would land in the wee hours of the night to collect the illegal marijuana grown in that region. I would be venturing into dangerous territory to complete my new task. Until then, I had been relatively fearless, but in those inky black mornings, when I had to sneak around in the mango fields, fear came at me from every direction. I feared being shot because I was trespassing, I feared being taken captive if I wandered into a marijuana operation or that the police would catch me. But that task was not optional and I had to do it to help keep my family alive. So it came to be, that most mornings while the community slept, I joined the other eldest children of neighbouring families to sneak around with torches in the darkness to find the mangoes. We collected the mangoes in baskets carried on our heads, which sat atop a 'catah', fashioned from a piece of folded cloth, normally old clothes, to help cushion our heads against the heavy load when the basket became heavy.

I hated my life at that stage. I wished that I were the baby of the family, so I could still be sleeping that early in the morning. We would try and get back from the mango walk before sunrise so that we could sort and wash the mangoes. Only the most bruised and unpleasantly soft fruits were kept for ourselves. As soon as the sorting was done, I would be sent anywhere that the mangoes might sell best that day; the location changed frequently. Most days I couldn't make it to school because the need to sell every mango so that my family could eat outweighed my desire to sit in a classroom.

Even after my contributions, our family's diet dwindled. We would eat rice or chicken back and turn cornmeal, a dish similar to the Nigerian 'ebba' or 'gari' or the Ghanaians 'banku'. The only cereal we knew was plain cornflakes and someone would have had to acquire a barrel sent from overseas (foreign) that we could get a small portion from.

Follow me on Twitter: @avabrown24

More regularly, we had oats; they were not the most flavourful food, but they were filling. My stepdad had cows, so he would milk them every morning for us. Milk was about the only consistent thing in our diet. I guess that's where my love for cornmeal porridge came from. Whatever we had for breakfast would have to last my family the whole day, until I came home with money from the mango sales. Yet, too often, I was only able to make enough to buy myself a snack for energy to continue the selling and to pay for my transportation back to our home when the market was far away. Sometimes, when the day's sales were slow, I would have to lower the price per dozen just to get rid of them and make some money; after all, any amount I made was good, since we didn't pay for the mangoes in the first place.

As I said, myself and others from my community would sell mangoes anywhere we thought there might be a demand; on the train rails, in the park, in the shopping plaza, and at any temporary attractions where people were gathering. If there was a fete, fair, or sports day, I tried to be right in the thick of it. There were days when we would be selling mangoes in the same region where my school was located and the kids from my class would recognize me in passing.

They rarely missed a chance to greet me with a mocking shout, saying, "Mango gal! You are so poor, you skull (skipped) school to sell mangoes."

At times, I felt like running away and abandoning my basket of mangoes. But I would force myself to sit there and endure their chants because I knew the consequences that I would be met with at home if I ever did such a thing. Back then, I would have been in grades four or five, when the students were preparing for the Scholastic Aptitude Tests (SAT). Since I attended school so irregularly, I didn't want to fall behind, so I asked my teachers for the books that were used in the classes to study on my own. I was told I would have to buy them, but our family couldn't afford the books.

I had heard about a man who would have been my uncle, if Dave was really my dad. To that date, however, no one, especially Dave, had acknowledged me as their daughter. Although by then, the word was out in our entire district about this possibility. It was close to Christmas that year and I boldly sent a message to my supposed uncle, to ask if he could buy me the books for the SATs. I explained that the exams were to be held in the summer and I needed to study. I was stunned when he sent the books. It was the first time anyone had shown me any outward love or kindness. Imagine a total stranger was the first to show me that; yet I saw my mum and stepdad every day, and although I knew they loved me, they never seemed able to show it. When I look back on that situation, myself a parent now, I am resolved to do everything in my power to ensure that my children know that I love them, not just by saying it (which I do often), but by showing them as well.As a child, I lived with the idea that my mum hated me. Every interaction we had left me feeling unloved and unwanted. I still carry traces of that painful emotion even now, as an adult, living far away from that small Jamaican village.

After I received the SAT books, I was inspired to rush through my chores each day so that I could sit under the trees to study them. Unfortunately, on my first glimpse of book one, I was completely bewildered. I realized that task was going to be incredibly challenging; even more so than my daily task of gathering and selling the stolen mangoes. My eleventh birthday was approaching and I saw no end in sight to my daily routine. Little did I know that very soon my life would again take another turn.

Dave, the man I believed to be my father, had begun living with a pretty woman named Sarah. Not only was she the most beautiful woman I had ever seen in my life, but she was also kind and gentle. One day, she invited me to her house. She was the first adult who had ever sought me out and spoken to me like I mattered. I was thrilled to accept her invitation and before long, I was at her house all the time. It was wonderful! She would comb my hair and feed me. We would attend the community's clothes washing day together. In those days, we would hand wash our clothes in the river and then hang them on the bushes to dry in the sunshine. Usually, the children would just swim and wait for the adults to finish. During one of these excursions, while Sarah and I sat side-by-side, washing in private, she told me that Dave was indeed my dad. I was thrilled to finally hear that validation, as the rumour had been flying all over the community for years. There, in that quiet moment, that beautiful woman had given me the answer to the very question my own mother was afraid to address.

Over the next few weeks, Sarah and I grew closer. I began to spend less and less time at my own house. Mind you, I still did all the household chores that my mother expected me to, and I made certain that I did them well, as I would have gotten a good beating if I didn't. But I loved being in my dad's house, especially because it was an actual house with two bedrooms, a living room, an indoor bathroom, and a veranda. To top it off, they also had a car. Their life seemed so luxurious to me, but my only comparison was the ever-more cramped one-room shack I lived in, where I still slept in a urine-soaked bed.

Although Sarah had confirmed that Dave was my father, he rarely spoke to me and he kept our interactions on the level of sending me to the shop. I felt hurt by the lack of recognition on his part, but I preferred that small bit of familiarity over none at all. After a few weeks, Sarah told me that she and my dad were going to be moving to the community where she had come from originally and she wanted me to go with them! I was thrilled beyond words, but was equally anxious about what my mother would say. When I approached her with the careful request, my mum surprised me by immediately agreeing. I would have thought that since I was now the main breadwinner of the family, my value would have been higher. But just like that, I was being hurried out of her front door.

I didn't have much to take with me; I had very few personal belongings. When I arrived at my dad's home, Sarah, my would-be step-mum expressed that the items I had really weren't worth taking with us. She set them aside and told me that she would replace them with new ones once we settled in at the new home. I had never had any 'new' clothes before. I thought to myself that if the way she dressed was any indicator, I was going to live out a dream. I was entering the happiest time in my life.

Changes can sometimes be laced with hidden journeys we would rather not have encountered.

Chapter Two

THE DARK

"We are scared of the dark, light is comforting as it helps us see shapes and forms. Light helps with recognition and shows what lies ahead of us. We yearn for the comfort of light as it provides silhouettes and form, allowing us to recognize and define what's before us. Are we afraid of the darkness, or is it the truth hiding behind it?"

––––––––––––

The drive to Sarah's old neighbourhood was filled with excitement and apprehension. I didn't know what to expect, and at times, I felt panicked and wanted to ask Sarah to turn the car around to take me back home. We had turned off the main road and were travelling along a windy road that seemed to go on forever. In my angst, the journey felt like it was taking an eternity. My mother's home was close to the main road, but now we were going farther and farther away from anything familiar to me and deeper into the hills; a meandering journey that seemed endless. I felt like we were

Follow me on Twitter: @avabrown24

leaving civilisation behind. I remember feeling the panic rising as I silently questioned myself, "What have I done? Why would anyone choose to live so far away from the lights and main civilisation?"

The roads continued to go round and round, climbing up into the mountains. When we turned from one road to another, I would look down and see the one we had just come off. I had never been so high up and it was scary. The mix of emotions I felt at leaving my mother's home for that unknown place made my anxiety about the height so poignant, it became a lifelong fear. We eventually arrived at Sarah's house. While there, she introduced me to her father, daughter, and son. My father was not there. His main home was back in the district I had just left. I was surprised to find such a ready-made family unit and I felt like the odd one out. I was unaware that Sarah even had children. She took me inside and showed me the room I would be sharing with her daughter, who was much younger than I was. That house wasn't nearly as crowded as the one I had just come from, and there was an inside bathroom and plenty of outside yard space. They had an outside kitchen and attached to it was a 'butchery,' which was like a spare room that farm produce was kept in.

My life settled into a routine quickly, but soon I began to realise that I was becoming a sort of housekeeper. I washed the clothes for everyone and cooked the family's meals. Sarah did register me at the local school and I started grade six. All of these changes; the new school, a new home and new family, were quite overwhelming. I had no way of communicating with my mother's family as there was no phone. As the days passed, I started to get a bit lonely and missed my old way of life. The walk to my new school was long, about two hours in a child's eyes, made harder by the fact that I was still making the journey without any shoes. I also found it challenging to adjust to my new classmates. These kids were brighter, and some of them much wealthier than those that had attended my old school. I decided that my best tactic was to keep quiet and not draw any attention to myself, but being the new girl, everyone noticed me right away.

Every day after lunch, the teachers would expect us to recite our times-tables. I remember the head teacher clearly and her ever-present cane that she carried as she walked down each row of students seated at their desks. She would randomly stop in front of a desk; point the cane at a student and bark out the quiz question, "What is 7x7?" That would go on for quite some time, with mixed up variations of the numbers. The students who had not yet memorized their times-tables completely; myself included, would just mumble some guessed answer or an ashamed admission that they didn't know the answer at all. I used to sit in dread of being called on, even when I knew the answer, because I was still trying to stay invisible among my new classmates.

I think the teacher recognised my apprehension because I was, thankfully, spared questioning for the first few weeks, but eventually my turn came. To me, it seemed to happen almost in slow motion; I saw her turn towards me and the world seemed to stop spinning as she pointed her steps towards my desk, raised the cane at me, and asked, "What is 9x6?" I can't remember if I didn't know the answer or if I was just smothered by the fear of having all eyes on me, but I do remember my tongue remained absolutely still. Out of the corner of my eye, I could see a multitude of hands popping up and the smirking grins on the faces of the kids who knew the answer. I was so angry with myself as I dutifully stretched out my hand to receive my caning. The pain was far worse than I had imagined; extremely sharp and nothing like the smacks my mum used to give me. When the first whack sent a jolt of pain rushing from my knuckles through my hand and up my arm, I nearly wet myself! The second one on my arm was even worse. I know for a fact that was a severe punishment because the scar is still on my arm. When I arrived home, I didn't tell anyone about that cruel experience; I was afraid that their concern over my silliness would be a source of a new problem for them. I needn't have had worried though, no one paid any attention to my nursing the unsightly wound, nor did they inquire about it when it turned into a scar. As the pain began to subside, I promised myself that I would never again get caned for not knowing something in school.

I felt sad to realise that there was no point in telling anyone at my new house about the punishment for my failing, because I wasn't sure if they would mete out another beating for my perceived transgression. I reminded myself, as I had many times before, that some things were best endured and left unsaid. I applied myself completely to the task of learning my times-tables. In every waking minute, while I ate, washed, cleaned, cooked, and bathed, I had the times-tables running through my mind. Time progressed and I learnt them perfectly and was able to recite them in class without a hitch. With that, I began to settle in more comfortably at school and, finally, I felt like I was getting on with my life.

There were times I could steal away from school during lunchtime. I would go to the mango market to look for anyone from my old district that could pass along a message of greeting to my mum and siblings. I was very keen to know how they were doing. Sometimes I would recognize my mum among the crowd, but she always disappeared before I reached her. Those close encounters always left me wondering how she could come so close to my new school but not look for me. However, these meetings with old neighbours became fewer and further between, and I heard less and less about my mother and her family. The fact that I had chosen to leave them to join a new family in search of a better life weighed heavily on me, and I constantly carried the longing for my mum's love in my heart.

Towards the end of my sixth grade year, Sarah gave birth to a baby boy, my brother, Chad, with whom I would cultivate a beautiful life-long relationship. To me, it seemed like my dad worshipped that new little life. The attention he poured on the baby made me a bit jealous. I yearned for Dave to give me just one-tenth of the gentle attention the baby received. After all, he had missed out on the first twelve years of my life and I felt due some level of affection. During that time, I was preparing to take my SAT exams. I was also anxious about the possibility of getting to sit for an extra post SAT preparatory test called the 'Twenty Percent'. That test was given to a select group of students chosen by the head teacher according to the expectation of their success in the SATs. I was crushed to find out that I wasn't chosen. But looking back, I should have realized that my chances were slim because I had no parent advocating for me; either at school or in the home.

Although my new home afforded me clean clothing, daily meals, and even lunch money, it did not provide anyone who parented me. There was no one journeying to my school to discuss my progress or prospects for the future of my education. I was acutely aware that many of my classmates who were chosen to sit for the extra placement exam were no smarter than me, but they had parents who would deliver coffee and yams to the teachers. At that time, it was well known that many teachers could be cajoled to show an extra bit of interest in your child if you 'greased their palms'. I took mental notes on the importance of social standing and once again told myself I was going to overcome that challenge.

I knew that I had to pass my SAT exam to further my education and without the aid of the post-test experience, it only served to motivate me to study harder. When the day came to sit for the exam, I gave it everything I had, barefoot and all. I left the test feeling confident that my studying would pay off with a passing score. In the weeks leading up to the delivery of the results, I saved up my lunch money every day, refusing to buy anything to eat because I planned to celebrate passing that hurdle. The day

Follow me on Twitter: @avabrown24

the results came out, I was eager to get into town and see my score. As I passed the local police station and turned towards the town square, I saw a friend of our family who was a policeman. He shouted out at me, "Girl, I told you I had faith in you!" That was all I the proof I needed to know that I had received passing marks. I threw myself in the middle of the road and started a 'piece a bawling' (very loud crying), as it's called in Jamaica. Inside me, I felt that something great was beginning to take shape in my life and I revelled in the fact that I could do anything I set my mind to...how naïve I was. I was so ecstatic that I didn't even hear the car horns honking at me. Two policemen came out and escorted me out of the road. As soon as I came to my senses, I turned tail and ran home, delirious with excitement to share my news. When I arrived at Sarah's house, I found that they all had already heard and had planned a little celebration with homemade cake and lemonade. They were so proud of me, and it was the first time I had heard such adulations aimed towards me.

On the following Monday, I went back to school with a strut like a peacock in my step. I was so happy to find that my passing marks had brought me a level of respect from some of my teachers who had previously looked straight through me. I also found out that my scores allowed for entrance into the DeCarteret College in Mandeville, which was in the neighbouring parish and over an hour's drive away. My excitement over my passing score was tempered by the very realistic concern about how I would afford to go to that new school.

My life back at Sarah's house was starting to change too. I had not been paying much attention to the changes occurring in my twelve-year-old pubescent body, but others certainly had. Sarah's son, who was about my age, started trying to fondle me and make advances towards me, but he was not the only one. Sarah had gotten involved with politics, and as a result, she was away frequently, but Dave was normally home, as he was then generally unemployed. One day, he did something that made me keenly aware of the fact that I needed to be more mindful of myself when I was alone with men, even ones I knew I should have been able to trust implicitly. It was so unexpected when he started a real conversation with me, and I had no misgivings when he led me back into his room to continue the talk. In fact, my heart soared with happiness over the attention I had so long yearned for. While he was speaking, though, he took my hands and pulled me close to him, only to lift my blouse and put my very small breast in his mouth. No one had ever spoken to me be about intimacy, sex, or even puberty, and I wasn't certain what he was doing. But I knew that whatever it was, it didn't feel right. I immediately pulled away and sprinted out of the house; I gasped in the fresh air outside and tried to dispel the sense of suffocation and the feel of vomit that rose in my throat.

My mind was racing; that wasn't what I had expected a father-daughter relationship to be. I could hear him yelling behind me, calling for me to come back. I felt so dirty and his voice had turned angry. He bellowed out, "I didn't do anything to you!" When I returned to the living room, he came at me and spoke in a quiet but stern voice. He told me that if I told anyone what had happened, they wouldn't understand or believe me and that I would be sent back to live at my mother's. I made the promise then, to not to tell anyone. That was a promise that I would keep simply because I was far too afraid of leaving the home I had now become accustomed to. Also, I feared the truth in what he said that no one would believe me. It wasn't until I was nineteen that I dared to tell that to anyone, sharing it with my first husband, Tobore.

As an adult, I still see my dad from time to time when I make the journey across the pond to visit Jamaica, but I have never been able to broach the subject with him. It has been only recently that I gathered the courage to tell my mum during one of her visits to London, where

I now live, and I could tell that was something even she finds hard conceptualising. But if I had the courage to face him, I would want to tell him that that single event altered my entire perspective on humanity and caused me to lose the ability to trust even those who were supposed to love me the most. More importantly, it has affected the relationships I've had with the opposite sex ever since. Instead, I would merely be civil with him. If someone were to ask me if I loved my father, I would not be able to give a simple answer. I do care for his wellbeing in general, but otherwise, there is only indifference. That event was to have an impact on my entire adult life, but it had little impact on my daily life at home. Certainly, I was more careful around all men, and I had to fight off the desire to run away to my mum's home every time I found myself alone in the house with my dad. But my being scared of him, even when others were around, was something I kept hidden from everyone. Our lives just went on as usual, as if nothing had happened.

My new school in Mandeville was too far away to walk to, so I had to start taking the bus to attend my classes. The cost of my bus fare soon became an irritating issue for Sarah. In addition, the bus I had to take left very early in the morning. That meant that it was nearly impossible to for me to complete my chores before I left for school. That too became a focus of annoyance for her. The grades from my first term were not very good, and I started to sense that going to high school wasn't going to work out as well as I had hoped. I was very aware of Sarah's annoyance with me and I became very nervous and edgy when I was at home. When the first term ended, I was informed that Sarah and Dave had decided to not send me back for the next term because they couldn't afford it. I received no further explanation on their decision, even though our financial situation seemed very stable. I wondered who had been paying for my bus fare and now felt the cost was unreasonable. Was it my mother, who Sarah demanded money from weekly or whenever she had it? Or was it my father, who pitched in a little something every now and again? It mattered not.

That summer, I received my first life lesson in puberty. I was home one afternoon, wearing one of my old school uniforms and playing in the yard with the other children. We were climbing up and sliding down the columns on the veranda. As I came down one of the columns, one of the boys told me that I was bleeding. I was frantic but couldn't see a cut anywhere on my legs or hands. I quickly turned my lavender skirt around and was met with the shocking sight of a bright red stain! I ran crying to Sarah. She gently shushed me into silence and ushered me back into the house to give me the lecture on the basics of puberty. One bit of the information she gave me that stood out was that I could now get pregnant. She explained that I needed to be careful, but at the time she didn't shed any light on how anyone actually got pregnant.

As the summer progressed, I wondered where I would be attending school when the new school year finally started. My inquiry, however, led to the suggestion that I should look around on my own and find a school that was nearer to our home. I was shocked by their answer. I was only a child, but there it was, revealing a deeper truth about my situation; that I was expected to assume responsibility for myself. I came up with a plan. I asked for bus fare to travel to my mum's and was given it. When I reached her house, I requested the fare to go to one of the high schools in my parish, to get registered for a transfer. At only twelve-years-old, I had made the first step into adulthood; I had to take responsibility for obtaining my own education.

I realised that even if I got accepted into the school, I would need to pay school fees and purchase the school's uniform. By the time the acceptance letter arrived, I had eight weeks to come up with the money and uniform. Sarah was not able to help out, citing the initial money problems that precluded my attendance at school in Mandeville. My father was a potential source of aid and, although he had done me wrong, I wanted to stay in his good graces so I passed on asking him. I went to my aunts, uncles, and everyone I knew to ask for money to help fund my second year of high school, but nothing came of it. I even tried to get help from a Member of Parliament who lived in our area, but that too produced nothing. It turned out to be my mum who was finally able to find the money for me. Just like Mandeville, my new school in Santa Cruz was a long bus ride from our house, but at least the fees were cheaper and it was in my parish. Every day was a challenge, but I was determined to stick with my decision to go back to school.

By the end of year nine, I started to notice the cute boys in my class. It was only a flirtatious interest and nothing more, especially because my mum had told me that if she got any inkling that I was having sex, she would rub scotch bonnet pepper in my private parts! That threat was enough to scare me into staying absolutely chaste.

While at secondary school in Santa Cruz, I struggled to eat as food was scarce. I recall loving practical lessons, as I would get food in abundance. So early on, from year nine, I decided that I would study food and nutrition, mainly because I already knew how to cook, but also because I would get to eat the day's lesson. My home economics teacher and my home management teachers were like my away-from-home mothers; they made me love going to school and I appreciated their care. I remember volunteering at the home economics block as they sold baked goods. I did so for two reasons. Firstly, it allowed me to get some food to eat, and secondly, I would steal some of the money to help me pay for my bus fare to be able to travel to and from school. I hated stealing but I felt I had no choice. It was either that or stay at home.

By now, my dad and Sarah had fallen out of sorts and there was no longer any consideration to assist me. In addition, due to her own needs, my mum was not consistent with her giving. There were aspects of how I was schooled that I wished my kids had experienced, such as teachers who acted as parents in absentia. High school was an uphill battle for me. It seemed it always was a toss-up between staying home, sitting on the roadside gambling, stealing from school, begging my Member of Parliament to help with my education, or simply going to school hungry, provided I even got a ride. In spite of all that, I made it through.

I had only one uniform for school, as I simply couldn't afford more. It was a navy blue tunic with four gores (panels). We ironed with a sad iron, which we heated in a wood fire. There was no ironing board; ironing was done on the bed. We would stupidly hold the iron near our faces to feel the heat to see how hot it was. It was our way of testing the temperature, but it shows how irresponsible we were at that age. One evening, when attempting to iron, I didn't bother to test, I just slapped it on my only tunic and 'bang, slap, damn' it left its shape burnt into my tunic on the front panel. I was left with a permanent sad iron imprint on my only tunic.

As a child in my mum's community, I always hated when the adult and teenage men would bathe at the community pipe. They would stand there in their briefs when we passed. Many would be disgusting enough to try to get our attention to look at their manhood, and when we refused, they would inform us that we were old enough to go on 'cutting table' (ready to lose our virginity).

It was revolting. I would cross the road and turn my face to the bushes to the disadvantage of 'bucking (stubbing) my toes'. When that failed, I would tell them to 'suck their mums' which were the worse swear words you could tell a Jamaican man. Mums were revered. I thought such practices were mentally child sexual abuse; it was torture.

One of my first crushes in high school was a boy who lived in my district. That, however, wore off rather quickly and I then began to like his brother. Looking back, I realised that I was trying to see if a boy would be interested in me; I had very low self-esteem and felt ugly and unlovable. I paid close attention in my guidance classes. The teacher explained that our class was at the age when kissing would become a point of interest, and I was no exception. I started looking forward to my first kiss and began planning how to get it. Soon, I had my first boyfriend and it felt wonderful when we were together. The two of us would walk the two mile journey from our homes to the bus stop together, sometimes we would walk back together in the evenings as well. However, whenever we got onto the bus, he would stop talking to me and that general disregard would continue at school. I reasoned that I must be really ugly and he was embarrassed to be seen with me in public places, so his love for me would only be acceptable in private. The truth was that I was merely too naive to realise that he had a real girlfriend. I was only a target for the sex he wasn't getting from that other girl. Thankfully, I never fully gave in to his requests and our 'affair' only consisted of a few kisses.

The next guy I fell for was nothing like that previous boy; in fact, he was a man. I was absolutely smitten by his age and his drop dead gorgeous, mature look. His name was James, and he was about twenty-five at the time. The fact that he was from the capital city, Kingston, which was far away from my rural community in St. Elizabeth, made him all the more alluring to me. I told my stepmother, Sarah, about him and I was delighted that subject seemed to pique her interest in me and my life. Looking back I realised what the source of that interest really was. I was still very young and naïve and at the time I didn't wonder why an older woman was suddenly so interested in the stories of a lovesick girl. By the time I realised what was really going on, it was too late and I just wound up feeling like a fool.

Every summer, the people in my stepmom's district would hold a summer party, and I loved to go. That particular summer I went with James as my date. When the festivities wound down, we stood close and he whispered a tantalizing promise to me that he would keep in touch with me. In the weeks after the party, my dad and Sarah began arguing frequently; I would hear her yelling about all the men she could have chosen instead of him, men who had a great deal more money than he did. In their last big argument, she called him a worthless swine and soon after, he moved away to Kingston to find better work. Things calmed down in our house and Sarah started visiting Kingston on the weekends. I naturally assumed that she was going to visit my father there. She would return and pass along a greeting to me from James. I wondered about that, but told myself that she must have just run into the object of my affection when she was visiting my father. Over time, the greetings became fewer and further between. I wanted to ask if she knew if he had a new girlfriend, but as a child who was barely coping with her own life, I had learnt to keep my silly questions to myself and not bother the adults.

Time passed and the so did the crush. Christmas came and there was a celebration on Christmas Eve, called the Grand Market. It was a huge street festival that gave us kids the chance to stay out really late; it was such a lovely celebration. I loved it when everyone was in a festive mood and the streets were laced with all the items for Christmas. I absolutely adored it. I felt like a child in a candy shop with a bit of freedom at last. It was my favourite night of the year, when I revelled in my freedom from chores and the watchful eyes of the adults. The evening of the Grand Market, I noticed a car in our drive that wasn't my dad's. When I peeked closer, I realised that it was James' and I thought he had come to see me. Yes, I know, stupid girl, but I was fourteen.

Without a word, my step-mum ushered him into her bedroom and asked that I get his bags. Although it wasn't said, it was obvious that they were together. I think that was my second heartbreak (after my dad's). I dutifully brought inside the bags of the man I had been so crazy about. Sarah then told us all to quickly get ourselves ready so that we could go to the Grand Market. She hurried us out of the house with a pocketful of money from 'Daddy James'. She didn't even give us a curfew. I was, however, given the task of babysitting my younger brother, Chad, and her two other kids. I was to be the responsible one in charge of our little group. With nothing else left to do, we headed off for the Grand Market and got caught up in the festivities until midnight. I finally gathered the younger ones and we started the walk back home. A short way into the walk, a car pulled up beside us and my dad's head popped out of the driver's side window. He was astonished to see us all by ourselves and quickly asked about my stepmother. The young ones answered in a chorus that she was at home, but my voice was a bit more timid because I knew that there was a showdown in the making. My father said to get into the car and drove us home in silence; even the young ones started to feel the tension of the situation, although they didn't understand it.

When we arrived, all of us quickly scampered out of the way, while dad stood at the front door trying his key in the lock. We could hear him angrily jiggling the key with no success. He called out to my stepmom, but there was no answer. She must have known that he had seen the strange car in the driveway and deduced what was going on. At that point, my dad was more than angered and was trying to kick the door down. Sarah shouted at him to leave because she was through with him and that she had told him this long ago! Things escalated into a screaming match between the two. They caused such a ruckus that they woke up the entire community and all the neighbours started coming out to witness the entire hullabaloo. It was so embarrassing. My dad broke some of the windows in the house, all the while screaming like a mad man. Finally, his energy left him and he got in his car and sped away. He had not paid any attention to me or Chad, and there was no invitation for us to go with him. Sure enough, the time of Sarah and my father being a couple was over and I no longer had any familial tie to that house.

I could never have anticipated how that break of a love affair between two people would have such a profound impact on my life. But Sarah immediately saw the consequence and told me that I would have to leave as soon as possible. I thought that if I worked harder, she would be convinced of my worth to her family and let me stay on, so I worked harder. Little did I know, I was about to be expected to work in a way that no girl or woman should ever have to resort to. Following my father's departure, our money situation got tighter and tighter. James did not stick around. Looking back at our situation now, I saw how my position in the family at that time was more that of a dutiful slave than of a daughter.

I was at the end of year nine in school, with all of my focus being on the excitement of what year ten was going to bring. I was certainly interested in boys, but I wasn't self-aware enough to appreciate the womanly figure I was developing. Our house at the time didn't have any electricity and Sarah decided it was high time that we got some. She found a man to wire the house, but his cost was beyond anything she could afford in our current situation. But she was crafty and knew of other ways to get the things in life that she needed.

Sarah had a male friend who would come over to the house occasionally. He was a tall, strapping man, about forty years old. He seemed like an old man to me. But that man had money, and she needed money to pay for the house to be wired and he was obviously interested in me. I would catch him eyeing me during his visits. In her mind, it must have seemed like an easy trade off. And so it began; she would allow that man to fondle me in exchange for the money she needed. The man started coming around more frequently, and each time I would be released from my chores and sent out to the veranda to entertain him. Sarah would always pick out my shortest shorts, telling me to wear them because they would keep me coolest in the heat. I hated those days when he came to visit. I would try to stall or even hide. When his visits became regular, I started coming home late from school so that I could at least limit the time I would have to endure his company. Each visit followed the same routine. He would sit on the veranda and Sarah would lock all the doors leading to the rest of the house. Thinking back, I believe that was her feeble way of protecting everyone else from having to deal with the fact that a lamb was being put to slaughter. Certainly, no one would have wanted to hear me constantly pleading with that man to not touch me in places I wasn't comfortable with. But my pleas fell on deaf ears. He would fondle me, touch my breasts, and grope me. Every time, I felt sick. I was transformed into the salary that was used to pay for the wiring of the house.

I was naïve, yes, but I was not stupid. Although it was never openly discussed that he was abusing me, I quickly realized the role my stepmother was playing in all of that and our relationship became strained. One day I just couldn't take it anymore, so I sent a message from school back to Sarah's house to say that I would be staying over at a friend's home. My friend's family understood my situation and did not have any problem with me staying there. I didn't even have a change of clothes with me, but my friend kindly offered me some of her own. The next day, when I returned to the house that had become my prison, I was flogged severely. I took the beating with dignity though, because in truth, it felt better than being fondled all evening. At least I wasn't being squeezed and probed by some old man's disgusting hands.

Luckily, my virginity was still intact and I was determined to keep it that way. The situation had become unbearable and I made a plan to escape back to my mum's house. Although her home was not as lavish as Sarah's, at least it was safer and devoid of that lecherous old man. By that time, my friends from school knew what was happening at my home, but there was nothing they could do to help. Jamaica did not have any proper social services to deal with such situations, so one just had to get on with it.

I surreptitiously packed a bag and hid it in the bushes outside. I didn't even feel guilty when I tucked in all the nice clothes Sarah had given me to replace the raggedy ones I had arrived with.

I was sure my plan would work, but I was sadly mistaken. Someone had obviously figured out my intent, because when I set off into the night to collect the bag with my things, I discovered it was gone. That didn't deter me though and I took off anyway. I headed towards my mum's place. I made it there without any obstructions. My mum was surprised to see me, but instead of greeting me with tears of joy and relief, she insisted that I go back to where I came from. Her mind was not changed, even after I tried to explain what had happened that had made me so desperate to leave. In her mind, my stepmother's home was still a better place for me. Through my mum's eyes, I looked healthier and better taken care of than any of the girls in my old district, and she wanted me to stay that way. I wound up leaving her house to travel to another friend's house, located in Southfield, St. Elizabeth, about twenty five miles from my mum's place. I was very relieved when my friend's family welcomed me in and allowed me to stay for a few days. I knew it was not a permanent solution to my situation and I couldn't stay there forever. I was still attending school every day and came up with the idea of trying to live secretly on the school compound. It's no surprise that plan didn't work out at all.

Eventually, I wound up at the house of one of my aunt's on my mum's side. She lived in a single-room house, which was about 10x13 square feet and was already filled with five people. I was in grade ten at the time and remember one night when I wet the bed because I was feeling so stressed. I felt embarrassed, but my aunt was extremely understanding about the situation. I stayed there for about two weeks until her husband started behaving inappropriately towards me. Thankfully, my aunt listened when I came to her with my concerns about her husband and she decided that her home was not a safe place for me anymore. Once again, I was let out into the world. I thought things couldn't get any worse, but boy was I wrong.

"Even without recognition, in the coldest part of us, fear has burnt from conception."

Chapter Three
THE REAL DAD STANDS UP

"True identity, for some, at times is hard to recognize, leading to questioning of characters and traits, for some even leads to questions about one's existence."

――――――

During those last days at my aunt's house, fate challenged me yet again. One day when I was in class, a message came for me that a man had come to the school to see me. I was perplexed and asked what he looked like, trying to place who could possibly be interested in visiting me mid-day. From the description, however, I had no idea who he could be and the girls delivering the message made it sound as if the man was mentally ill. They told me that he was waiting at the front of the school and loudly refusing to leave. Apparently he was convinced I was his child! I was torn as to what to do, but the situation was turning into a ruckus, and the longer I dawdled in indecision, the more embarrassment I was causing myself and the school.

At the front of the school, I found a short, dishevelled man walking in agitated circles. I was with some friends for support and we had decided to gingerly walk by him to first check out the situation, but as soon as we neared him, he immediately rushed towards me. His story came pouring forth, like he was in urgent need of claiming his stake as my father. He told me his name was Ralf and he was certain that I was his child. He was even able to provide me with quite a convincing history to support his claim. By the time he finished speaking and fell into an expectant silence, my thoughts, too, were swayed and I began to think that man could really be my father. In fact, I still carry a suspicion that that man planted the seed from which I grew, but time has consumed my chances of finding out the truth. However, he represented a new world of promising possibilities, namely that I had a whole other family that could love me and treat me with respect. I had never received that in Sarah's house and my disgusting experience with Dave overshadowed everything. I didn't want another father to cope with. I could survive without one! When I went home that evening, I relayed the experience to my aunt. As our community was relatively small, she knew exactly who Ralf was. My aunt surprised me by confiding that she long thought he was my real father. That was all too much for me at the time and I simply put the thought aside and never explored the possibility in earnest. I had more pressing issues to worry about at that time. My days of safety in my aunt's home were dwindling and I needed to take my meagre belongings - a few pieces of clothing and my single school uniform - and find a place to live.

As my aunt and I had feared, her husband's inappropriate behaviour continued to escalate in both frequency and aggressiveness. My aunt suggested that I travel the short distance to one of my uncles on my father's side - meaning Dave's side, as he had played the role of father to me for much longer than Ralf. I was terrified at the thought of having to put my life in the hands of yet another man. On the day of my departure, she helped me pack my belongings into a small plastic bag and assured me that man could help me. Despite the awkward nature of the situation in her own house that she was not strong enough to oppose, I could hear the sincerity in her voice and began to let my guard down to trust my aunt's judgment.

My aunt made the walk with me to a nearby garage that my uncle frequently took his work vehicles to for maintenance. It was a Saturday morning and the garage was buzzing with activities, all of which only served to make me pull further into my shell. We waited for about twenty minutes until he arrived. My aunt approached him first, alone. After speaking to him briefly, she beckoned for me to come and meet him. I remember that my heart was filled with such trepidation; I had to force myself to move forward. Due to my previous experiences with the older men in my life, all of whom were supposed to be my protectors, I had developed a general mistrust for the opposite sex. As I moved one foot in front of the other, my mind was racing with the question of what I was getting myself into that time. But what other choice did I have? I had nowhere to go and I had to rely on myself for protection. Hopefully, he would not be an enemy and another attacker from which I would have to flee.

My aunt introduced me to Gregory, but using the simple familiar term 'uncle', which I was to call him by. I was only slightly relieved to find that he had a very gentle and polite manner. In front of me, he agreed to assume responsibility of me and I felt a greater sense of relief that I was finally in the presence of two people who might actually care for my wellbeing. Needless to say, I was quite surprised when my aunt suddenly turned and left, without even a parting word or offering to come along with me to his house to settle me in. I had thought she would at least want to see the home where he would be taking me, so if anything happened, she would know where to find me. It was as if a business transaction had been completed; an inanimate object had been delivered and there was nothing left to do but to head home.

Not knowing what else to do, I waited quietly until my uncle finished

Follow me on Twitter: @avabrown24

his evening work at the garage. We carried out the trip to his home in awkward silence; it was a nerve-wracking experience. I was only fifteen years old and on my way to my fourth home. Gregory had actually tried to make small conversation with me as we travelled, but I was too busy making mental notes of where we were going, just in case I needed to retrace my steps. I was slightly comforted by the fact that the distance from his home to my aunt's did not seem to be too great; I could make it on foot if necessary.

We arrived at a tidy two-bedroom house that could have passed for a cottage. Although it was smaller than Sarah's house, it was still bigger than my mother's and I was in no position to be picky. When we entered, the house was still and quiet. He showed me to the room next to his and said that it would be mine. The room appeared to be set up for one person and I couldn't sense anyone else living in it. My heart skipped a beat when I realized that I was going to have a room of my own for the first time in my life! However, my excitement was tempered by the nagging curiosity about where this man's family was; where was the wife, or girlfriend, or even boyfriend, for that matter? Panic began to rise in me but I held silent as my mind raced frantically to find a trace anywhere in the house of anyone who might be his partner. There was a faint glimmer of hope when he said that a lady washed for him, but it was dashed when I found out that she only worked there in the daytime. At night, it would just be the two of us. He told me that his brother and family lived next door and that they had two daughters; I focused all of my attention on that fact to calm myself down. The tour ended and he retired to his room and me to mine. I slept fitfully, but the morning came and my fears had gone unrealized. More importantly, though, my trust in the opposite sex was starting to gradually be restored.

I quickly befriended the two young girls next door, and in no time, I trusted them. I pretended to be afraid of the dark so that they could come and sleep in the house with me at night. Soon, it became a regular thing

Follow me on Twitter: @avabrown24

for them to sleep over - the three of us sharing a room, and me sleeping soundly with their presence as protection. After being there for a few weeks, I realised that my uncle was prepared to be the father I never had. I became more relaxed about my living situation. Uncle started to teach me how to drive and trained me in the accounting practice so that I could help out with his business. He was concerned about my education, provided me with food, and gave me my first room by myself. Even though he was now the breadwinner for two, he never showed that he begrudged the financial assistance he gave to me. Because I handled his accounting, I knew that he wasn't hiding anything from me in regards to his money, and I flourished, having someone trust me so completely.

In many ways, that time in my life was like a dream. The two of us established a daughter-father relationship that I had never thought possible, and it was one that everyone admired. I was finally content with life and able to have the childhood I had been denied for so long; eating full meals, going to school and sleeping with ease. As with all things in life, though, that time was only temporary. For all of his responsible actions, my uncle was still a bachelor and wanted a partner to share his life with. An introduction to a young woman named Clementine brought that to fruition. Unfortunately, it also ushered in the end of our harmonious times.

Clementine wanted to become more involved in every aspect of his life, as new lovers often do. Soon, she started campaigning to take over the accounting from me. She quickly grew more courageous in her interrogations of me. She constantly questioned me about the real reason I was doing his accounts; hoping to discover that I was collecting money from his business for my personal benefit. I was extremely uncomfortable in her presence and started staying at my friend's house in the same district. Even though my uncle wasn't happy with me staying away so much, I needed to escape the intense atmosphere that Clementine was creating at his house.

Follow me on Twitter: @avabrown24

Eventually, I made the move to my friend's house permanent. I knew that broke my uncle's heart, but I felt it was for the best. I felt that I needed to be somewhere more stable and Clementine was securing her position even more firmly in my uncle's home, which did not promise to go well for me. I found out later that the relationship between my uncle and Clementine broke down irretrievably and that he had moved to the Cayman Island to find better work. That revelation helped to ease my conscience, since I knew that his situation would be better.

Meanwhile, I finished high school and started to plan for getting into college. The only person who came to mind to help me on that ambitious venture was my father, Dave; after all he owed me that much. I had heard from a friend that he was still living in Kingston, having made his residence there since Sarah had kicked him out of the house that fateful Christmas. I made the journey to Kingston by bus in search of Dave, with the hope that he would want to take any opportunity to make right the father-daughter relationship that he had treated so carelessly. Once there, I was surprised to find that he lived in a ghetto. He resided in a small hovel with his new partner and a whole new set of children. The conditions were dreadful! I felt awkward telling him my reason for coming to see him; I had finished high school and was there to seek his help to start college. I braved it anyway; after all, what did I have to lose by asking? His advice was to find a man who could look after me and send me to school. In his opinion, having a 'sugar daddy' was my only option. He had no sense of obligation to me; he felt he had done enough for me in my younger years. Night had fallen by the time we finished talking and it was too late for me to return home to St. Elizabeth. I ended up sleeping at his house on the filthy floor, atop a dirty mattress covered by a thin sheet. The pungent smell of faeces and stagnant water wafted in from the street outside through all the cracks in the doors and windows. The smell was so strong that you could taste it and I wondered how the rest of the family could breathe that putrid

Follow me on Twitter: @avabrown24

air every day.

While I slept that night, I dreamt that I went to the Ministry of Education and when I told them my plight, they helped me. I woke the next morning with full recollection of my dream, and a burning excitement about that possibility in my belly. I left the house, un-bathed and still in my clothes from the day before. My old yellow, rayon challis trousers and shirt were crushed like a spinach leaf, but I didn't let my dishevelled look deter me from my mission to go to the Ministry of Education. I was in Kingston, and I was a sixteen year-old girl with no fear of failure in her head. When I am in Kingston today, I am a scared wimp, even though I have the life experiences of my thirty-three years beneath me! I quickly boarded a bus and made my way to downtown Kingston with determination in my soul. As I boarded, I took one last look back in the direction of the pathetic ghetto where my father was living and thought, 'Well dad, that was your last chance to be in my life and fuck you! You blew it!'

The bus arrived in front of the Ministry at seven thirty am, far too early for a governmental office to be open. I posted myself in front of the Minister's office to wait for him to arrive. Every time the security guard passed me, he would give me a strange look; the intensity of my determination must have made me look as if I was crazy, but he never harassed me. The Ministry's staff was beginning to trickle in and they were not happy with my loitering. They tried every trick in the book to get me to leave, but I refused to budge, telling them that I had an urgent matter to discuss with Minister Burchell Whiteman.

It wasn't until about four in the afternoon that the staff finally realised I was not going to leave without seeing the Minister. A lady came out and told me that he had made time for me to come in and speak to him. I could see him in about half an hour. I began to consider my dishevelled, physical state. Man, my mouth stank! I could smell it each time I breathed out. I hadn't eaten since the day before and there was nothing around that I could use to wash it out or clear it of that bad smell. I bucked up and reminded myself that I had come that far and had no time for embarrassment over something as silly as my outward appearance. Soon enough, Minister Whiteman stepped out into the hallway where I was sitting, and kindly invited me to take a seat in his clean and comfy office.

I remember his calm voice putting me at ease as he expressed his admiration of my intense resilience. He said that he was intrigued to hear what I had to say that had given me the patience to wait so long while he finished the urgent duties of his post. I started to tell him my whole life story, leading up to what caused me to travel the long distance to Kingston and even how my dad had received me and what advice he had given me. I ended my plea by expressing my desire to become a lawyer and how it was necessary for me to go to college to make my dream come true, so that I can help others who were in my situation. He listened attentively and then gently told me the unfortunate news that their office couldn't provide any help for that particular desire of mine, but that he could offer me training to enter the career of teaching.

I was not interested in that field and began to reiterate my initial intended career path in law, but he quickly pointed out to me that I was not in a bargaining position. Instead of getting mad or asking me to leave his office, he briefly outlined the positive aspects of his offer and the reality of my situation. His words were not unkind when he told me that I could either take or leave the offer. Well, I was stubborn but I was not stupid; I grabbed at it! Since it was my hope to start my life anew and attend school in a different parish from the one I currently resided in, I asked if he could recommend me for matriculation at a Teacher's College in Montego Bay, St. James. To my utter delight, he agreed! I left his office with his promise that I would be going to college in September. My heart was so full of gratitude towards that kind man; a man who was asking nothing of me in return except my promise to live a full and productive life. The relief accompanying that momentous occasion in my life erupted in big wet tears. I had seen what perseverance could accomplish and I set it as my life's guiding light.

I went back to St. Elizabeth to give the great news to my uncle and the rest of my family. Since I would be living on campus, I asked different members of my family to help me procure each item I was going to need for my time there. That was just before my uncle left for Cayman, and he was kind enough to contact someone he knew in the local bank, Jamaica National, to secure a job for me. Beneath it all, he was sceptical of the Minister's promise and only wanted me to have something more secure so that I could make a living if everything fell through. I was touched by his continued show of genuine care for me, but I was certain that my dream was going to come true and I declined the job offer when it came through. Certainly, that path could have provided me a salary and some prestige among our largely unemployed community, but I wanted an education and a greater stability for my future.

I readied myself for the long trip to the Teacher's College to put in my formal application. It was a testament to how eager I was that I had already collected everything that I would need for attending the college before I had even applied! On arrival in Montego Bay, I went directly to the admissions office of the college and again started the waiting game. A secretary finally asked me what my purpose was and became furious when I told her that I had arrived to complete an application for the upcoming semester. She asked loudly, "Who do you think you are? Everyone applied back in April. You are two months too late." Her tone with those last words was final and she was set to walk away from me, but I wasn't about to let that rude and unpleasant woman push me aside and hinder me from reaching my goal. I trailed behind her; I apologised profusely and did not respond in anger to her insults. She laughed mockingly, stating that even if she allowed me to fill out the form, my application would only wind up in the waste bin. I offered her my reasoning that trying was all I could do and explained that it was really only her conscience that she would be dealing with if she chose to put my application in the trash.

She relented and gave the form to me with a flick of her wrist. I summoned my courage yet again to bravely ask for a pen, which she provided with an audible murmur. She told me not to spoil the forms and you can be as sure as hell I did just that. Suddenly, the enormity of what I was undertaking hit me; I became extremely nervous, my mind racing with the realisation that I was the first of my mother's children to even apply for college. But I remembered my lesson from the Minister's office about perseverance and I put the pen to paper.

When I had finished, I handed the document to the secretary and I could tell she was expecting a bunch of rubbish. Instead, I saw a great change come over her hardened face as she read. My stomach somersaulted as her mouth relaxed from its downturned pursing into an easy and calm form. She stood and ushered me from the waiting room into a more formal room, deeper inside the office, and there she helped me fill out a new form. It was during that time that I discovered the reason for her attitude change - we were from the same parish, St. Elizabeth. We finished the application session with her telling me that when I received my end of high school exam results, CXC or GCSE equivalent, I was to take them straight to her. When my results finally arrived in the following weeks, I was delighted to see that I had passed enough subjects to support my application for college, even though my English and Math scores were very low. However, when I delivered the results, I was elated to find out that I would be accepted to major in Secondary Education with specialisations in Home Economics and General Science.

Follow me on Twitter: @avabrown24

The rest of the summer flew by and September came along faster than any other time in my entire life. On the morning of my departure from St. Elizabeth to Montego Bay, I woke up with a stomach full of butterflies because I couldn't believe I was actually about to start college. I was full of anticipation for the next chapter of my life where peers who loved learning and were focused on bettering themselves and the world around them would surround me. Yet, when I arrived, it almost felt like primary school all over again. It was painfully obvious how much I stood out. I felt myself being transformed back into that poverty-stricken, mango-selling girl. Everyone else was dressed in the appropriate college uniform, but I was still wearing my old high school uniform, as the proper uniform was the one thing I could not acquire back home before I moved. I looked around the campus on my first day, I felt so small and insignificant. But a small voice in my head urged me forward, reminding me to never let such negative feelings overcome my ambitions.

I was relieved to see that the secretary from my previous visit to the college was the one now processing the new students. I quickly jumped into the line to get registered; however, I immediately noticed that everyone was carrying a pink slip that I had never seen before. I quietly asked the girl ahead of me, "What are these slips for?" In response, she loudly announced that it was the payment-of-fees slip and then asked how I could not know that, with an incredulous ring to her voice. Squinting her eyes at me, she asked, "Where is yours?" I mumbled some excuse and she turned her attention away from me. When I reached the top of the line, I spoke to the secretary about that issue, assuming that I would again find understanding and favour in how to rectify that new situation. That day, however, she exercised no tolerance and excused me from the line of students being processed.

As the day wore on, I stood with my belongings and watched everyone receive the assignment for their rooms and class schedules. I had hung around hoping that after all of the other students had been processed, the staff would find time to be sympathetic to my case and help me get everything resolved. While I waited, I met a girl who, realising my plight, offered to keep my luggage for me until I was able to sort out the situation. I accepted and then made my way to the office upstairs to ask if I could make a telephone call. That was before mobile phones, oh how times have changed! The office staff were busy with their registration duties and were not interested in listening to my distracting request.

Whenever a lady became available at one of the service windows, I would ask for the favour of using one of the office phones to make an emergency call. The response I got was a slamming of the glass window in my face. It happened so many times that afternoon that I lost count. As the evening hour approached, I had to change tactics. I went into the village to make the call to Minister Whiteman from a public phone box. The call rang through just as he was about to leave his office for the day. Looking back, I recognized that as just one of the many small miracles that have occurred throughout my life, and I know unmistakably that I should be returning the service back to Christ, who has never failed me. Even though I was crying hysterically into the phone, the Minister's secretary recognised me right away and quickly assured me that I had no need to worry. She told me that I just needed to calm down and take deep breaths.

Even after I quelled the tears, I could not fully let go of the overwhelming fear that my situation was falling apart before my eyes. I was frantic to get her to understand that I had no place to go back to in my district, telling her that the uncle I had lived with had gone to Cayman and I had no place to live. I reiterated that college was my only hope and registration was closing in the next few hours. She reassured me that she was going to call the school immediately and get everything sorted out.

Follow me on Twitter: @avabrown24

I finally calmed down and went back to the school's registration office.

The same rude lady who had slammed her window shut on me multiple times faced me when I returned. As I approached, her phone began to ring and she again slammed the window shut. I stood in stillness and waited. Eventually, she gently reopened the window and handed the telephone handset through to me. I was afraid to take the phone from her at first, in case she was planning to slam the window down onto my hand in an effort to make me go away once and for all. But instead, she simply handed it over to me. My timid "hello" was answered by the most important voice I had heard to date. It was Minister Whiteman on the line telling me not to worry and reassuring me that everything would be all right.

The lady at the window beckoned for the handset to be returned and, without any preamble, provided me with a room assignment. I didn't know what Minister Whiteman told the registration staff, but whatever it was landed me in college. I felt as if I had been lifted by the wings of angels, even more so when I arrived at the door of my room to find my roommate was that very same girl who had earlier taken my bags for safekeeping. Whether that was a mere coincidence or God in action, you decide. I was finally starting college and it was the most joyous event that had ever occurred in my young life.

"Our entry into the world is most met with laughter and tears of joy; do we cry as we are fearful or hopeful?"

Follow me on Twitter: @avabrown24

Chapter Four

COMFORT ZONE

"Far too often we hide behind that which makes us comfortable,

looking for a shelter from the truth of our pain and sadness

as they are too difficult and devastating to confront."

———————

Campus life provided a degree of freedom I hadn't yet known. It was a new and different environment and I liked it. I felt like I had a place to call home now, with a new family consisting of my classmates and teachers. All freshmen went through an initiation called 'grubbing', a form of hazing, which occurred during the first two weeks of college and was headed by the seniors. The senior students would come into the dorm rooms and wake freshmen up at five in the morning. The activities they would have us do varied each day. Sometimes it was running laps, sometimes it was enduring toothpaste being placed on our eyelids. There were all sorts of crazy things they came up with to torture us, but it was all done in good nature and to foster camaraderie between us and the older students. I wound up making friends with several of the seniors, one who even gave me a uniform to wear so that I could immediately start to blend in and understand what it was like to be one of a group.

As the term progressed, I came to realise that the students who had grubbed us at the beginning of the term were the very same ones who were most willing to share their food and their knowledge. They were the ones who were available to give advice on how to cope with exam stress and campus life; many of us were not accustomed to the workload our teachers were piling on us, or living away from home. All of the students were expected to return home at the end of term for a break from the burdens of campus life, but I had no real home to go to and the impending event made me extremely anxious.

When the day finally came, my classmates were all packing their things excitedly. They chattered about whom they were going to see and the home cooked meals they were going to eat. I stayed quiet and lingered around until I was the last one left. Of course, the housemother noticed and I had to explain to her that unlike all the other girls, I really had nowhere else to go. I was so relieved when she took pity on me and allowed me to stay in my room during the Christmas break, but she warned me that was a one-time thing and I couldn't count on it to become my regular situation during the term breaks. I didn't care about anything so far in the future at that moment and I just thanked her profusely for saving me that day.

Despite the grant I received from the Ministry of Education to pay my tuition, I still had to come up with money for all the miscellaneous things that come along with living on campus and attending classes. Occasionally, my mother would send a small amount of money, but it was so little and infrequent that many times I couldn't even afford sanitary napkins for

Follow me on Twitter: @avabrown24

my monthly flow. I would save up some old pieces of cloth, which I would carefully roll around the crotch of my underwear to catch the blood; these didn't work very well and it was an embarrassing chore to wash them out at the end of each day so that they could be reused. I was sure everyone knew when I was menstruating, especially because I would only wear my royal blue skirt during those days of bleeding to hide the stain better if there happened to be a leak. On the occasions when that happened, I could always feel it before I saw it. So, I would wait until the classroom had emptied and then I would walk by myself to my room, using my books to cover my bottom.

While on campus I made friends quickly and involved myself in all sorts of activities, which helped keep me occupied during my free hours. After all, I didn't have the hours of chores to attend to that I used to have when I was attending secondary or primary school. I found that the social activities served to keep all of my negative thoughts at bay. My closest friend at that time was Jenn. She quickly proved herself to be someone I could trust and confide in. We were like kindred spirits, as we had come from similar backgrounds. I was shocked and a bit thrilled to find out that she, too, had nowhere to live. She made me feel not so alone in my circumstance. My loneliness was soon to take a turn. One day I was on campus, rushing to get to class, when I met the man who was to become my first husband; though I had no clue of it at the time. His name was Tobore and he was an extremely attractive guy, with freckles and just the most handsome, youthful face I had ever seen.

Soon we were hanging out as friends and although I thought he was terribly handsome, I did not see him as someone I would have a relationship with. As a matter of fact, I didn't think a guy like that would have any interest in someone like me. At that stage of my life, my self-esteem was non-existent. Jenn, however, was convinced that he liked me from the very start. I had even tried to set him up with one of my other classmates; a pretty girl named Syria - just to prove Jenn wrong. I was steadfastly refusing to let anything interfere with my college education, as it was all I could count on to secure my future.

When the summer arrived that year, Jenn and I were literally chased off campus by our housemother. With neither of us having any need to return to our districts, together we rented a single room in a house owned by a Mr. Brown in Catherine Hall, Montego Bay. Over the next few months, he grew to be a surrogate father to the both of us. He knew that we could not afford the rent or food, but he let us stay and fed us anyway, accepting any amount that we could afford to pay him from the odd jobs we found around the city.

That was how we survived the summer of 1994. At times, we would laugh or cry at the irony of our situation. Here we were, training to educate the next generations of our communities so that they could be successful and live full lives, but we were practically homeless. We would stay up late at night and talk about our dreams and goals, and how we looked forward to the start of our second year. I knew that my grant from the Ministry of Education was limited to my first year, so I had to start applying for grants and tuition assistance. In a short time, I secured a student loan from the Students' Loan Bureau. Even though it was not free money and the loan was not to be paid back until after I graduated, securing it eased my fears about not being able to complete my education.

A few weeks into my second year, my mum contacted me to say that the man I had always claimed as my father, Dave, was petitioning the courts to have a change made on my birth certificate. I immediately assumed that somehow it had to do with him denying me, but instead she told me that he wanted to give me his last name. What was the need I wondered? I had always used my mother's last name, the shameful mark of a truly fatherless child that no man wanted to claim as his own flesh and blood. Now, at seventeen years old, I considered the idea with a more rational mind.

I realised that I had survived that long without having a paternal family name or the favours that I thought that would have brought. While this gesture was not the cause of any great celebration on my part, I could not bring myself to object to it. Looking back, I suppose I let the change happen for sentimental reasons... to respect the child I had once been who would have rejoiced at that moment. My new birth certificate arrived by mail and I felt nothing when I saw my new name boldly printed on the official document; Ava-Gaye Beckford became Ava-Gaye Brown. I filed the paper away without another thought, having no idea how that change would haunt me in my adult years.

Academically speaking, I was doing well and my grades were higher than many of my peers. I think my successes in the classroom were largely due to the fact that I stayed on campus over the weekends, with nothing else to do but study, while many of the other girls went on trips or travelled home. One evening, I was completing some coursework in the computer lab when Tobore appeared. I asked why he was not out with our friend Syria. I had arranged a date with her for him, and was shocked by his bold reply, "I'm not interested in her. Don't you know that you are the one I am interested in?"

Tobore's confession awoke something inside of me and I almost instantaneously realised that I had feelings for him too. The fact that we immediately started dating came as no surprise to Jenn. My relationship with Tobore had many unexpected benefits. My whole life seemed to become easier, more pleasurable, and I was now seeing the sunshine in the sky instead of the clouds, and the flowers covering the ground instead of the weeds. We spent all of our spare time together. He was my escape, my new everything. My friends started teasing me, saying that I was no longer available.

Follow me on Twitter: @avabrown24

At the beginning, I worried that my newfound relationship might act as a distraction from my studies, but I managed to remain focused. On Tobore's part, he supported me and helped me with my coursework. He was extremely caring and treated me with the utmost respect. In those times of the month when I would experience chronic pain from uterine cramping during my menstruation, due to a condition I later learned is called dysmenorrhoea, he was my nurse. I was so touched by his careful attention to me that I could not help but tell him how much I loved him. That was my first experience of love in any shape or form in my mind. We took our relationship to the next level and I was comfortable and ready; I felt safe, loved, and complete.

It did not escape me that the reason I gravitated towards that man and felt so at ease in his presence was because of the healthy affection he showed me, all without expecting anything in return except for my happiness. It was so refreshingly different from the previous concept I'd had of men. He was in no hurry to be involved with me sexually and I felt such a relief to not have that expectation weighing down our time together. We cultivated a deep and trusting relationship and I felt secure in the knowledge that he genuinely cared for me.

As any new couple would be, we were curious about one another's history. When he would ask about my family, though, I found it difficult to openly share that information, as it was a source of embarrassment for me. He was also from St. Elizabeth, and I suppose that fact made me guard my tongue as well. After we had been dating for a few months, we took a long weekend trip back to visit our home parish. During our travels, I plucked up the courage to tell him about my family and my trials growing up among them. I was uncertain of how he would react, but I believed that if he truly loved me, he would not see my past as tarnishing my present character.

Follow me on Twitter: @avabrown24

He listened intently and was very understanding. We played the song 'Somewhere Out There', by Linda Ronstadt, and sang along to it at the top of our lungs. It was such a cathartic release and he fully claimed my heart.

Tobore and I fell into an easy routine after we returned from St. Elizabeth. He would pick me up after classes and I would stay some nights at his place. He cooked for the both of us and we grew closer. I was doing well in school and I was in love with a man who was also in love with me. He would send me roses for no particular reason and there was nothing expected of me in return. I never had to ask him for money; he would somehow know when I needed it and never begrudged helping me. I had finally found comfort and stability in my life and I wanted it to stay that way forever.

My third and final year of college arrived before I knew it. Part of the senior year curriculum included teaching in assigned schools for a term, after which our practical skills would be assessed by an external examiner for certification to obtain employment upon graduation. When the term of the teaching internship came to a close, we threw the traditional celebration that was called 'burying the TP' (teaching practice). That event was carried out as a symbolic burying of all the stress from our teaching practice, with the hope that we would all pass the evaluation and successfully move forward into our adult lives.

Tobore had moved to Kingston to find employment in the latter part of my third year. I was dismayed that we weren't able to keep in regular contact, but I was busy enough with my own responsibilities of finishing my education. I was able to visit him in Kingston once or twice during that time, but the fact that he was living at his sister's house was an added strain on our relationship because it was inappropriate for us to stay there together. When my graduation day came, Tobore was busy at work in

Kingston and could not attend. Even though my mum and sister were there to support me, my heart was broken by his absence.

I felt blessed to have my mum there with me and I told her so. She was proud of me, and I could see it on her face. I took the time to reflect on what I had achieved over those past three years and I was even more proud of myself. Graduating from college was the single greatest achievement in my life. I returned to St. Elizabeth with my diploma in hand and settled myself back in my aunt's house.

My relationship with Tobore had begun to see challenges and began to deteriorate, but I had to focus my energies on finding a job to support myself. After more than one hundred and twenty applications and one hundred and twenty turndowns or non-replies, I was losing hope. Finally, I applied for a position at the school where my aunt worked and was offered the job (with a little help from my Aunt). Someone finally believed that a nineteen year-old college graduate could be an effective teacher! The job was only for one term, but to me it was better than nothing. My student loan repayments were coming due and I didn't want to be a burden to my aunt for much longer.

The evening before I was to start my first day of work, a call came from the head teacher of the school. Thinking she was calling with last minute instructions for me, I was shocked to hear her say that the teacher whose position I was going to take had reconsidered quitting and wanted her job back. The bottom line was that there was no job for me.

How could that be? My heart sank further with every word. The lady apologised but said that there wasn't anything else she could do. I hung up the phone and crumbled into deep cries of despair. I had my loans to repay and wanted desperately to have my own place. After all, hadn't I achieved my qualification to escape that exact situation?

When the tears finally stopped, I began to plan a re-start of my job search to begin immediately in the morning. However, God must have heard my cry, because before the moon came out, I received another phone call. The call was from the head of Food and Nutrition of Ardenne High School in Kingston. She said that she was looking for someone to fill a teaching position immediately and that she had heard from my education officer that I was a capable young graduate. The job would be mine if I could make it to Kingston by eight a.m. the next morning.

I owned only one interview suit, which was currently in the wash because, just hours before, I had believed my job hunt was finished. I jumped into action, washed it and placed it behind the fridge to dry. I didn't know how I was going to be able to make the eight a.m. deadline, but that wasn't about to stop me from trying! I woke before the crack of dawn and by 5:30a.m I was on the bus heading to Kingston. I arrived at the school right on time.

Again, the job that was offered was short-term, but I took it anyway. I hadn't had time to find anywhere to stay in Kingston. I considered finding Tobore and asking to stay with him, but quickly decided against it. Instead, I remembered an uncle who was living in Portmore, a town near enough to Kingston that I could travel to work every day without much hassle. The minute I arrived at his place, I was given approval to stay, but knew it would not be an enjoyable time. As I looked around the dilapidated room, I heard a voice telling me 'beggars can't be choosers' and I resolved to make the best of my situation. After all, I had a job and I would be making my own money.

I worked at Ardenne for only a few days before the same lady who had hired me told me about a new vacancy at a nearby High School. She explained that the job would be 'a bit more permanent' than the one I was currently in at her school. I told her that I was interested and she called to arrange the interview. She even drove me to the interview. Her kindness made me wonder if she was an angel sent to guide me. I wound up getting the job at the high school and started immediately. I had felt torn and disloyal accepting the job, but she encouraged me to look at my long-term future. The new job would put me in a better position, both financially and in terms of experience.

Tobore and I had reconnected since my arrival in the city and he helped me look for a place that I could afford on my own. Soon after we started looking, I rented a room in a house that was close to my new workplace. My move to Kingston seemed to be a double blessing, as it also helped Tobore and I mend our relationship. Even though we had not officially ended things, we definitely had drifted apart. Over time, he began staying over at my place and I remembered why I loved being with him and recognised that I was ready to take our relationship to the next level. Things moved on well for Tobore and me during that time in our young adult lives. I even became friends with the girl who was dating Tobore's older brother. Her name was Constance and she was very kind, funny, principled, and just a genuine girl. We are still friends, almost like sisters. She now lives in Africa, where she works as a missionary, but that hasn't affected our bond.

Tobore and I took one more trip to St. Elizabeth, and this time, I was to meet his parents. For me, it was an uncomfortable introduction. My eyes grew wide when we drove up to their house; it was what I considered to be a mansion! I immediately felt inadequate and out of place. Of course, his parents inquired about my family and background, but I had no idea what to say. In my head I played out the honest conversation: "Well, my mum is unemployed, has kids with two different fathers, and lives in a one room shack where we all used to wake up wet with pee because someone was always wetting the single bed that we shared. My stepdad is also unemployed and has been ever since his job was made redundant at the rice factory, which happened about ten years ago. I really didn't even know who my real father is, but the man who has claimed me as his daughter tried to molest me when I was twelve."

Just imagining the looks on their faces was enough to make me shiver! Here I was, trying to make a good first impression, and all I could do was try my best to sidestep their questions about my family. The entire visit was awkward. On our journey back to Kingston, Tobore assured me that they would warm up to me in time, but I was sceptical. To me, it seemed as if his parents and sister did not think I was good enough for him. I was torn and confused, wondering if I should just break it off immediately to spare us both the disaster that was sure to come in the future. In all seriousness, though, I did begin to question the realistic chances of our relationship lasting long-term.

When my year teaching at the high school came to an end, I found out that the post would not be renewed and that it was time for me to start looking for another job. Finding another teaching job in Kingston proved to be a difficult task, and soon I was applying for jobs outside of the region. I was finally offered a job to teach Home Economics in Manchester. The thought of a move was not appealing to me and even less so to Tobore, who said that he might not be able to follow me because of his steady job in Kingston. But we both realised the reality of our situation; he could not afford to have me at home as a kept girlfriend and it wasn't my ambition either. I also felt the break would do us good.

Accepting that new job bolstered my sense of independence. I would be moving to a new place and starting my life anew. As soon as I got settled, I purchased my first set of furniture on hire. I chose a rather luxurious sofa, dining table, and bed, along with a few other pieces. In my heart, I was intending to make my flat comfortable for my man and myself. My hope that Tobore would soon visit me was ever present in my mind. I strived to make my apartment look like the home I had always dreamed of.

In time, I realised that I liked being on my own, but some parts of me desperately missed Tobore's company. I looked forward to every one of his visits. He always arrived bearing tons of presents, but most importantly, he would bring his love to me. Our lovemaking in these times was passionate, and every minute I spent tightly pressed up against his naked body was no less than amazing. We were carefree but committed to each other.

My new job was challenging but exciting; I was learning a lot and enjoying it immensely. When October came around though, I was starting to feel very tired and was having a hard time making it through the days. Then, I started feeling frequently nauseous. One day I entered my food and nutrition practical room not feeling well. I couldn't figure out what was wrong with me. My students started to tease me about being pregnant. I laughed with them, thinking how ridiculous the idea of me being a mum was; it was unimaginable!

I was still at that age when you thought you were invincible, the age when something as adult as pregnancy can't happen to you. Tobore and I had never really discussed having children, and frankly, it was the furthest thing from my mind at that time in my life. I was having fun, we just loved our time and I didn't want anything to change that. However, one day when I fainted in the middle of teaching one of my classes, my friend Gloria took matters into her own hands and insisted that I go on a doctor's visit. I relented and made an appointment for that evening after work. In all honesty, I was avoiding the situation because I was scared of what the doctor might say. What if he discovered I had a mysterious illness or a brain tumour? How would I afford all of the medical care and time off work? What would Tobore do if he had to take care of me every day while I wasted away until I died? Such silly thoughts from a silly girl! Would he even stay with me?

When the doctor asked my symptoms, he immediately ordered a

pregnancy test, which I thought was preposterous. I kindly declined, not wanting to waste my money on something that I didn't need, but when he insisted, I complied. The doctor returned with the results in a few minutes. I was all ready to roll my eyes at him, but when he delivered the news that I was pregnant, I felt the earth move beneath me. I was confused and disorientated. The silliest questions spilled from my mouth. "How could that be?", "When did that happen?" It was the doctor's turn to roll his eyes. After a few calming words, he dismissed me home. Yet, he had not answered my most important question: "Why now?!"

"What makes us ultimately happy is sometimes disguised in shadows of turmoil."

Chapter Five

NEW LIFE APPEARS

"Hidden happiness awaits us if we stop to see beyond the now,

only that is most times almost impossible."

The doctor's office was far from my home and I was so distraught that I couldn't think straight, so I hailed a taxi. That trip home seemed much longer than it was in reality. I sat in the back of the car, not speaking to the driver and simply overwhelmed with panicked thoughts. Being pregnant and unwed meant that I was going to lose my job, which in turn meant that I would have no way to pay for all the furniture I had just bought or the rent on my apartment, which meant that I was going to be homeless! Not only would my grand attempt at independence be an absolute failure, I would also be an utter embarrassment to my family and everyone who had faith enough in me to help me along the way. I couldn't stop the tears when a thought struck me: There is no way to break the cycle you were born into, girl.

Follow me on Twitter: @avabrown24

As soon as I reached my home, I phoned Tobore and told him that he needed to come see me. While I waited for his arrival, I paced the floor of my apartment. The doctor estimated that I was about two or three months along already, which meant that I had already been pregnant when I moved into that place. My thoughts quickly turned into a petulant conversation with God. I asked why He couldn't have let me know earlier, so I wouldn't have wasted my time on the move, wasted my money on the furniture. I asked why He didn't care enough to help save me the hassle, why He had allowed me to finally feel a bit of comfort in the false knowledge that my life was finally coming together. A mocking little voice crept into my head, reminding me of where I was from and that I needed to just accept the sad life laid out for me; a life of being considered a community's property and serving without question. The voice grew stronger and more challenging, asking, who do you think you are? Just how stupid are you to believe that you can change the history and lineage of so many women that came before you?

Tobore arrived very quickly, although to me it felt like hours had passed. I blurted out the news, my thoughts having worked me into a complete frenzy and my beaten spirit was just waiting for the next awful thing to happen...for him to leave me. To my great surprise, however, he took the news much better than I had. A giant smile spread across his face. He was excited, but I was baffled about what he could possibly find exciting about my predicament. As he said soothing words to calm me down, my mind continued to work. I reflected on the opposite roles that a man and a woman played in that situation of life. Really, a man had nothing to lose when a girlfriend (not a wife) told him she was pregnant with his child. He would still have his job and he wouldn't lose his figure. Oh, I hadn't even thought about that aspect yet; I was about to lose the perfect, taut young body and wicked curves that I suddenly realised I had and never truly appreciated. I instinctively put my hand on my belly and thought about how men didn't have to face the massive changes that come with carrying a baby. I wondered if he would love me after I became all pudgy and round, after giving birth to his child.

As Tobore continued to hold me close and reassure me, I began to calm down. That night, he made such tender love to me that I felt my heart might burst. His arms made me feel secure and I began to believe that things would work out after all. We lay in bed deep into the night, tangled in each other's arms, discussing what would happen next. As the morning hours came upon us, we came to the decision that I would move back to Kingston; there really was no other option, but a part of me resented it because I still desperately wanted to be independent and live on my own. I was also confused and a bit ashamed by my childish desire to simply run home to a mum that could give me the nurturing that I needed at that moment, but that wasn't an option either, since my mother wasn't a loving, empathetic, or encouraging type of mum.

Tobore was the person I would have to rely on through that situation and I recognised the truth in his words when he said that I would eventually have to move from Christiana back to Kingston. I was resolved to that decision the next morning when I went to my school and delivered the news to my head of department that I was pregnant. She listened quietly and then informed me that I would have to give up the job as my time there hadn't even exceeded a single term of classes yet. She reminded me that I had signed the contract acceding to the school policy, which forbade employment in that exact type of situation. Inwardly, I was screaming out about the gross unfairness of it all, but outwardly, I kept my mouth shut because I knew there was nothing to be done.

Tobore and I immediately made plans for my move and, before I knew it, I was moved out of my little apartment and back in Kingston. On arrival,

Tobore brought me to the large house he was still sharing with his sister. His plan was for me to spend at least a few nights there while we got an independent living arrangement established. However, that was short lived as his sister wasn't very happy with the idea, and my heart sank when Tobore made no attempt to sway the decision.

I sat in tears, again overwhelmed by my situation; I was jobless, pregnant, and now homeless, without the protection of the man whose child I was carrying. I was so disappointed with Tobore, even though he continued to try to find a place for me to live without him. Tobore approached a friend who lived with his girlfriend and their child and they agreed to take me in. Lucky for me, they turned out to be lovely people and they treated me well and welcomed me warmly into their small home. But their kindness made me sad and I felt as if I was invading their privacy and adding an unnecessary burden to their lives.

When my friends found out about my situation, many of them couldn't understand why I was living in these strangers' home when my man was living in a large house that could have easily accommodated me, as well as our imminent child. I was always filled with shame when I had to explain the circumstance of his sister's disapproval that had brought us to that situation. A few weeks after I began staying with his friends, I was surprised and delighted when Tobore suggested that we find somewhere for the two of us to live together. As soon as we settled into our new place, he sent word back to his family in St. Elizabeth that we were living together and I was pregnant with his child; they received the news tentatively. I understood the reasoning behind their hesitation. I was certain they were harbouring an unexpressed belief that I had become pregnant on purpose to trap him. Nothing was further from the truth.

I was still worrying that by starting a family so young, I would be wasting my bachelor's degree and impeding my chances of getting anywhere in life. But life moves on. Tobore and I settled into our life together and started preparing for the birth of our child. However, his family did not warm up to the situation too well. I felt a deep sense of guilt as I watched his relationship with them become strained and contentious. I remember on New Year's Eve that year, Tobore phoned his parents to send season's greetings, but after the discussion, he seemed sad. I knew that something negative had been said about our situation and I felt like running away so that he could be rid of that burden and find peace again with his family. I knew that they were really disappointed with how everything was turning out between us and with the baby on the way. Tobore would often try to hide their disappointment and disapproval from me, but I could always tell what was being said on the other end of the phone just by the look on his face. Even though he had finally started standing up for us as a couple, it pained me to realise why he hadn't in the first place; the emotional beating he was taking for me was almost unbearable.

I was still working on finding ways to improve my standing in the world, and another step towards independence was learning to drive a car. Tobore had one but never taught me how to operate it, so I took it upon myself to learn. I remembered what little my uncle had taught me years ago. I began to sneak the car out at night while Tobore slept. Even with my growing belly in the way, I was soon able to expertly manoeuvre the vehicle. Although I was pretty certain that Tobore wouldn't get mad at me if I crashed the car, I was constantly worried that the police would be on my back if I got into an accident. Luckily, that never happened.

After living in our first rented place for only three months, Tobore and I had to move out of it because the landlord absolutely refused to fix anything and the place rapidly became unliveable. We started thinking about the need to have more space once our little one arrived. We were blessed to find a two-bedroom house in a much cleaner and safer neighbourhood. Our lives continued to move along and we found more comfort in one another with each passing day. Soon, we began to talk about marriage and that turned into a formal engagement, even though we had no idea when a wedding would be feasible.

At that time, Tobore was working as a shipping agent, that meant that he had to travel frequently and I was at home by myself most of the time. To stave off the feelings of isolation and loneliness, I began writing. Putting my life's story down on paper proved to be therapeutic. I finally got the nerve to tell my mum about my pregnancy and engagement, but her response, as always, was rather unemotional and I wasn't sure how she really felt. Her lack of response made me feel so anxious I lost my appetite. Looking back, I can now see that I was in fact in a deep depression during this time. Not having the support of my family, nor of my future in-laws or their extended family, some of whom lived a mere ten minutes walk away from our place, weighed heavily on me. I wondered if that situation was hinting at how they would treat my child when it finally arrived into the world.

I tried reaching out to the few friends that I had in Kingston, but they were busy with work. I had no one to talk to about my concerns and anxieties about being a new mother and successfully caring for that new life that would be entrusted to me. There was no one to help me strategize how I was to restart my career after the pregnancy was over. Tobore was as supportive as he could be, but it wasn't enough, I needed a female who understood the challenges facing the fairer sex.

During that time, however, Tobore was my whole world, and I couldn't have asked for a better partner. He had grown very courageous, standing up to anyone who insulted or challenged me and our unborn child. He made sure that I didn't miss a single doctor's visit, paying for all of them and even attending them with me whenever his work schedule allowed. I had become confident in his love for me; all of his efforts made me feel happy and secure. Despite the challenges we faced on a daily basis, we still had fun. The days and nights inside our little home were filled with laughter, playfulness, and utter joy. Oh, how I loved him!

I would sometimes get to travel with him when he went out of town for work. I loved these trips; for me, they were a vacation. On one such trip to Ocho Rios, I got the chance to meet a famous female songstress who was my favourite Jamaican artiste at the time. I had been wandering around the hallway outside our hotel room moaning about wanting to go with Tobore to the concert she would be performing at that night, when she happened to walk past us! I had no idea she was staying at the same hotel as we were. Tobore was bold enough to strike up a conversation with her and ask her to talk some sense into to me about the fact that I was too far into my pregnancy to go to a concert full of jostling people. She was so kind and offered me an autographed card as consolation for not being in any condition to go see her perform. That placated me enough so that I didn't hassle Tobore when he left with his work colleagues to see the show.

We decided that it was best to get married before the baby arrived and began planning the ceremony in earnest. When we decided on the date and made the announcement to everyone, time went by with no word from his family to say that they were coming. I didn't know if they contacted Tobore separately to deny or accept the request; he was too kind to tell me. I resigned myself to the possibility that he and I might be the only ones there.

We were wed in March of 1998 in a simple ceremony, surrounded by about twenty friends and family, including Tobore's parents! I wore a white wedding dress that had been made by one of my friends who worked in a nearby embassy, whose daughter I had taught in high school. We had to use a ton of fabric to accommodate my ever-expanding belly, as my due date was only two months away. The wedding was nice, but it was nothing like I had dreamt of as a child. Like so many other women, I had always pictured myself surrounded by a grand court of bridesmaids, my groom supported by his court of groomsmen, the maid of honour next to my side, the best man next to his, and a ring bearer and flower girls. My wedding was far from the fairy tale. We did get to have the ceremony in a church though, which I had worried about, since most churches frowned on marrying a woman so obviously full of child. We even had a small reception at a well-respected heritage site in Kingston that Tobore had been able to secure because of his family name.

I remember being so relieved when I saw Tobore's parents sitting in the church. The dread that had been gripping my heart in the weeks before, finally relaxed. His sister didn't attend though, and her failure to come, even though her residence was in the same town, was a show of her disapproval. As for my family, only a distant cousin made it to the wedding. I remember looking around at the small crowd that had gathered for the ceremony and feeling utter happiness at marrying someone as wonderful as Tobore while feeling our baby kicking in my belly. However, that was tempered by the realisation that so few members of our families were present to share in the celebration with us. I began to grow anxious again about the reality of our situation; we were setting out in life on our own, without a strong support system behind us to help if we faltered.

We never planned to take a formal honeymoon. In some ways, the wedding itself was mainly carried out to help ease some of the shame our families, more so his, must have been feeling because of my pregnancy. I remember someone asking me if I would have married Tobore if I hadn't been pregnant. My answer was a solid yes; I was madly in love with him. The pregnancy rushed our timing, but I like to think that we were such a good fit that our relationship would have survived and we would have eventually made it to the altar.

The close and easy relationship that I craved to have with his parents did not come about, even after we were married. I had hoped that once I became Tobore's wife and a legal member of his family, they would finally let their guard down and accept me, but that was just a dream.

"They say nothing worth having comes easily, yet we could benefit from balls thrown at us that weren't always curved."

Chapter Six
BROKEN

"Sometimes we go through life feeling broken and something magical happens to change that, like the birth of an innocent life."

I was in my third trimester and still very ill on a regular basis. I had to carry a paper bag full of medicine wherever I went, to help keep the nausea from turning into violent vomiting. When we were in the car, I would have to ask Tobore to pull over so I could throw up on the side of the road. Certain smells, like Irish Spring soap or the Styrofoam cups from Wendy's and Burger King would trigger a severe nausea. The doctor even prescribed Gravol injections, but they were painful and the trip to the office to get the injection made it almost not worth the relief that they brought.

I was so tired of all the medication and the continued feeling of illness. I tried on several occasions to reach out to my in-laws, hoping that I would hear some excitement in their voices about the upcoming birth or comfort about the natural state of my condition. But there was little advice or support offered through kind words. My doctor often told me that my illness wasn't entirely physical, but a result of the extreme emotional and psychological torment I was feeling at the time. I tried to force myself to overcome the feeling of rejection and my desperate need to feel accepted. But my efforts were to no avail. I believed that if I were nicer or more solicitous they would grow to love me. But each visit to their house ended with me feeling even more like an uninvited and unwanted guest. In reflection, some of these feeling were my own insecurities. Tobore worked hard to make me feel included, and eventually he got his parents and sister to ease up on their cold attitude towards me. My illness got milder when the tension from his family eased. I was filled with hope that our relationship would only continue to progress, especially for the sake of our child, who would certainly need the love and acceptance of both sides of the family.

A few weeks after our wedding, Tobore's sister announced that she was expecting a baby also. I was thrilled to hear the news because I was sure that our shared condition would help to improve our relationship. After all, she and I were now in the same boat, at least somewhat. One day, when I was home alone, I felt a strange calmness in my belly; the baby wasn't moving. In a panic, I checked myself into one of our discussed private Christian hospitals and the emergency staff went into overdrive. The number of injections I got was shocking! I had no idea what was wrong, but it seemed serious by their treatment of me. When I became stabilized, the consultant at the hospital discharged me to home with the advice that I needed absolute rest and strict instructions for no solid foods; I was only allowed broth.

Tobore was in the middle of a big project at work and felt that I was not fit to be on my own, so he took me to his sister's home. He outlined to her that I needed to just be on broth and no solid food and I was left to rest in my husband's old room. However, when dinner was prepared, there was no broth in sight. I was shocked to find that dinner was fried chicken from a local fast food chain restaurant. The chicken broth and olive branch of peace I was expecting wasn't offered and I retreated back to my room and cried silently. Did she disapprove of me so badly that she would risk my life, as well as that of her future niece or nephew? I left and went back to my own home as I knew that sort of rejection would only make me feel worse since I was continuing to be so severely ill.

Nearly eight months into my pregnancy, we decided to change my doctor. We had become increasingly concerned for his lack of care and professionalism that we thought it best to make a change. That added a new stress to the end of my pregnancy, but I did start to feel a bit better under the new doctor's care.

We were busy planning for the baby's impending arrival. Tobore and I started writing down baby names we both liked. We had a good set of options for either sex; if it was a boy, we thought of Matthew or Michael, and if it was a girl we liked Jasmine, Tempest, Tonya (after a student of mine, who was the daughter of the lady who'd made my wedding dress), April, or Ginell. I particularly loved the names Tonya and Jasmine. Our excitement was contagious and my friends Jenna, Arlete, Janiz and Violet organised a baby shower for me. When I arrived at the room full of my friends, I felt such a strong sense of love. I realised that I had finally cultivated a family of friends who cared for me and loved me as much as a blood family should.

One day, shortly after the shower, I began to feel unwell. I had a suspicion that something was wrong and I soon had convinced myself that I hadn't felt the baby move in three days. Tobore was working in town and I didn't want to alarm him, so I went to see my doctor on my own and she advised that I get checked into the hospital right away. Tobore and I had already decided that we would have the baby in a private hospital and we had chosen one which was not far from our home and the doctor's office. On arrival, I was admitted for observation. The initial examination revealed that my blood pressure was far too high and within minutes, the consultant informed me that they needed to perform an emergency caesarean section. At that point, I knew I had to phone Tobore and tell him what was about to happen. When I reached him, he assured me that he was on his way and would arrive at the hospital as soon as possible. I was very scared at the prospect of having to undergo surgery. The situation was extremely daunting and I wished there was a friend's hand to hold.

The hospital staff changed me into an open dressing gown that provided no privacy. But my embarrassment was soon overshadowed by the discomfort of having to lay spread-eagle and the extreme pain of having a urinary catheter inserted without any aesthetic. I cried and prayed for it all to be over soon. Just as they finished prepping me for surgery, Tobore arrived. He was allowed to walk alongside my gurney, holding my hand, up to the entrance of the surgical theatre. I will never forget the feel of his kiss or the smell of his sweet sweaty brow as he leaned over to kiss me. He whispered that he loved me and assured me that he would see me in a bit. I was sure I was going to die and that was my goodbye kiss.

The anaesthesiologist told me she would give me something that would make me feel sleepy and that I would soon fall into a deep sleep. As she started her work on me, I anxiously looked around the room and was horrified to see all the various apparatuses waiting for unknown uses. I broke out in a cold sweat. I had never been given an anaesthetic before and I kept thinking of the stories of people who were given a general aesthetic and never woke up. I tried desperately to calm myself down by thinking about the moment I was going to see the beautiful face of my child for the first time. Everyone had speculated that I was going to have a son, based on their assessment of the shape of my belly and other body signs that I didn't understand. I conjured up the image of my beautiful baby boy and welcoming him into the world and that was the last thought I had before everything went dark.

I awoke in a haze. My thoughts were so muddled, but there was a definite recognition of pain in my belly. It felt like I had been chopped with a machete right through my lower abdomen wall. I could tell that someone was talking to me but the words being spoken made no sense to me. I could make out a jolly voice saying, "You have a lovely girl!" I told myself I must be dreaming and that I should go back to sleep to await the announcement of a boy. I fell back into the solid darkness of unconsciousness. I was aware of the jostling of the bed as a porter transported me to a room for post-surgery recovery. I awoke just long enough to ask that person to please slow down and be gentle, only to hear a soothing voice tell me that we were going very slowly and smoothly, but I would feel the discomfort because I had a fresh wound.

Discomfort was not the word to describe the feeling I awoke to. Never before had I experienced such immense pain! I gritted my teeth and held back from sobbing as my loving husband leaned over me and began telling me all about the beautiful baby girl we had. He was so excited; his whole outlook on the world seemed changed. He gushed unashamedly at what a proud father he was. I was overcome with happiness and my reason for weeping was now because of our shared experience. I was finally happy, he was finally happy, we were finally happy together without the restraints that had been holding us back from one another and our blessed life together.

I told Tobore that I wanted to name our little miracle Winter, but when my father-in-law phoned the hospital to check in, he expressed his strong displeasure with the name. He asked to speak directly to me and inquired why I wanted to name his granddaughter after the coldest season of the year? I didn't have any satisfactory answer to give him. In the end, we named our daughter Jasmine but acquiesced to his family's instructions that her middle name be the one that had already been established in his family for several generations, Elizabeth. I felt as if naming our child should be our decision alone. I seemingly had little say in giving my daughter her name, but to keep the peace I agreed. Again, I was made to feel like an outsider in my own life story.

In the hours following the birth, my hospital room was flooded with gifts for the baby and well wishes from visiting friends of both Tobore and myself. When the room finally quieted down, Tobore took the opportunity to go home and freshen up while I took a nap. He was one proud and happy dad, and I was just relieved that our little girl was healthy and breathing. When I woke up, I found that I was afraid to look at her as I feared that all the medicine I had been given while pregnant might have caused some abnormalities. I screwed up my courage and said a pleading prayer to God. I was so grateful when I peeked into the bassinette and saw a perfectly formed baby girl. She was a pink bundle of joy!

My heart melted when I held her; I had never felt such a rush of unconditional love for anything before in my life. The nurse instructed me on how to breastfeed her. I was a little scared at first and felt anxious about how it would feel, but I watched in amazement as she latched onto my breast. Unlike me, she had not needed any instructions and knew exactly how to do it. The feeling was strange, but so full of emotion that my life bond to her was strengthened beyond anything I could have imagined. I looked up to the heavens and thought, "God you have made my life so amazing with this one miracle."

About two days after our daughter was born, we were told that the doctors had detected a heart murmur and needed to have an echocardiogram to confirm the health of her heart. I was still all terribly sore from the C-section and could hardly move, but when they told me that my little girl might not be well, I was determined to stay by her side for any testing she was to undergo. They told me that she needed to go to a different hospital for the tests. The best place for her was the public hospital attached to the university which we would need to travel to by car. Even though I had dreaded the pain associated with walking, talking, and even coughing in the days prior, when I heard that my child needed me, I got up and started doing all of the necessary activities. I didn't know where the strength and courage came from, but they were there and there was no keeping me down. Tobore also became infused with a sense of protectiveness, nothing like I had seen before. He helped get us ready for the trip to the hospital, making sure we were quickly discharged and safely in his hands for the travel. Thankfully, the test showed that nothing was to be feared and that the heart murmur would disappear with time.

We settled into our home with our new little bundle of joy. I basked in the love of our small family and wanted to shut out the world and all of its hassles. Just one of our daughter's smiles made all of my insecurities and negative feelings disappear. I started to view my worries over how my in-laws felt about me as silliness. I realised that I didn't need to be accepted by anyone else's family, I had my own family now and my life was complete.

Our little girl developed a bit of jaundice in the first week at home, so I sunned her as it was recommended as the best remedy. I was still learning to walk standing straight up and cough without wincing in pain, but the duties of motherhood provided the strength to overcome my physical ailments without complaint. I was very distraught when I developed an infection that made breastfeeding difficult; I missed the bonding time with my daughter. Tobore had been able to employ a daytime helper, but he remained extremely attentive and helpful. He even washed the dirty cloth nappies, bathed, and changed our little girl without being asked. His enthusiasm for fatherhood was like nothing I had ever seen. Then again, who did I have to compare him against?

Tobore's parents and sister visited periodically, and they all seemed excited about the baby. I was so taken aback by their interest and tried to hide my confusion so I wouldn't come off as offensive. When I had been pregnant, they'd barely paid any attention to me, so all that time together and easy conversation was very new. I remembered how people had said that a baby changes everything, and for that moment, it seemed like that was exactly what was happening in my life.

My sweet little girl, Jasmine, was growing into a fine specimen of a perfect life. When she was a few months old, I decided it was time to start looking for a job as our money was dwindling. I initially tried for teaching jobs, but they were scarce and nothing came of my efforts. Then, I heard of a job with the daughter of a famous singer from Jamaica who still had strong ties with the local community. I found out as much as I could about the available position, which turned out to be for the guidance of disaffected young people, and took it upon myself to write a sample curriculum for what I could carry out as the teacher/student supervisor. I became involved unofficially on the periphery of the project. I would often visit the Museum where some of the initial work was being done. Eventually, I was offered a formal position to work on the project and I immediately found that I loved being back at work, although my duties weren't exactly what I was expecting.

I started to feel anxious and disgruntled about the work I was expected to do. For the most part, my dissatisfaction was stemming from the fact that another person was home taking care of my baby and I was not by her side. I felt guilty that I was somehow abandoning my child and I had to remind myself that I was doing that job to feed and clothe her and help Tobore, who had done a stalwart job of looking after both of us so far. Every day, I would have to take a fresh blouse to change into during mid-day because my breasts would constantly leak. No amount of breast pads worked for me! My body seemed to know that my daughter was at home waiting to be fed.

I would pump enough milk each morning before I left and leave it in the fridge. I was very concerned about her health and would not allow any type of formula to be used, since it was mixed with the local water and I worried about her hygiene. Before I left for work each morning, I would lie in bed and Tobore would fetch Jasmine for me so that I could feed her a good first meal for the day. She would stay on the breast for two hours sometimes, but the routine would get tiresome when she was on a marathon-feeding streak. The intimacy of bonding with my child through breastfeeding clashed with the intimacy that my husband and I used to enjoy.

I began to hate my husband being on my breast; something inside told me that for now they belonged to my child. I shunned his requests to be together sexually as I felt it was inappropriate somehow with an innocent new child in our house. I had no idea if that feeling was normal for new mothers because I had no close friends with children to ask such a personal question. I looked back at that time and realized that was the same point when the bonds of our marriage started unravelling. I am certain now that I had some postpartum depression, but I had always tried to disguise my feelings of sadness, especially because everyone around me was so happy about the baby.

There was such a tumult of emotions coursing through me at the time. I wanted to recapture the carefree love I shared with my husband, but I was also aware of my time with my child. I would often come home more anxious to see her than to see him. I would be at work and become overwhelmed with the sense that my baby girl was crying out in hunger and that she needed me. At those times, it was such a relief to drive the car up into the driveway, run inside and wash my hands, throw a blanket across my lap and let my daughter feed until her heart was contented. I just wanted her to know that her mum loved her and would never abandon her.

"Sometimes our lives have to be turned upside down and rebuilt in an effort to take us to the God given place we were meant to be."

Chapter Seven

PUSHING FORWARD

"I have realised that we can directly measure life by our will to endure,

persevere, and survive."

———————

Jasmine grew so fast in her first year of life and we soon realized that she needed more space than our current house provided. We found a slightly larger home where she could have more freedom to move around and she could continue to express herself in her boisterous baby language. I was still working with the project associated with a popular Museum, but was starting to yearn for a different challenge. I saw an ad in our local paper for a sales representative role with a telecom provider. I took the plunge and applied, thinking it would be exciting to work in a field that was so different from anything I had done before. Something about all the challenges I had faced and overcome during my first year of motherhood had given me a lot of courage and self-confidence.

Follow me on Twitter: @avabrown24

Still, I was a bit shocked when I got called for the interview. When I arrived, I was interviewed by a man who held a long career in the telephone industry. Even though he readily agreed that I was a long shot for the job, he treated me with respect and conducted the interview as if he was talking to a respected potential employee. He drilled me with questions about how to conduct sales in the field, as well as about general customer service issues. I had never done sales before, but I knew that being friendly and easy to converse with was my strong suit. People used to tell me that I was a chatterbox, and in this interview, I chatted myself into a job! There was only one problem, it required me to have a car at my disposal all day long, and Tobore and I were still sharing the one.

I admitted my dilemma to the interviewer, but he could not see a way of us getting around that requirement. I sat up straight and looked that man square in the eyes, saying that if I had passed the interview and it was only the lack of a car that was holding me back from getting the job offer, then he needed only to give me three days to get a car. In my mind I recalled sitting in another office; begging the Minister of Education for his belief in me. I was confident that I could find a way in three days' time to overcome that obstacle. I was thrilled when the interviewer agreed to my request.

I phoned Tobore at work with the good news of the job offer and the requirement of a personal car in order for me to accept it. As always, my husband delivered. He immediately went out and found an affordable car that would help me secure my new job. He arrived home that evening with my first car, a blue Geo Metro. I was so overwhelmed with love for my husband. He believed in me and supported my dreams. I felt as if my life was back on track; I had a new job and my own car.

I had already taken the test and paid the fee for my driver's license. At that time in Jamaica, there were a lot of under-the-counter schemes run by the civil servants. There was little oversight and many times you would pay the fee only to be failed and told to return to take the test the next day, no matter how well you had driven, this was how the instructor made his salary. I had attained my license though and I relished the new feeling of independence that having a car gave me.

Shortly after acquiring the car, Tobore was in St. Elizabeth, visiting his parents, and I was at home in Kingston with the baby. I decided on a whim to make the drive down during the night so we could be with him when he woke in the morning. Now that I had the option, I wasn't about to settle for staying home alone to care for the baby on my own. I wanted to talk to him about the anxiety I felt about starting my new job and how it would affect my being a wife and a mother.

I think I wanted to prove to him that I was capable of driving and taking care of myself outside of our house. It never occurred to me how stupid, how very stupid I was being by heading out into the darkness all alone with little experience behind the wheel. If I'd had a lick of sense, I would have never endangered my child and my life for such a petty reason. Needless to say, when I arrived at his parents' in the wee hours, they were incredibly angry and Tobore gave me a proper telling off. I did not rise to their anger, as I quickly saw why they were so upset with me. I deserved Tobore's tirade, and his words of anger that were solely borne from his love and concern for me and our child.

I started my new job, and although the money coming in was good, I again started feeling that same sense of guilt over being away from home for such long hours. I had thought I was gone from my baby too much with the previous job, but it was nothing compared to now. I was constantly on the road, travelling from customer to customer to sell advertising space in the telephone directory. The company itself had a monopoly in Jamaica, so the locals didn't always look on it favourably, but took the space if they needed it because there was no other alternative.

One of the clients they sent me out to deal with was a large international paint company, and when I arrived at their local headquarters, they wanted nothing to do with the company I was representing. They pointed out all of the non-working telephone equipment that they had already paid for and all of their issues with trying to get the company to resolve even the simplest of problems. And here I was trying to sell them an expensive glossy ad! They were having none of it.

I decided to take a different approach and transformed my sales pitch into a customer service offering. In the end, I helped them to fix their existing problems and they showed their gratitude by placing one of the biggest sales I ever secured. That experience taught me the skills in customer service that I would use to excel later on in my career.

That year, I made money like I had never seen before. Our little family wanted for nothing. I began to not mind the expectations of the job so much because I was now able to collaborate with Tobore to provide for our daughter. Tobore and I would always pool our earnings by sitting together to plan our budget whenever I got my pay cheque. Even after paying all of our bills, we were able to afford all the gadgets we wanted. We were only in our early twenties and we were doing better than anyone I knew of in my family or our age group.

Things were going so well that I suggested a family holiday somewhere exotic. I felt guilty that I was away from Jasmine so much and realised that Tobore was starting to think I was away from home more than our society saw fit for any woman with a husband and child. I had also started formulating an idea for a new business, thinking that we could start something in the clothing trade, either in exporting or importing. I chose Panama for our vacation that year and it was a wonderful experience, one that I had never dreamed would be a part of my life when I was a young girl

living in the ramshackle homes of my family and friends back
in St. Elizabeth.

Things continued to go well at work. I was at the top of my game,
and that year I won the company contest for the largest sale, having
secured the contract for the Caribbean and South Florida telephone
directory that netted the company over eight million Jamaican dollars in
profit. The prize was an all-expense paid holiday to a large theme park in
Florida to attend a company-wide conference with winners from all the
other international offices. Since it was technically a working holiday,
families could not attend. I stayed at the resort itself and was driven
everywhere by a private golf cart. I hate to admit it, but I found the time
away from the hectic life of daily work and family to be wonderful. Even
though I had to attend day-long meetings, I could go back to the quiet of
my private room that had been serviced by the cleaning staff and wait for
room service to deliver a hot meal.

Like any accomplishment in life, however, my success only served to
set the bar higher for the next year. The pressure at work was intense and
the upper management expected me to exceed my prize-winning record,
which put further pressure on my home life, especially my marriage. I came
home one day during regular work hours to find my husband busy doing
the daily chores. He had given notice and left his job, feeling that one of us
needed to be at home. To date, the reasons as to why Tobore and I differed
on him being a stay-at-home dad are still blurry. I felt terrible; I had never
intended him to become the stay-at-home spouse, but he felt I had left him
no option but to stay at home.

At that point, our communication had broken down completely.
Neither of us understood what the other wanted and we were making
decisions based on our misunderstandings of each other. There was nothing
to do now, he could not go asking for his job back and I had to work even

harder since I was now the sole breadwinner. So we drifted even further apart. He began to feel the same isolation and dissatisfaction with life that I had felt in that first year after our daughter was born and I felt the stress he must had felt to get home to a lonely spouse and growing child. We both recognised that our roles weren't balanced, but we couldn't figure out how to resolve it and we had no one to help point us in the right direction.

Tobore was a wonderful father to Jasmine, as well as a wonderful husband. He had dinner on the table very often and every time I would see the plates set out, heaped with nourishing and delicious food, my heart would ache because I knew he needed me at home. It was killing me because even though our marriage was so young, it was also frail and brittle from the tribulations of our lives. To make matters worse, clients would often present urgent and complicating issues at the end of the work day that required me to work late; often missing dinner time at our house completely. I would try to make up for it by cutting some of my days short, but it interfered with my work to the point that my performance was suffering and my bosses were starting to take notice.

I felt trapped in a no-win situation. Leaving my job was not an option because one of us needed to work. But my extended hours away with clients, coupled with the growing discord between Tobore and myself at home, led to jealousy and distrust. Tobore started accusing me of cheating because he could not imagine how someone could be busy with clients for so many hours of the day. We were constantly quarrelling and I had a short temper that was then being set off by the smallest of things.

I had not given up on my marriage though. I made a concerted effort to be encouraging towards Tobore to restart his career. He admitted that he had been looking for jobs, but his old firm was not hiring and no other industry showed interest in his application. I suggested that he go back to school to bulk up his qualifications. These conversations didn't yield much.

We never seemed to finish them with a productive plan that we both agreed on and could work towards. I think we both expected the other to do their part, and we didn't see that teamwork required sacrifices on both ends.

I thought our problems might be solved when my company offered me a promotion. The new position had the same duties, but was based in a different location and offered a bit more money. I interpreted that opportunity to mean less work time and more time with the family. We moved to Mobay and used the compensation I had received the previous year from my large prize-winning contract, along with some help from Tobore's father, to purchase a piece of land. We saw that empty piece of bush land as the tool to restore our marriage; working together to build our dream home would heal our wounds and bind us together again. We rented a two-bedroom flat near the regional hospital and started making the architectural drawings and interviewing the necessary contractors. We were both relieved to realize that the project was indeed strengthening our bond and we started feeling closer than we had in months.

I was doing well at my new job and my successes soon got the attention of another large company in the wireless communication industry. I received an offer from a competitor and it was too good to turn down. Meanwhile, Tobore had secured a job with a supplier of aircraft food and was now working at the nearby airport. Jasmine was now old enough to attend a nursery and we no longer required a full-time caretaker in the house. While Tobore and I struggled to make our daily life an easy and happy existence, Jasmine existed in a carefree world.

When I was offered the position with the new company, I consulted with not only my husband but also his family to discuss all aspects of the new job to help us make the decision. I told them I had carefully considered it and recognised it as a great opportunity, but was careful to verify that I wasn't blinded to some key issues that could be detrimental to our family's situation. Tobore's parents had always believed a woman should have the more traditional role within the family. I was thrilled when they agreed with my assessment and I quickly accepted the offer.

At that time, my sister Kem had sent word from St. Elizabeth asking to come to live with us. She was the third child born to my mum after me (mum's favourite child, as she had a heart condition that made her fragile and more cared for) and I had loving memories of playing with her when she was a toddler. I knew that we could offer her a stable home life and opportunities that were not available to her back in the one room home that they were all still living in. I felt like the salary at my new job afforded us the luxury of taking on that responsibility, and because Tobore and I were bonding again, I felt no anxiety about the presence of another person in our house.

The new company was relatively new in the industry but very successful and growing at a rapid rate. The output and demand for its services was much greater than anyone expected, which is great for income, but also a substantial burden on its employees' time. I began travelling a lot again. There was no formal office space in our region, so I worked out of my home and sometimes out of the car. On paper, my job responsibilities were clear-cut. In the initial stages, one of my responsibilities was for a colleague and me to negotiate with local landowners so the company could acquire their land for our operational equipment to be erected . Basically, I saw my job as wining and dining people while I sold them the company's concept, maintaining compliance, and being the face of the company in that region. I was good at it and soon was internally promoted to the position of Dealer Account Executive.

But the same problem arose as with my last job. My time at home was limited and I carried out my job responsibilities under a cloud of private shame over my family suffering from my absence. Tobore and I talked about it from time to time and I was aware that his family wasn't happy with the outcome. I felt like I was being torn in two directions; my heart wanted to be a full-time wife and mother, but my mind craved the challenges that only my career could provide. Perhaps I was a bit over zealous at the time because of my roots being in a community where very few people went to work or had a career; especially the women.

My job satisfied something deep within me that was almost pathological. My talent at what I did only further fed the fire that was consuming me. Yet, that wonderful aspect of my life was causing my family to fall apart. I was fully aware of the whispers around me, telling me that I was selfishly sacrificing my family for my career. Unfortunately, I didn't know how to confront them and tell them that I wasn't doing it purposefully; I just didn't know how to balance both. My family wasn't going hungry, we were secure financially, and I used these facts to justify my being away from them far too often.

Before I knew it, the relationship between Tobore and I had again deteriorated into fighting and dislike. He reinitiated the blatant accusations of my cheating and I responded by losing respect for him for believing that I had such low character. We both recognised yet tried to ignore the fact that the fracture in our relationship was rapidly reaching an irreparable point. Tobore was convinced that I had a lover tucked away somewhere, and I began to suspect him of the same. We grew so far apart that even though we lived in the same house, we communicated as if we were separated by continents.

Our rented home was a good distance from the land on which our dream house was being constructed. Tobore had lost interest in the project and it was I who kept it going. I would travel alone to spend hours at the site and oversee the workmen to catch the common mistakes that would have otherwise cost us so much money. Soon, I took over the whole project in earnest, travelling to the hardware store for items and taking on the entire payments for the construction crew and materials. Even though I didn't want to admit it, I was building a house for a family with no husband or father.

Jasmine would often accompany me on these trips to the construction site and it was our time to bond. I would tell her about all the dreams her dad and I had for our family house, how we would all live there in a bubble of love and happiness. The workers recognised Tobore's absence as an opportunity to slack off. One day, I arrived to find that the workers had erected a column on the veranda that leaned and was clearly unstable. I immediately pointed that out, citing that it would not support the weight it needed to and told them that they needed to remove it and start again. They challenged me in an obvious way that related to me being a woman. I was used to these arguments by now, and I had grown clever at making up some story to cover my husband's absence and assuring them that he was still overseeing all of their work.

Finally, our house was completed enough for us to move in. I was still hoping that this residence would magically heal our family, but when we moved in, it was even more painfully clear that Tobore and I were over as a couple. I started dreading going home to the arguments and tense silences. If it weren't for my daughter, I would have never returned to that house. The silence gradually took over and there was no longer any communication. We were married in name only. I felt utterly abandoned and was sure he did too. Even though my husband and I slept under the same roof (but in separate rooms sometimes), our relationship became so broken that soon after, we both found comfort in someone else.

We quarrelled and fought, but knew we had to discuss our indiscretions and figure out how we could move past it in the healthiest way possible for both of us and for our child. Even though I was guilty of the same offence, his admission nearly killed me. We both knew there was nothing to be done but for one of us to move out. His brother arrived one Sunday afternoon and helped him pack his belongings and removed them and him from our lives while I sat in silence on the veranda, combing our daughter's hair. Before they left, Tobore came and said goodbye to our daughter. I felt as if my world had crashed down around me, but I couldn't fall apart in front of our child.

That night, after I put Jasmine to bed, I cried until my eyes were swollen. I had no idea how much I would miss Tobore's presence in our house and in our lives. I realised that despite the undercurrent of anger and dissatisfaction, I loved him deeply and relied on him for our family's stability. We had just lost our way as a couple. I realised that Tobore had been a part of my life since I was a teenager. I started to feel ashamed that I hadn't properly appreciated him. The fact was neither of us had appreciated each other at the end. I thought about how I had lost sight of what was truly important over the past couple of years. We really were still too young to be able to handle all of the events that life had presented us with. I thought of how we might have benefited from more emotional support from our extended families, but that time had passed and there was no going back and no blaming anyone except ourselves. My primary concern then had to be our child; I had to protect her from the pain that Tobore and I were feeling during our uncoupling.

Even though my sister was still living with us, it was challenging to keep the house together without Tobore around. I had to hire workers to do many of the routine chores that were too cumbersome for me and my sister, such as maintaining the yard. Hiring men for certain jobs served another purpose of bringing a male presence to our house that gave us a sense of protection. We gradually adjusted to life without Tobore. He would arrive every weekend to pick Jasmine up for her overnight visits with him and there was never a problem during these hand-offs. He maintained a fabulous relationship with our daughter.

Jasmine was a very clever little girl. She took notice of everything, and would catch the importance of even the subtlest experiences. One day, when she and I were out running errands, she pointed out a house and told me that that was the girl's house that her dad would take her to. I was confused by that designation and asked her what she meant. When I asked, "What girl?" she answered with a sense of impatience, "Mummy, that's where Aunty Femi lives." I eyed the place suspiciously, but when I asked who Aunty Femi was, Jasmine simply replied, "Daddy's friend." I did some investigating and found out that 'Aunty Femi' was a topless bartender who worked at the local joints, and indeed, she had lived in that very house that Jasmine had pointed out. So, I began to get some insight into what Tobore's post-marital life consisted of.

Shortly after that encounter, the company I worked for organised a grand function in Montego Bay at which two internationally acclaimed songstresses would be entertaining. The invited clientele came from my territory so I also got an invite, but I knew it would be a working evening. I dressed in one of my finest gowns and waited for Tobore to come and pick up our daughter to watch her for the evening. He arrived with a young woman in the car who he introduced as his friend. Jasmine seemed well acquainted with her, so I decided not to worry. Besides, I was so excited about the night's concert that I simply accepted his explanation.

The isolated life that Jasmine, my sister and I led in our house passed by without much incident, but I continued to miss Tobore and the relationship we once had. I started attending counselling and decided to ask Tobore to come back home for Christmas that year with the intent of initiating a reconciliation. I had the entire plan laid out, and at first everything went as expected. We attended Jasmine's kindergarten Christmas play, where I leaned in close to tell him in an intimate whisper that I had something to talk to him about afterwards. He walked me to the car and stood by my side as I strapped our sleepy daughter into her car seat. I became suddenly shy and my awkward movements showed it.

In my head, I was dying to ask him to come home, to spend Christmas with us, to lie next to me until the dawn, to talk and rekindle our love for one another. I knew we could work this out. He then filled the silence by saying that he wanted to tell me something. My heart leapt. I was flooded with relief, thinking that he wanted the same thing and that we were really going to be a family again.

My relief turned to shock, though, when he said, "I have gotten someone pregnant, the girl you met the other day, in fact. I wanted to tell you myself. I didn't want you to hear it first from someone else."

I didn't think I even responded. I was so shocked, I couldn't even speak. I started the drive home and that was when the tears and anger came. I didn't know what to do, but like a child tattling on a friend who had offended me, I phoned my mother-in-law and told her that her son had gotten someone else pregnant. Her response made me fume even more, but I had no argument to counter her when she said, "Until I hear it from my son, I won't believe it." I hung up the phone. Suddenly, certain things from our past became clearer to me. Our separation was no surprise to many of our friends and family, and neither would the news of his impending fatherhood.

When we arrived back at the house, I handed Jasmine over to the care of our house-helper and my sister. I then made my way to the kitchen and began drinking every bit of alcohol I could find. Within hours, I was an incoherent mess, on the edge of eternal unconsciousness. My sister got me to the hospital, where the doctors pumped my stomach to remove what alcohol hadn't yet been absorbed and in doing so they probably saved my life. They kept me in the hospital under observation for a few days. I found out they were going to discharge me on a day that my sister was working and our helper had off. A friend of mine brought my car and Jasmine to the hospital to pick me up, I was ready to go home but I needed to drop my friend back home first.

The next day, another female friend of mine called me in great distress. She wanted to talk, so I invited her over. Not only did I have something to tell her too; but I also needed a distraction. We spent the entire day cooking, laughing, crying, talking about men and burying our sorrows in each other's friendship. It was getting late, so Jasmine and I dropped her home and rushed back to start preparation for work the next day.

It was around 7:00 pm when Jasmine and I pulled into the driveway of our house. I had been talking on the mobile phone with another friend and I told him that I would call back as soon as I got inside and got Jasmine settled down. I had the phone still cradled between my shoulder and my ear and was holding a sleeping Jasmine in one arm, while trying to open the front door with the other. Suddenly I felt something cold and metal press hard against the side of my neck. My eyes swung to the side and saw the muzzle of a gun and four men with their eyes trained on my frightened face. In a quick second, one of them swiped the phone from my ear while another took Jasmine from my grasp; it was a miracle she didn't wake. The one with the gun pointed at me grabbed my arm harshly and pushed me forward, instructing me in a quiet, sadistic voice to open the grill by our front door. The two other men, who had been silent so far, stepped forward and told me to give them the cash card for my bank account. As soon as they had the card they left and the other two hustled me into the house. I was escorted at gunpoint to the bedroom and I saw one man put Jasmine down on the sofa, where she just curled up and continued sleeping.

The two men were hurling all sorts of insults at me and started recklessly wandering throughout the rest of the house. They stopped occasionally and poured out little packets of cocaine, which they snorted in front of me unashamedly. I was absolutely certain that I was going to die and my thoughts turned to how I could save the live of my daughter and of my sister who would be coming home from work at any moment. When the men were out of the room on one of their rampages through the house, I snuck a call through to her and left a message to not come home and to call the police. I hung up just in time before the men returned to ask me for the keys to unlock all of the stores that my company owned. I began then to think that this was a robbery based on my job.

I told the men that I didn't have any of the store keys, explaining that I wasn't responsible for that part of the operations. I told them that I only supervised the stores. I went into a babbling explanation of how the company was structured but the taller one cut me off with a sharp laugh. "We're not interested in your work!" he yelled. I was shocked into silence, my mouth hung open mid-sentence. He became very serious, looked me straight in the eye, and told me in a hissing voice that they had been sent to kill me. I made a panicked plea for my life; I told him that I would pay him more than the person who sent them, if only he would spare my life. He said that he had already accepted the payment to kill me and he was a man of his word and would not renege on his contract.

The man with the gun then started asking me about a man he had been told I was seeing. I told him I wasn't seeing anyone, but he said that he didn't believe me. He stalked around the bedroom, he said that I must have pictures of that man and me together, but there weren't any pictures of that imagined relationship to be found. Then he said that I seemed like a nice girl, nothing like the cold bitch he was told that I was. The other man pushed me back onto the bed and pointed his gun directly at my chest; I was certain my life was about to end. Back in the living room, however, my daughter had finally awakened. She was so innocent. Curious as any two-year-old would be; she came running into the room to see what her mummy was doing. The guy with the gun aimed at me spun around and trained his gun on her. My heart skipped a beat; I thought he was going to shoot her.

I fell off the bed and onto my knees and screamed out for him to hold his fire and not to kill my child. The scene was tense, but everyone managed to remain calm in the seconds that followed. The man allowed Jasmine to come to me. She came into my open arms; tears were streaming down my cheeks. She was such a sweet babe, and as I held her tightly to me, she told me not to cry. I knew that the situation was growing dimmer as each moment passed. The men were obviously agitated and their whispered conversations with one another were becoming more aggressive. I heard some of the words creep through and I knew what was being planned.

One of the men left the room to go rummaging again and the other turned his attention back to me. Fearing I knew what was about to happen I told him that there were condoms in the drawer next to where he stood. I was thinking if I somehow survived this night, I didn't want to come out of it with HIV. A smile crept across his face and he said he didn't need one; he had come prepared. I panicked and blurted out a feeble lie that I had a sexual disease hoping it would deter him. His jolly mood continued, though, and he laughed and told me that he knew clean women like me were always careful, he was confident I didn't have anything transmissible.

There was no hiding the danger of the situation from my daughter then and she had begun screaming and crying in a hysterical manner. I was still holding her and trying to comfort her when that man came close, leaned in and stroked Jasmine's face in a blatantly sexual way. He nearly cooed when he asked her to tell him how old she was. I answered for her, telling him sternly that she was only two years old. He kept his eyes trained on her only and told her in a soft voice that it was too bad; if she were three he would have to fuck her too. My body convulsed and I nearly threw up. My conscience was crying out to me that she had been spared; it was only me who was to be subjected to his violation.

Everything happened rather quickly, or maybe I just thought it did. The mind protects you from the horrors you experience by erasing them from your memory sometimes. What I do remember was during the course of that violation there was a phone being answered and I remember the two men waiting at the cash point were angrily demanding my security code to get access to my accounts. Some days I remember much more.

Let me be very clear; the bastard held me down at gunpoint and raped and molested me inches from where my daughter sat cowering on the floor. My baby, Jasmine, was crying hysterically and I could not reach out to comfort her. That horrid man teased and taunted me in some kind of sadistic dance he played in his mind. He grabbed my breast hard and licked my face; boasting how lucky I was going to be. I was so disgusted I could feel the vomit rising in my throat. I called out to Jasmine to turn her head and close her eyes. I told her to put her hands over her ears. I promised her everything would be okay. But I knew better. Nothing would ever be okay again.

All at once, that vile man was on top of me. He kissed me; trying to shove his tongue into my mouth. I spat at him. He hit me hard; telling me if I did that again I would pay. I was so terrified. I took that to mean he would do something to my child, my baby, my light in the darkness. I looked to see Jasmine sobbing in the corner between the bed and the wall. My heart was breaking. I then decided the best I could do was to endure whatever was to happen in silence. He pulled the clothes from my body. He bit down hard on my nipple; exclaiming how aroused I was. Aroused? In terror, perhaps. I wanted to scream and cry out from the pain; but dared not. He shoved his fist inside of me. That pain was almost unbearable. I thought I might lose consciousness. The entire time I heard his heinous laughter as he waved his gun in my face.

My mind and body had gone numb. Like I was in some horror film, I could only watch myself. He waved a condom in my face telling me I was not worthy of a child of his. I thank god for that. He entered me and that time I could not stop the vomit. But I made no sound as the tears streamed down my face. My only thoughts were that I had to do everything to protect my daughter. He enjoyed himself immensely at my expense. I just laid there cold; feeling a part of me was dying.

The other man came back into the room with a bunch of keys that he had found somewhere in the house. He assumed they were keys to the stores. He told his accomplice that we all needed to go to the shops so I could let them in. I felt broken. I felt as if they had torn my soul right out of my body. Then they told me how angry they were at me for making them wait so many nights. They said that they had been waiting for me since I had been in the hospital. They mocked me for taking so long to recover before I was discharged. I got a sick feeling in my stomach when I then realised that really couldn't be merely a robbery gone badly. The Mayor and his family lived next door and had far more money and exploitable power than I did. I was only twenty-four years old. How much did they really expect get from me? I thought could it be true that they were hired to simply kill me?

The two men then told me to get dressed. They then forced my daughter and me into my car outside at gunpoint. As we drove, the two who had gone to the bank called again and I could overhear them talking casually about how they would get rid of me shortly. They made me take the driver's seat and ordered me to start driving. I felt a glimmer of hope when they instructed me to drive down a road where I knew the police station was. I nearly got caught by the speed trap set up there, I was so grateful to have the chance to be rescued by putting my foot down a bit harder on the gas pedal. But there was no such luck tonight; there were no policemen sitting and waiting to catch a speeder.

One of the men sat next to me in the front passenger seat and kept his gun aimed at my knees the whole time. He told me not to do anything stupid. If I had been alone, I might have crashed the car or driven it right into the police station, but the other man sat in the back seat with his gun aimed at my baby. I didn't give up though and tried appealing to their conscience. During the earlier part of the night, I had given them nearly sixty five thousand in cash that had been kept in a safe at the house. I offered them more money if they would just let me and my baby go. They merely instructed me to keep driving.

We drove through the mountainous and gully regions of Montego Bay, Jamaica, and we final ended up in the city centre. They directed me to one of my company's stores, but I had been telling the truth when I told them that I had no keys to open the shops. They were livid when they realised that. One of them slapped me hard across the face as he grunted in frustration. The one who I had begun to think of as their leader was upset too, but he remained calmer than the other and told him there was nothing to be done; that I had told them the truth.

We were hustled back into the car and they instructed me to drive them to a well-known place by the seaside. By then all of their cell phone credits had run out and they started using my mobile phone to make contact with their two accomplices at the bank. They set up a rendezvous point and made me drive to a shadowed area. I sat in stunned silence and listened as the men told me that I was to leave Jamaica. "Go abroad," they said. One of them stifled a little chuckle and told me that when my daughter was grown, I should tell her, "Life is fucked up." But then they pointed their guns again and told us to get out of the car. My mind went crazy; I started to remember all of the recent news reports from the Middle East, where women were being executed in open areas to send a message to the public.

I stood trembling in the darkness, holding my child to my breast and prayed to God for his mercy. The first shot was so loud it nearly burst my eardrums, but the volley of shots that followed made me realise the men were firing into the air above us. They jumped into the car of their accomplices, who had finally arrived, shouted a final warning that I was to leave Jamaica immediately, and drove off. They just left us standing there.

A part of me thought that Jasmine and I must be dead and that if I looked down I would see our bloodied bodies lying beneath us and realise we were just ghosts, doomed to haunt that beach for eternity. I frantically searched Jasmine's tiny body for gunshot wounds and could hardly breathe when I found none. My entire body...my entire spirit...was numb. I couldn't believe we were rid of the men and still alive after that dreadful ordeal. By some miracle, the men had left my phone behind, and I called the police and the friend I had dropped off at home before that nightmare had started. The police had told me to stay put, but I was afraid that the men were going to come back and finish the job. I put Jasmine back in the car and drove myself to the closest police station I could think of. I was trembling the entire way and could hardly keep straight on the road. I didn't even recall arriving at the station; the police later told me that they found me outside in the parking lot, collapsed over the steering wheel.

"Watered baptism is said to be the only thing to cleanse original sin, thus sins are stained and embedded in us. However, forgiveness is saved for the contrite, making it hard to erase the embedded evil."

Follow me on Twitter: @avabrown24

Chapter Eight

YOUR GUT

"I've learnt to let my instincts and gut guide me in all I do,

regardless of how things seem. "

———————

The days that followed our ordeal were miserable and confusing. The police sent a team out to my house to dust for fingerprints among the ransacked rooms and in my car. They said that they would only be able match a person to any evidence once they found a suspect that they could use for comparisons. I was shocked to hear that the chances for swift justice were so slim! The officer explained that our assailants must have worn gloves or cleaned up the evidence. He also explained that since the men didn't steal any physical objects from the home, besides the cash I gave them to ransom our lives, it wasn't really considered a straight-forward robbery case, according to the legal definition at the time. I had walked from room to room with the officer to make an inventory of what had been stolen, but found everything still present. They had not taken a thing; not the fancy electronics, the TV or stereo, none of my jewellery, and even the mass of cash I had hidden secretly were all still in the house.

The realisation that the robbers had truly had no interest in our belongings shook me to my very core. I was trembling like a leaf and could hardly breathe when I remembered the man sneering at me that they were simply sent there to kill me. Earlier, the police had sent me to a hospital in Montego Bay for treatment of my physical wounds. There too, the doctors had given the grim news that there was little to no physical evidence from my attackers they could retrieve from my damaged body. Even though the house was released from its status as an active crime scene, I could not return to living in it. I got assistance from an organisation I was close to that put the three of us; my sister, my daughter and me up in a hotel. I worked with the police to trace the calls made by the assailants from my cell phone that night. Unfortunately, that was a time when tracing technology was still new in Jamaica, so the only information they managed to get was that one of the calls had been made to a well-known ghetto area; August Town, St. Andrew.

We stayed at the hotel for a few days, just long enough to finish dealing with the police. As soon as that was completed, I felt compelled to flee so that I could gather my wits. The only place I could think of that would provide a calming and safe environment was Florida, probably because of my recent experience there with my previous company. Jasmine and I flew out a few days later; as soon as we secured our visas. I wasn't sure where my sister went that night, but she re-joined the next day. However, the distance did not calm my nerves the way I had expected. I was an emotional wreck. I couldn't eat and my nights were spent either sleeplessly pacing the room, or jolting up from a nightmare that would force me to relive the trauma once again.

Follow me on Twitter: @avabrown24

A friend called and told me that Tobore had moved from Montego Bay back to his parents place in St. Elizabeth. I was told he quit his job without giving a reason for his sudden departure. I wondered if he'd left out of fear for his own safety after hearing what had happened to me or if he simply feared being questioned about our separation and his impending fatherhood. With that in mind, the fact that my attacker had said they had been sent to kill me by someone I knew kept playing over and over again in my head.

The time in Florida was doing no good and I knew Jasmine and I couldn't hide out there forever. I needed to figure out how I was going to move on with my life. I wondered if I could simply force my mind to shut out the trauma and return to my home and my daily work schedule. My assailants' final warning to me was to leave Jamaica; would I dare go against it? I could not help but to fear they would come back to finish the job. Regardless of what my ultimate decision would be, I knew I couldn't make it and carry it out from my cousin's home in Florida where we had been staying. I steeled my nerves, packed up Jasmine and headed back home to Jamaica to face the situation head-on.

I was surprised to find that the love for my family home that I had built with my ex-husband was now dead. I stood at the front door and realized our home was really just an object made of brick and wood, nothing more. My life within its walls had been ended by those four men and I walked its hallways like a ghost. I employed a security guard, but still could not find solace. My sister moved back in and the three of us stayed in a single bedroom. However, I was still too terrified to sleep the whole night through. One night when I couldn't calm down, I called the friend whom I had spent the day with prior to the attack; the one whom I had been on the phone with when the attackers had arrived. My sister and Jasmine were beside me in the bed fast asleep. While talking to her, my heart nearly

Follow me on Twitter: @avabrown24

seized when my ears picked up an unusual sound, almost like footsteps on the roof of the house. I told her I would call her right back.

At first, I thought I must have been hallucinating because of my hypersensitive state. I ensured the two girls beside me were still sound asleep; I didn't want to alarm them. I was sweating and really beginning to panic. As I gently opened the curtain to see if I could get a peek of what was happening, I saw the barrel of a gun. Panicked, I shook my sister awake; I quickly stifled her gasp of surprise by cupping my hand over her mouth. I whispered that someone was outside. I was certain it was the men coming back to kill me. I feared there was no escape for me that time and my imagination went into overdrive. I imagined these coke-fuelled fiends with spy-level skills which allowed them to disable the guard and my sister and make their way inside to shoot me in front of my baby girl. I gently got off the bed and tried to get everyone on the floor without any sound, my hand was still over my sister's mouth to keep her from panicking.

I grabbed for my cell phone and frantically dialled a friend of mine on the police force who had been at the house earlier that evening. I gave him the pre-arranged signal we had come up with earlier to alert him that there was an immediate danger to my life. He understood and rang off. I then used my shaking fingers to dial the local police station, which was only a seven minute walk from my house. Within moments, I heard the scream of a siren and my police friend calling to say that he was the one pulling up outside. He instructed us to stay in the house while he surveyed the perimeter of the building along with the security guard, whom he found unharmed, too afraid to move and frozen on the sofa in the front room. Several minutes later, I heard the noises of several cars alerting us that the local police were finally arriving.

The sirens had chased the men off and we were safe for another few hours, but I knew they were not going to let up. I knew that was the last night I would spend in that home. The next day, I went to Santa Cruz to stay with a friend and started looking for somewhere to live. Not long after, I found a house to rent in Santa Cruz with enough bedrooms for myself, Jasmine, and my sister. However, as we finished packing up the old house and started loading the car with our personal belongings, my sister Kem told me that she was not going to join us. I could not blame her. I was disheartened that I was going to take on that new phase of my life completely alone, without any help to take care of Jasmine. I was frustrated at her timing, too, since I had already committed to the massive rent for a larger place that she was supposed to contribute to while living there with us.

I completed the move in a daze. Everything was happening so quickly and I still hadn't had time to process the trauma of the events or what they really meant to my life and my sanity. When we arrived in Santa Cruz, I contacted the lady who had been employed as my helper right before the attack. I was so stressed that I hadn't had time to consider the frightening implications of the suspicious circumstances under which she had requested the day off on the evening that the men showed up to begin their reign of terror.

My new life in Santa Cruz was the same as it had been in Florida. Every night when the sun set, I would be besieged by the normal noises of the boisterous city around me. I would pick out individual sounds and convince myself they were whispers of the men coming to kill me. The entire trauma of that night in Montego Bay replayed constantly in my mind. I was becoming a shell of the woman I used to be. I knew I couldn't continue that way and be an effective mother to Jasmine. I had to do something.

I had an aunt living in London who invited me to come visit her. I jumped at that idea, especially because I was set to complete an exam for my Bachelor's degree and I had been struggling to complete it. I could not concentrate. A complete change of scenery sounded good. London was far away, but she was family. She had left Jamaica many years ago to emigrate there. She and I weren't close at all. In fact, my only interactions with her had occurred when I was a young child. But when I wrote to tell her that I wanted to accept her invitation, her response was positive and warm. I couldn't afford to take Jasmine out of school at that time, but I needed time and space to myself to think and unfreeze my zombie-like state. My in-laws volunteered to keep Jasmine and she was excited about the prospect of staying there because her daddy was also living in their house. I felt certain that despite the threats that were being aimed towards my life, no one would seek to harm an innocent child, so I entrusted my daughter to them.

Having passed all of my exams, I made the trip to London. My aunt was such a blessing; in the downtimes she lifted my spirits. She took me all over the city; we even attended the wedding of some very distant relatives. Before then, I didn't even know I knew other Jamaicans who had relocated to the UK. The whirlwind social schedule helped me begin to forget about the stresses that awaited me back home. I began to see that as long as I had my daughter with me, I could build a fulfilling life anywhere, even there in that new country. Though the people and certainly the weather in that country were vastly different from my home country, I felt a sense of safety. The news reports on the TV reported crimes that were nowhere near as heinous as those that had become routine in some parts of Jamaica at that time. Certainly, I didn't hear of anything as blatantly violent as the attack I had just experienced in my own home.

I began to dread going back to the life that Jasmine and I had been living back in Santa Cruz. Even on the nights that my mind calmed enough to allow sleep, I would be awoken by the intermittent flashes of lights being shown in our windows by the police who were still making routine patrols of our house to assure our continued safety. My auntie recognised my internal torment and suggested that I register with some local employment agencies just to see what opportunities there might be in London if I decided to stay.

I thought very carefully about the reality of our situation in Jamaica now. I thought of how I could no longer stand to drive the car with anyone sitting in the back seat, as I would suddenly fear that person might pull a gun on me or Jasmine. I thought of how I would drive far out of my way, meandering to get to my destination, all to avoid any crowded areas where my attackers might see me and force their way into my car. I thought of how I could no longer make myself drive anywhere as the hour of sunset neared, since the dark was much too frightening a reminder of our plight. This was no way to live and I knew it. I acquiesced to my auntie's wisdom and registered with several agencies before making the trip back home.

I left London with a bittersweet feeling. That city was so completely different from any place I had ever visited before, yet I felt safer there than in the country I had spent my entire life. When I returned home to Santa Cruz, I did my best to settle into life again. My company rearranged my responsibilities so that my territory alignment was to include the parish I lived in and the adjoining ones. That meant that I was now responsible for the parishes of St. Elizabeth, Hanover, Westmoreland, Manchester, Trelawny, and St. James. That was June of 2002, and I was doing my best to return to my normal life of hard work and taking care of my growing daughter.

One day, as I was travelling from an appointment in Manchester, back to our rented home in Santa Cruz, my cell phone began to ring incessantly. I had purposefully ignored the first barrage of ringing because the hill I was driving up was particularly steep and treacherous, the site of frequent accidents. Yet, when the phone started ringing a third time, I pulled to the side of the road, panicked with the thought that there may be an emergency at my daughter's school or the house.

When I answered, I found that the person on the other end of the line was indeed calling with life changing news, but not in the way I had imagined at all. The caller was in fact a secondary school principal from the Mitcham borough in London. She stated that she had received my credentials from one of the job agencies and she was anxious to speak with me about current and upcoming employment opportunities with her school. I was slightly taken aback by her interest in me; after all, I had not taught in four years. It must be divine intervention, I thought. God's favour must finally be turning towards me again! I refocused my attention to the words being spoken into my ear from so far away. She was already starting to conduct the interview with me right there on the side of the Spur Tree Hill.

I hadn't really expected anything to come of my registering with the job agencies back in London, let alone to get an interview for a position in a field I had left so long ago. It was all happening so suddenly. My mind started to buzz with excuses to get out of the interview. What if at the end of my interview she was to offer me the position and expect me to commit to moving there? A pessimistic voice in my head reminded me that teaching was not something I had a flair for, like I did with sales. It was not something that I would even enjoy at that point in my life, as it couldn't afford me the lifestyle that I had grown accustomed to. Mentally, I wasn't in a good place to absorb the stress of working with children. That same little voice told me that even considering a move into the teaching field would be a step back. After all, teaching was something I had used to get a start in life and it had never been my dream job.

In the background, I could hear the woman's continued questions. Somehow, I was managing to answer them coherently and, based on the tone of her voice, she appeared to be pleased with my responses. Then it seemed to me the conversation was ended abruptly, with her making a firm job offer and asking when I could start. I was dumbfounded and searched for how to answer that last important question. There was so much to consider! I mumbled some platitudes to give myself time to think. A part of me thought I must be crazy to not just hang up on her absurd offer and go about my daily business. That part of me was seized by the fear of leaving my country. After all, the job I held now gave me financial stability and the ability to afford much more than Jasmine and I could ever need. I had just imported a fancy new car from Japan, which was my weekend car. Very few people at my age could afford such a luxury, so who was I to throw it all away? I still owned the house in Montego Bay but it was now rented, so it was not a financial burden and I could count it as a solid investment for my future. I was now living closer to my mother and she was providing a new type of emotional support I had not known before. Finally, I was still legally married, even though I only saw my husband occasionally and he had started another family with another woman. My feelings for him were certainly tangled and complex.

But then another part of me began to intrude on my torrent of thoughts, and it was the voice of logic. Despite all of the successful contracts I was still managing to secure in my fragile post-trauma state, I lived every moment of my life with fear and paranoia. Jasmine and I still lived under constant police surveillance and our activities were restricted. That was really no sort of life, no matter how many amenities and gadgets I could afford to buy.

With that final realisation, I made an impulsive decision to accept the job. The voice on the other end of the line was filled with happy relief as she rolled out the details of my employment and told me the agency would finalize the details. My first day was to be on September 20th. I hung up the phone and sat in awed silence for a moment. It appeared to me that

God had just opened the door leading to the next chapter of my life. I called my mum and told her the news. She was shocked but mostly unsure if I should move to another country or stay close by to her, where she could essentially watch over me. I also called Tobore to tell him I had accepted a job in London. He expressed elation at my decision and told me that was the best way for me to move forward. The sincerity in his voice reminded me of what it had been like in those years during college when he was my staunchest supporter.

Alone, I sat silently in my car on the side of that steep hill for some time, trying to gather my emotions. A part of me felt afraid of the unknown. I wondered what life would be like once I moved to the UK. Granted, London had looked inviting while I was on my short visit, but what could I really tell about a place after just a two-week visit? In reality though, it didn't matter what my fears were, I had accepted the job and now needed to get Jasmine and myself ready for the big move.

Within days, the job agency forwarded the various documents that I would need to send to the British Embassy to obtain my work visa. They informed me of the vaccinations that I would require to teach in the UK. Before I knew it, I had an appointment with a nearby doctor in Santa Cruz and left his office completely up to date on my immunisations. Everything was happening so fast I couldn't keep up. My new job did not supply an allowance for moving all of my household belongings, so I made quick sales of the largest items I owned. My sewing machine, a treadmill, our beds, and the large American-style appliances were quickly snapped up or given on credit.

A few weeks later, Tobore accompanied Jasmine and me to the visa interview session, which was conducted in Kingston. That day, it was raining in sheets and I phoned the Embassy ahead of our travel to ask if it was necessary to make the trip due to the rain. The woman who answered

Follow me on Twitter: @avabrown24

my call laughed good-naturedly at my question and told me that if I intended to live in the UK, I needed to understand that rain stops nothing. We hastily jumped into my car and made the trip to collect our visas.

Jasmine and I got our visas and I was scurrying around trying to get all the family's affairs in order before we left. Now, the family here did not just mean my daughter and Tobore, it meant all my siblings as well; all my mother's and stepfather's children combined. Before I left for the city of gold and honey, how we referred to England; one of my obligations (or what I felt like was my obligation because I was the eldest) was to ensure all my siblings were what we say in Jamaica "set up". That meant I would ensure that each one had something to help insure his or her future while I was gone. After all, taking care of everyone seemed to have always been my job, even until today.

Part of me felt guilty to be leaving them knowing they didn't seem to possess my resilience to survive; or so I felt. I didn't know what was waiting for me in the UK but I felt I needed to ensure all my siblings had a start for their lives. So that was what I did. For my eldest brother I had a shop stocked with inventory. It was what he said he wanted, he wanted to be an entrepreneur. The sister that followed him was given money to pay for hairdressing courses; she said she wanted to be hairdresser. The sister that lived with me, her school fees were paid off .The sister after her was also given money to go back to a full-time education. I gave Kem the option to come with me to England and remain a part of my house. Essentially in my mind, I had done the best for each of them. I gave them all a start in the lives they wanted; something someone had done once for me and that I had used to the best of my ability.

I had to leave the house in Montego untenanted while we were gone. That meant the mortgage still had to be paid and obviously that too was my responsibility. There was the car I had just recently purchased, my Honda

Accord with the 3-litre engine, it was no baby car as it was all glammed up. That was a massive loss of money; I hadn't envisaged having to leave Jamaica anytime soon. If I had known; I wouldn't have bought a new weekend car. During the week I drove the company car, a Honda CRV.

As my migration was so sudden, I ended up selling all that I could of my belongings for little or no money. I sold everything at a bottom dollar price; some items were given to people who promised to pay me later. Little did I know that even before I had ascended into the sky, these people had no plans of repaying me. That is how most of my money was diminished. Even with all that, I still felt I had more than enough to start a new life across the pond. After all, I had a job waiting for me and new found family and friends there for support. However, when I later landed in the UK I had a very rude awakening, at the time the conversion rate was £1 British = $15 Jamaican dollars. That was roughly 6-7 cents on the dollar. As you can imagine, there was very little I now had left after converting. Alas, unknown at the time, I would be broke and on my face.

With everything in place for our emigration, I resigned from my job with the company that had been so much a part of my life over the past few years. My heart was heavy and I began doubting my decision as I delivered the news to my supervisors. I constantly reminded myself of the promise of the new life awaiting me in London, one that would bring me out of the fear I lived in currently.

The plan was for me to move to London first, where I would set up a home for my daughter and sister to join me later in October, as my sister had decided she would join us on our grand new adventure. Moreover, Tobore had told me that he would like to come with us as well. His plan was to join us there in December of that year; things had not played out well with the new woman. In the meantime, Jasmine would stay with her paternal grandparents. Although I knew Tobore's parents would look after my daughter well, it was difficult for me to leave her behind. I kept my focus on the knowledge that it was the best decision for us as a family and, eventually, we would all be together again. I was more excited to finally have the opportunity for Tobore and me to work on our marriage again, away from all the stresses of our families and the demands that we were surrounded by at the time, including his newborn. A fresh new environment may do us some good, I thought.

In August, only a few weeks before my scheduled departure, Tobore's girlfriend gave birth to their daughter. The news of her birth ripped my soul in two. It felt as if someone had defiled the one sacred event that he and I shared. It was a difficult period for everyone involved because Tobore and I had begun seeing each other on a regular basis. The tension was thick between everyone; Tobore and I, and Tobore and the mother of his new child. I could only imagine the torment he felt, or how it compared to my own, because we never spoke directly of it.

Here we were, Tobore and I, with a child who, in essence, was the core of our relationship and she needed her father. But, at the same time, he had just brought a new child into the world, and that child needed a father just as much as mine did. I was torn with the shame that I would be taking the father away from his child, like someone had taken mine away from me at one point. I was beginning to feel like I should start a blog about my life and make the domain name Confused.com, with a capital 'C'.

I stayed with Tobore in Montego Bay the night before my flight to London. I awoke in his arms feeling extremely nervous. I pulled myself from the bed, forced myself into the shower, and started getting ready to leave. All of a sudden, there was a great commotion at the door of his flat. His girlfriend had arrived at the doorstep and was demanding entrance. The scene was heart wrenching and I felt an unexpected wave of guilt and shame, even though Tobore was still my husband. She was crying and shouting at the two of us, clutching at her heart and screaming out in pain as if it was breaking. I felt guilt grip my heart that the cost of my husband and I restarting our married life would be the destruction of this other woman and the future of her newborn baby.

Finally, things calmed down when she realised that her pleas to Tobore were falling on deaf ears. He had not even let her in the door. Eventually she just left. I stood in the silence that followed and collapsed in his arms, sobbing. I felt like our marriage had been broken in so many ways. Not just by that situation, but by everything the two us had been through in the past year, together and separately. Our ride to the airport left me feeling that we were facing so many uncertainties as a couple and I wondered how we could possibly survive. I could not bring myself to voice all of the questions that were swirling in my head. Could I bear the guilt of separating a man from his newborn child? Was I making a mistake by trying to reconcile with him? Would moving our family to an unknown country be our downfall? I remained silent.

As I boarded the plane, I looked back at the landscape I was leaving. I bid farewell to the country that I had known my entire life. The nine-hour flight seemed to last for an eternity. I watched movies, walked around the plane, and even slept. It was frustrating to wake up and still be thousands of miles up in the sky, with hours left until I was to reach my destination. I fought the urge to stand up screaming for the pilots to turn around and take me home! I was reminded of the feeling I'd had as a child, living at the will of everyone else in control. I reminded myself that I had made the choice to get on that plane and to take the chance of restarting our lives away from everyone we knew and loved.

The airline served lovely Jamaican food and I greedily wolfed down my meal, not realising that these authentic flavours tantalizing my tongue would only be tasted again when I someday returned home to Jamaica.

Follow me on Twitter: @avabrown24

Finally, the announcement was made that we would be landing in thirty minutes. Even though it was the same airport I had flown in and out of for my first visit to London, I was utterly disoriented and overwhelmed when I disembarked from the plane. In my anxious state, the airport seemed to have grown by miles since my visit a few months ago. My ears were blocked and I couldn't hear the announcements directing people to customs, and the entire ground I stood on felt unsteady. I thought maybe there was an earthquake starting, but realised that everyone else around me was moving with calm purpose.

I was surprised by the cold chill in the air, even though we were inside. It was most certainly the wet chilly weather that London was famous for in the autumn that was sneaking into the building. I snapped out of my daze and tried to catch up with the other passengers from my flight; I assumed the direction they were all going was the correct one. I knew it wasn't snowing outside that early in the season, but all of the other passengers were retrieving heavy coats from their luggage; I was not prepared for that at all.

I joined the queue to clear customs and followed the instructions for those without UK citizenship; the line was much longer than the one for the British citizens. It was obvious that our flight was not the only one that had landed at that time. There was a great assortment of people in my queue. I took in the various shades of skin colours, the assortment of traditional clothing I had never seen before, and the cacophony of strange languages. I was relieved to finally recognise some of my native people, a family who had travelled on the same flight I had been on, but I breathed a sharp intake of breath as they were gathered up by the stern authorities and taken away. I wondered what they had done because they didn't look suspicious to me at all and seemed much more relaxed than I was. I was struck with panic; would they come and detain me as well? Another lady from the flight must have sensed my anxiety and confusion because she leaned over and whispered, "Drug mules." I was surprised at my ignorance but breathed a sigh of relief and realised that my hypersensitive state was more the norm for people legally immigrating to a new country.

I reached the customs window without incident. The officer hardly looked at me, simply stamping my passport and telling me in a bored voice, "Have a good day." I settled myself in the arrivals section of the airport. I was so anxious to call home and tell Tobore I had arrived safely and hear my daughter's sweet voice, but my Jamaica-based service was unable to pick up a signal and I realised I really was on my own.

"Sometimes it's best to be unsure of what lies ahead of us because if we knew, there wouldn't be any great adventure or ability to build resilience."

Follow me on Twitter: @avabrown24

Chapter Nine

THE UNKNOWN

"The unknown is sometimes started with excitement and anticipation that isn't realised at first. It's then that we have to accept we weren't prepared for the unknown."

I had been told that a representative from the employment agency would meet me in the arrivals area of the airport and take me to the home they had arranged for me to stay in while I settled into my new life and job. But as I looked around, I couldn't make out any particular person among the hundreds of people who were crowded, waving frantically to loved ones and rushing around to hug long-missed parents and lovers. To me, the room was cavernous and filled with laughing, chatting people whose lives had just been completed by the dear ones now in their arms.

On the edge of that melee were a few men standing sombrely and holding up placards with arriving passengers' names printed on them.

I was so relieved to realise that maybe one of these men might be from the agency and waiting patiently to collect me. I walked past each man in turn, carefully reading each card to find the one bearing my name. When I reached the end of the line, I doubled back to look again, thinking I must have somehow missed the one with my name on it. But my second search was as fruitless as the first. I began to think I might have landed at a different airport than the one where they were expecting to pick me up. I rechecked all of my notes from my previous conversation with the agency. I even rechecked my boarding tickets, which clearly read Heathrow Airport, and when I asked an employee walking past, he confirmed that I had landed at the right place.

I began to think that the agency representative might simply be running late. I settled myself in a chair close to the area where the pick-up gathered for each arriving flight, so as not to miss my person when they arrived. After thirty minutes ticked by, I found another airport employee and explained my situation of just having arrived and finding no one to pick me up and having no service on my mobile. The employee directed me to a bank of public phones, but when I went to use one, I remembered that I had yet to exchange my Jamaican dollars for British pounds. Luckily, someone nearby noticed my plight and graciously handed me some coins and I immediately dialled the agency.

The woman who answered the phone was surprised to hear that I was waiting at the airport and admitted they had overlooked the fact that I was landing that day. I breathed a sigh of relief when she said to sit tight because they would send someone to come get me right away. In that case, however, 'right away' really meant another hour and a half and the representative I was expecting turned out to be a cab driver who barely spoke English. I felt a rush of camaraderie for a fellow immigrant, but soon understood that our conversation would be limited to monosyllabic words.

The driver took me to a hotel and gestured for me to go inside and check-in while he waited with my luggage outside. When I went to the reception desk, though, I was told that there was no Ava Brown on their guest list. At first I assumed that the agency may have used a variation on the spelling of my full name that was causing confusion, but after the receptionist checked the guest list again, with every possible variation of my name, she still came up with nothing. A sense of panic flooded over me; here I was in the middle of London, homeless, with nothing that the agency promised, when I could have been easing into my king-sized bed with the knowledge that my house-helper had taken care of all my family's needs.

When I expressed my predicament to the cab driver, he understood and made some calls back to the agency. As he chattered away in a mix of English and some foreign language I didn't understand, I had begun to feel like I was a product being bartered in the human slave trade. I realised I was at the mercy of the employment agency. I had trusted them to bring me to another country and I knew I already owed them something for getting me my work permit. Little did I know how the process worked; the school I would be working for had paid thousands of pounds to the agency as a "finder's fee" for me. The cab driver finally finished the call and told me that we were at the wrong hotel and he would take me to the right one.

We drove in pensive silence to the north of London and stopped in front of a tall building with the term 'hostel' in big white letters above the door. I had no idea what a hostel was, but I learned exactly how it was different from a hotel as soon as I entered it. The communal living atmosphere reminded me of the dorms I had lived in while at college. But, here I was, a woman with a husband, a child, and a successful career behind me; I was no longer a teenager who was comfortable sharing a single bathroom down the hall and noisy, tightly packed bedrooms.

That time, the cab driver brought my luggage inside and drove off after gesturing me towards the reception desk. There my name was on the guest list. I was given the key to my room and informed that I would be sharing a room with eight other people. I could hardly believe what I was hearing...eight other people? How could that be? Even when I lived in the cramped single room house as a child, we didn't have nine people in it. My quick assessment of the lobby did not bode well and, as expected, when I reached the living quarters, I found filth and chaos. The bathrooms looked like they hadn't been cleaned in years and there was a buzz of activity, with people of many different colours, races, and languages jostling about the narrow hallways, in and out of our room.

In Jamaica, the language was either Patios or English, but here there was Russian, French, Italian, and Polish. I soon realised that the many people of different origins were interacting as one group, and that made me feel like even more of an outsider. In addition, I was keenly aware that I was the only black person and that made me feel even more isolated. "What have I gotten myself into?" I asked myself out loud, but either the people around me hadn't understood me, or they were just far too busy getting on with their own lives to care about a new addition to their already crowded home.

The room we all shared was about 14x15 metres with three-tiered bunk beds along the two side walls and two flat beds in the centre. There was absolutely no privacy. I had been assigned one of the bunk beds, which was covered in the filth of an unknown amount of people who had slept on it before me. I envisioned myself in prison and couldn't believe that I had condemned myself to that sentence of suffering. I tucked my belongings in the small space that had been spared for me and went to bed that night in a state of complete disillusionment. I cried myself to sleep lying on the disgusting pillow. I missed my home, my daughter, and my husband. I felt so cheated and misled.

Settling into my new life in London quickly proved to be more emotionally difficult than I could have ever imagined. Every night as I lay down to sleep, I lamented the life I had left behind in Jamaica, blinding myself to all of the difficulties I had endured; remembering only the good times and all my successes. I berated myself for having left an excellent paying job, my friends, and family. I would constantly cry myself to sleep thinking about how I had abandoned the simplest pleasures of life in my home country. I missed being able to knock on a neighbour's door just to say good morning or the ability to ask friends and family for a favour and being confident of the laid-back response being a kind "no problem irie mon" in our friendly sing-song accent. I consoled myself by remembering a piece of advice that my dear friend Dee had given me during a particularly difficult period of my life: God doesn't take us through dirty water to drown us, but to cleanse us.

I had arrived in London with nothing more than what had fit into my single piece of luggage, bringing minimal clothing and only what I thought would protect me against the intense wet and cold weather I imagined existed year-round. Establishing my new life with these relatively few possessions was a daily reminder that I had consciously chosen to leave behind a lifestyle of luxury and certainty to start all over again. I felt as if I was back in the first week of college, the poor girl without the appropriate items to do my work and without any friends. However, the fear that still lurked in my heart about the men who had attacked me on that fateful night compelled me to reflect on the justifications I had given myself for moving to London in the first place. I reminded myself that Jamaica had once been a colony of England and of its significant influences on our culture that were still evident even today. I told myself I was just being a silly girl. How different could the two countries really be?

My roommates seemed to be settled into the hostel lifestyle. But I found it very difficult to adjust, especially with the lack of privacy and the requirement to share a toilet and a shower with so many strangers. The shower was on the third floor, and I had to take six flights of stairs to get there, carrying with me all of the toiletries I would need. I would wearily climb the stairs every morning, my arms loaded with my towel, toothbrush, soap, toothpaste, lotion, underwear, and most importantly, bath slippers to protect myself from contracting the fungal skin diseases that were rampant among the community. I would also take my clothes to get dressed for the day, since the shower room provided the only privacy and I was incredibly uncomfortable with the sexually liberal attitude that I was seeing all around me.

The hostel provided meals for all of its residents, but I had an extremely hard time eating the daily dinner rations of bland mashed potatoes, runny brown gravy, and fatty English sausages. Sleep was never easy and an undisturbed eight hours was impossible. I soon found out that my roommates all worked different jobs and kept different hours. Some worked in the food service and others at the twenty-four hour cab dispatch offices. As such, we all kept different schedules and the lights in the room were going on and off at all hours of the night. It seemed as if we were all in a constant overlap of going-to-work and coming-home schedules, with someone coming in at dawn, exhausted from the late night shift, just as somebody else was crawling out of bed, exhausted from lack of sleep, to get dressed and join the morning commute. It felt like I was simultaneously living out a multitude of scenes in a movie that was set in fast-forward.

Another difficulty in that living situation was the potpourri of smells that assaulted the nose throughout the day and night. I was sure that I smelled as strange to the others in the hostel as they did to me. We were such a mismatch of body odours that revealed our cultural beliefs of how much bathing was appropriate and what kind of foods were eaten in our varying nations. Almost everyone sought out their native foods when they were outside of the hostel. The breakfast menu was not much better than the dinner menu, and just as unchanging.

The smell of eggs frying in stale oil permeated the entire building every morning as the sun rose. I would drag myself down to the breakfast area, because if you missed breakfast, you were on your own until dinner. Whatever wealth I had acquired remained back in Jamaica for the time and with money being tight, the food at the hostel was my only option.

The cleanliness of the dishes we ate from was equal to that of the rest of the hostel and the food was of very low quality. My first morning at the hostel, I looked down at my plate and imagined it shouting "Don't eat from me! I am not clean!" The bread looked as if it had been obtained on sale after being rejected from the production line, the eggs were runny and barely warm, and the sausage was undercooked to the point of being nearly raw. My stomach knotted and I nearly gagged at the thought of eating that meal, but I knew I needed sustenance for the day ahead of me. My most important duty was to find a place where I could get my phone activated so I could hear the voice of my sweet daughter and remember the reasons I must endure that situation; to create a safer life for her and me and to create a more stable home life for our family.

"Being in the wilderness without a familiar object is like being left to die, but faith will allow you to survive until rescue can come."

Follow me on Twitter: @avabrown24

Chapter Ten

DEEP END

"The mundane things in modern life, like technology, can be one's best friend in the desert."

———————

I found a mobile phone shop about twenty metres from the hostel that sold SIM cards, which I hoped would allow me to access international calling on my phone. The price was steep, especially considering the very few pounds I had to survive on until I started to receive my salary from the teaching job. I was incredibly hopeful as I handed over the non-refundable money and watched the salesperson insert the card into my phone. I was practically breathing down his neck as he held up the phone in the air and together we watched the screen as it searched for a signal. I laughed out loud with glee when the signal bars filled up to the highest range, showing strong connectivity. Finally, I was returning back to civilisation!

It was my second day in London and the agency had not left any messages at the hostel. I checked to see if they may have been trying to contact me through my mobile phone, but there were no messages on it either. It was strange; prior to my arrival, they had been in routine contact, constantly reassuring me that they would take care of me when I arrived in that new country. After the debacle at the airport, I couldn't imagine them forgetting me again so soon. I called the agency's main office, but only got a receptionist. She had no power but could only promise to pass on my message to an upper-level staff member. I left my mobile number and asked for a return call. My anxiety was again beginning to heighten. I thought in panic of how much I was at the mercy of these people whom I had no reason to trust. I only had their word. Again, I thought of all the stories I had heard of unsuspecting immigrants landing in a county only to be placed in indentured servitude or outright slavery.

A tense two hours later, my mobile rang and I was greeted by the branch manager of the agency. He apologized profusely for all the messy planning up to that point but I couldn't get a word in edgewise. When he finished his jovial rant promising that everything would be well from then on, I was finally able to express myself. And express myself I did! I let out a barrage of complaints starting with the disgust I felt about being treated as nothing more than an after-thought and finishing with the horrible living conditions at the hostel.. He waited on the other end of the line in patient silence and then told me I needed to collect my belongings and find my way over to the office in south London to discuss the details of starting my job right away and to get settled into a better living environment. I was still fuming, though, and yelled into the phone, "I am in the north right now! Don't you have an office nearby that could find me a more tolerable place to live?!" His reply was curt. He told me again that I needed to find my way to their office, which was located on the south side of the city. He capped it off with a biting comment, "You said in your interview that you were a dedicated employee, who wasn't lazy."

I was so offended. I wanted to end the conversation right then by telling him to just fuck off. Instead, I bit my tongue and kicked the wall. We both knew that I needed his help due to the predicament I was in. I took a deep breath and thought to approach the situation like I would have with any cantankerous client in my old sales job. I kindly asked if the agency would send another cab to come and get me, but felt like I hit a wall when he snapped, "I would imagine you can read and in doing so get yourself from point A to point B. You mentioned in our chat that you travelled to the US frequently; well it is the same here, just a different country. That was what working adults do, and I trust you are not a child. We don't employ children either." He cleverly placed a chuckle here to break the tension.

I stood in stunned silence and then thought about how I was to accomplish that feat. I mumbled something about getting a cab, and he replied by telling me to have the cab drop me off in Mitcham Town Centre, then to give him a call and he would provide me with the necessary walking directions from that point. He then hung up and all of the frustration at the indignities he had thrown at me came boiling to the surface. I let out a giant scream and stomped like a two-year-old. The passersby must have thought I was a mad woman!

I steeled myself for the travel to the Mitcham Town Centre, wherever that was. I consoled myself with the thought that at least I would be leaving that disgusting hostel. However, when I went back up to my room to gather my things, I found my bag lying open and broken on the floor. My things were strewn about and all the money I had brought was gone, along with the more expensive items of clothing and desirable personal care items. Thank God I had tucked some money away in my purse and taken it with me when I left on my errands. There was no way to know who had done it, as everyone had access to where the tenants' luggage was kept. My only recourse was to pack up what was left, improvise a quick fix to the latch so that it would be semi-functional, and check out.

I didn't know where I would be sleeping that night, but I didn't even care at that point. As I dragged my broken bag through the hostel's front doors, I felt as if I was wearing all of its grime on my skin. A white man, whom I recognised as one of the young immigrants from Kosovo that was living at the hostel, noticed my struggle and offered to help me. I almost wept at his simple gesture of kindness. I realised then that the cold personalities I had encountered so far in London were almost more than I could bear. In that moment, my heart ached so much for my home country that I thought it might break. Never in your wildest dreams would a Jamaican man stand by and ignore a female in need of physical help. The young man could see my turmoil, and without a word, he took the bag from me and carried it down to the curb.

I didn't have to wait long for the cab that had been called by the front desk to arrive. I loaded my things into the back and directed the driver to Mitcham Town Centre. Before we set off, I asked him how much it would cost, but he said he couldn't say for certain as the cab fares were based on the mileage covered. All I knew was that London was large. I had no clue how far my destination was from that point, and I prayed that the money I still had in my purse was enough to cover the fare. My body and mind were so drained from the emotional turmoil of my first few days in London that the movement of the car lulled me into a deep sleep. I remember clearly how I dreamt about Jamaica, imagining that I was seated on a plane and on my way back home. I felt a gentle tap on my shoulder and smiled, thinking it was my baby Jasmine waking me up as she normally would do. But when I opened my eyes to see only the Rastafarian immigrant face of the cabbie, tears streamed from my eyes.

Follow me on Twitter: @avabrown24

"Madam," he said, "we are in Mitcham." I was still very groggy and looked around; searching desperately for scenes that would tell me I was really alighting in Jamaica. But there was only the drizzly London weather and people tightly wrapped against the chill with their heads down and hands tucked firmly in their pockets as they stalked through the town square. The shock of that scene was too much and I started bawling outright. The driver was at a loss about what to do with me. He stepped away and instead busied himself with removing my luggage from the car and setting it carefully on the sidewalk. I finally gathered myself enough to ask him what the fare was; forty pounds. It would take nearly half of all the money I had in my wallet.

When I handed the money over, the cab driver asked me what was wrong. I shrugged off his question and told him that I was fine, but in a hurry to make an appointment. I did not want to air all of my complaints in the middle of a public street to a perfect stranger. Still, he placed an empathetic hand on my shoulder and told me to be strong. As he handed me a card with his number on it, he said, "It all comes together at some stage. I meet new immigrants from the Caribbean all the time and they were always overwhelmed by that massive city. With time, it will get better." I felt like God had sent an angel to deliver just the right message to strengthen my resolve to go forward.

I tucked his card in a safe place in my purse. I felt like I was no longer a complete stranger in that country, I now had met one person who was willing to offer the hand of friendship. As he got back into his cab, he gave me one last piece of advice, he told me the quicker I picked myself up, the better it would be for me, because the path to my future in that new country was going to be rocky. And soon, I discovered that he was right on both of these points.

I finally snapped back to reality and made the call to the agency to

Follow me on Twitter: @avabrown24

tell my handler, whom I had begun to think of as my owner, I had arrived in the town centre. He asked me to tell him a landmark near my location and then told me that I was a short twenty-minute walk from where he was currently doing some business, which was closer than the office. When I arrived at the destination, I found the man was a tall, white Briton. He formally introduced himself for the first time and I learned his name was James Tuckader; I could call him Mr. Tuckader. In an unexpected gesture of kindness, he said that he had driven near to the town centre to do some business and pick me up. The drive to the office in Clapham was completed in absolute silence, and that time, I was much too anxious to fall asleep.

When we arrived, he directed me to a small room with a desk and quickly got down to the business of explaining the details of my employment - where I would be working, what hours I was expected to be there, and to whom I would be reporting. Without any unnecessary pleasantries, he then took me back to his car and drove me to the school that I would be working in - a large public high school. We sat in the main reception area, on hard plastic chairs, for a good forty-five minutes. All that time, there was a din of boisterous teenaged shouting and jostling in the surrounding corridors. I was utterly confused because the schools in Jamaica were so strict and the children were expected to be well behaved in all grades.

Finally, the door to one of the inner offices burst open and a thin, sallow-skinned white woman rushed in and made a beeline straight for us with a stern look on her face. She introduced herself as the deputy head teacher. Even though she was brisk and unfriendly, I was impressed with her efficiency. She spoke with us briefly and handed us over to the school's financial officer, who then surreptitiously handed an envelope to Mr Tuckader. I assumed it was the agency's finder's fee that was paid for me and which made me really feel like I was being sold like a slave. I realised

Follow me on Twitter: @avabrown24

from my eavesdropping on their jovial yet argumentative conversation that the school was paying quite a tidy sum for me. The financier was an obese white woman, who wore a tent-like, bright yellow, floppy housecoat with frills and flapped her arms about when she spoke so that she looked like the giant talking bird character from a popular children's show back home. I did not realise then that was her regular daily attire and that the students and staff alike secretly referred to her by the name of that very same character.

When what I imagined to be the financial transaction was completed, she stood and shook hands with me, commenting on how smartly dressed I was for their humble school. I thanked her, but soon realised that it wasn't really the compliment I had assumed it to be. I was wearing one of my power suits, which I was so accustomed to wearing in my executive job in Jamaica to convey a sense of professionalism. I had thought it was appropriate because the teachers in Jamaica always dressed professionally and modestly, with all unnecessary skin covered up and tattoos hidden. The concept back home was that teachers were supposed to be models for the students to emulate.

I had dressed in my suit out of respect for the teaching profession and for the children I would be mentoring. But as I started paying attention to the students and teachers who were going back and forth in the corridor, I realised that I was terribly overdressed. I lamented the fact that even the dress that made me feel successful and capable in Jamaica only made me feel awkward and uncomfortable in a first world country. I buried these feelings and held my head high as I was given the grand tour of the school. At the end, I felt totally lost in that new world and thought that I was intruding where I so clearly didn't belong. We passed classroom after classroom filled with screaming teenagers who were left on their own and were jumping around the room. At first, I thought we must be in the drama department, where pupils were practicing for an upcoming play, but as the tour continued, I realised that these were just regular classes and that the teachers simply had no control over their pupils. The tour guide must have noticed my surprise because she told me not to worry because the wild behaviour was only expected at the beginning and end of the school year, when the children were still hyperactive from summer break.

The guide told us that the next stop would be the technology department of the school, where I would be working. She gave an embarrassed titter and admitted that the school was so large that even though she had been there for two years and was a senior manager, she didn't know where that block of classrooms was. I knew right then that the rocky path in England the cab driver had predicted would not include only my personal life, but my professional one as well.

"Sometimes we end up in situations where running is our best option, but when we find that there is nowhere to run, we just stand."

Chapter Eleven
TRANSITION

"Life can sometimes toss, shove, and send you into the wilderness before it brings you back to civilization, the place you ideally want to be at."

———————

The transition from being an employee in the private corporate sector to becoming one in the state-run school system was a shock, to say the least. In addition, the school's curriculum and teaching role was completely different to what I had been trained for in my home country. I was confused as to how two countries that spoke a similar language and had a shared history could be so different. My fellow teachers and the school staff turned out to be very polite and eager to help me get settled in to my new teaching post, but I could not shake my homesickness and the feeling of culture shock. I struggled to overcome my subdued mood and match the enthusiasm of my colleagues, but my smiles never reached my eyes and belied my belief in the Jamaican proverb to be weary of overly friendly people.

Follow me on Twitter: @avabrown24

My general disorientation in that new setting only strengthened my paranoia that had been born on the night I was attacked. I remained on high alert in any situation involving strangers, including all of my colleagues and pupils. My inability to form any bonds within that social group pushed me deeper into a depression. For the first week, I would start each day in my classroom by arriving early, before the students, so that I could gather myself to be an effective instructor. Inevitably, as I would look around the empty room filled with desks, my resolve would crumble and I would sink into a ten-minute sob fest. My crying was so intense in those days that I would hear myself gasping for breath and moaning out loud. I remember the horror that would strike my heart when I heard myself and it would make me cry harder. I also worried about what my colleagues would think if they heard me, so I would bury my head in my handbag to suffocate the noises of deep emotional pain that were escaping from within me.

I could not escape my misery. I wanted to be gone from that strange place where I did not fit in. I wanted to be back at home with my daughter and my husband by my side. I wanted the past year to have been only a bad dream. I began to convince myself that the threats to my life were not real after all, that I had somehow misunderstood my attackers' parting words, or dreamed their second visit to my home. I was desperate to return to the familiar world that I now felt foolish to have fled. There were so few black people in that new town and my uniquely dark skin colour made me feel even more isolated. I yearned for the days when I could have simply walked around my local community and found any number of extended family members to complain to or commiserate with. Here, I didn't even get a simple good morning from passers-by on the street. I even began to miss the distant and sometimes tenuous relationships that I had with my mum and siblings.

On that first day at the school, the man from the agency had excused himself shortly after my tour of the building had begun. As he tried to sneak off, I grabbed him by the jacket so that he wouldn't get away without telling me where I was to be staying that night; after all, I had checked out of the hostel and my luggage was still in his car. He told me that he would drop my bag off in the school's main office and I could find it there at the end of the day. For the second time that day, I found out that it would be up to me to take care of myself.

When the tour ended, the ladies in the school's main office were kind enough to make some calls to various B&Bs in the area. After several calls, they found one with a vacancy in the south of London. When the secretary asked me to approve the price of twenty pounds per night so that she could make my reservation, I agreed with trepidation in my heart; twenty pounds was almost the exact amount of money I had left in my wallet. The secretary also provided me with the bus schedule so that I could catch a ride directly from the front of the school to my new lodgings. The bus was crowded with people travelling home from the end of the workday across the city, and in the entire hubbub, I missed my stop. I was relieved to find that the next stop was only a five-minute walk from the one where I should have got off.

I found the B&B rather easily and felt like my luck was finally changing. The building was a paradise compared to the hostel. As I approached the shining oak reception desk, I wondered just what would have happened if I had had no money left to pay for it? I shuddered to think that the agency would have just abandoned me to sleep on the street at that point; with their commission in hand; there was no need for them to concern themselves with me any more. The receptionist took my money as prepayment for the night and informed me that there was no access to a phone line. I smiled, because for once today, a challenge was not insurmountable; my phone was still showing a strong signal and I would be able to call home as soon as I got settled.

The collective cost of my taxi fare, the bus fare, and the lodging fee left me nearly broke, remembering the money that had been stolen that morning. I had no money for a proper meal before bed that night, so I focused my energies on taking a much-needed shower in the B&B's clean bathroom. Then I found a small shop where I could purchase a loaf of sliced bread and a two-litre cream soda. Those items would serve as my dinner until I managed to get some money wired from my account in Jamaica or my first paycheque arrived. I retired to the privacy of my well-kept room at the B&B and picked at the inadequate meal. In Jamaica, I was accustomed to a hearty dinner each night, which would include everything from oxtail, rice and peas, coleslaw, and potato salad, to fried chicken, bacon, and eggs; my help had been a lavish cook! My new life in England was so different to that in Jamaica that I felt as if I had been transported to another world and not just another country.

Having that little bit of bread and soda in my stomach fortified my spirit more than it did my physical state. Despite my situation being nothing as I had imagined it to be, I recalled my natural strength of perseverance. I resolved to make the move work, no matter what, by reminding myself of the fact that my daughter and sister were coming to join me in October. There was no way I was going to allow them to arrive to the same frightening uncertainty that I had.

When I drifted off to sleep that night, I had serene dreams, filled with my daughter's sweet laughter and the sensation of her little arms hugging me. Before I knew it, the alarm was jolting me awake, alerting me to the impending workday ahead of me. I had slept so deeply that I was disoriented by my surroundings for a few moments. Finally, the realisation that I was in London, about to start teaching at the high school and needing to check out of the B&B, crept into my mind. I took another long shower, luxuriating in the extreme cleanliness of that bathroom compared to that of the hostel. As the hot water cascaded over my head, covering my body like a blanket, my brain and soul woke up and I steeled myself to handle all of the new challenges that lay ahead of me that day. The B&B served a hot and hearty breakfast and I ate as much as my stomach could hold, knowing that my next meals would only consist of the leftover bread and soda that were now tucked among my belongings in my luggage.

Even though my heart was aching to hear the voices of my daughter, my sister, and Tobore, I hesitated to call them with only complaints about my first few days in the place that was soon to be their new home. Instead, I placed a call to a childhood friend, Jos, who offered to provide me with a quick loan of British pounds so that I could rent a place before my financial matters were settled. Since I was expected to be at work all day, I would have to use the evening to look for a place to live permanently. I hoped I would find something immediately and not have to return to the B&B, as night-by-night lodging was always more expensive than a monthly rental.

I borrowed a local newspaper from the reception desk and scanned the advertisements as I finished my breakfast. Without thinking, I immediately started to seek out houses that matched what we had in Jamaica, but the exorbitant rates that were published next to each listing quickly jolted me back to reality. There was no way I would be able to afford a dwelling large enough for each of us to have a separate room and extra space for socialising. I scanned the adverts until I reached the section at the end that was more 'poor man's housing' and I took a sharp intake of breath when I realised that even these prices were incredibly high by Jamaican standards. In all my considerations about accepting the teaching job in London, it had never occurred to me to consider the drastic difference in cost of living, which reduced my already low pay to nearly nothing. I cursed myself for having made such a rash decision to immigrate; clearly, I had not thought it through adequately.

I caught the bus to work and was again overwhelmed by the newness of my surroundings. The buildings were tall and crowded together. Everything looked the same to me, including the people on the streets, who all wore dour expressions and kept to themselves. When I arrived in my classroom that morning, I met the first of my students. The informal interactions between pupils and teachers struck me as it had the day before. I planned to overcome this and establish a sense of decorum in my classroom by instructing my students to take their seats and give me their attention while I gave a very formal introduction about myself.

I stood straight up in front of the class and gave a proper oration about who I was, where I was from, and what my hopes were in regards to helping guide their lives and enriching their education. I asked the pupils to introduce themselves one-by-one.

When we got to one boy who was of Caribbean descent, he concluded his introduction by saying to me, "Hey, I have seen you somewhere before."

I immediately labelled that boy as the class clown, and I was more than ready to put a stop to his attention-seeking behaviour. I brushed his comment off with ease, but was thrown off balance when the boy stood up, pointed at me and exclaimed, "Oh yes! I have seen you before, in the paper! My mum and dad just came back from the big reggae show in Jamaica, and you were in the paper they brought back."

I laughed his words off, but that just riled him up more.

He looked me straight in the eye and said, "I will bring that paper tomorrow and prove you wrong."

He was so emphatic that I agreed that he should bring the paper in so that I could see myself in print.

Turns out, he was right. When he came in the next day with the paper, there I was staring out from the front page, dressed to the nines at one of the last big galas I had attended for the telecom company. The fact that I was standing next to a singer who was very popular worldwide at the time impressed my students and gave me a bit of respect in their eyes. I silently thanked God that was the story in which I was headlining, and not a report of the brutal crime that I had just survived.

The resources at the new school were nothing like I had ever seen before. I felt like the students were being educated in the lap of luxury. Back at my high school in Jamaica, we had learned about photosynthesis by picking leaves off of trees outside and holding them up to the sun to squint at the structures that the bright light made semi-translucent. The school was full of the latest technology and clever exaggerated representations of even the smallest of molecules and elements. Even though these resources were advanced, I lamented that, as a teacher here, I wouldn't have the opportunity to teach the children the important life lesson of improvising and using their creativity to overcome a challenge.

My strict demeanour allowed me to gain some semblance of control over the pupils in my classroom. However, on the whole, my impression from the first day in the school was correct and most of the other classrooms seemed completely out of control. I found out that the lower grade feeder schools for that high school were all same-sex schools, so for many students, it was their first experience attending school with the opposite sex. The titillation that these students felt at being in a co-ed structure meant that many teachers were merely policing the hormone-driven students rather than teaching them. I noticed the sexual tension even in my own classroom, which was visible in the way that the children sat themselves on opposite sides of the room according to gender. I laughed inwardly because the room looked like a community ruled by two rival gangs who had no trust in each other.

Follow me on Twitter: @avabrown24

I made a concerted effort to help the girls and boys begin to interact with one another more naturally by formally assigning seating that mixed up the two. That arrangement was met with much loud grumbling, but I overruled it all and the classroom benefited from it in the end. Sooner than I had dared to hope, I found my footing in the classroom and the lessons started to interest the students. I did make an attempt to instil the importance of smart dressing, but that was largely a failure. The style for boys at the time was to wear their trousers down past their hips, so that their ass was literally hanging out, covered by thin cotton boxer shorts with wild prints on them. It was also the style to look a bit grungy, but boys of that age need to bathe and they often smelled rather 'ripe' from their boisterous activities.

I was continually surprised when the students would show up completely unprepared for lessons, carrying no pens, pencils, or books. There was a particular group of boys and girls who were already quite hardened to life and who accepted no amount of guidance. The boys would almost always skip class, and instead wander the corridors in search of their own entertainment. Unfortunately, that entertainment consisted of accosting anyone they found alone and that even included the staff and teachers, who they harassed relentlessly because they knew that the law would favour them if they made any false accusation of abuse. I soon found that I was not immune to their torments. On one particular occasion, one of the rougher girls in this gang shoved me up against a window and threatened to thrust me straight through the glass in retaliation for my having reprimanded her during class. When I made a complaint to the administration, I was told there was no recourse since it had happened without any witnesses besides her group of friends, who, they assured me, would lie for her.

My personal living situation got settled pretty quickly. I found a small flat to rent in a multi-storied building in an ideal location. It was near the train station and bus depot, as well as several fruiterers and banks. The floor plan consisted of a front social room (which also served as a second bedroom), a proper bedroom, kitchen, and bathroom. My flat was on the ground floor, and the flat below ground level was occupied by a number of African men living together in a place of similar design and size. The men, though packed in together and sometimes rowdy, were courteous whenever we met. But I was still very fearful of strange men, especially when they were in groups, so I always kept a far distance.

While the place was cramped and dingy, it served my purpose. I dismissed my disappointment by reminding myself that the flat was simply a stopgap along the journey to my great life in London. Still, I greatly missed all the luxuries of the home I had abandoned back in Jamaica and I began to worry about what my family would be expecting to live in when they finally arrived. Would they condemn me as a failure when they found no king size bed with Egyptian cotton sheets, en-suite bathroom, or walk in closet?

When I moved in, I got a better appreciation for just how dirty the last tenants had left the place. The carpets were thoroughly soiled and there was a prevalent underlying odour of mould that began to cling to everything I owned. I had no money to clean it, but I was also working so many extended hours at the school that I had no time to care about it. I had also managed to make a friend among my colleagues at the school; another young teacher named Soha, who immediately proved herself a trustworthy confidant. It was she who recognised that the struggle with my finances could be resolved by getting a flatmate to share the cost of rent. My first reaction to her recommendation was horror. Without thinking, I argued that it was impossible. I was a woman, I was a mother and a wife, I owned my own luxurious home back in Jamaica; communal living was for youngsters who were just starting out, I stated flatly. She simply looked me straight in the eye and asked me if I had really just described myself. She also explained that she knew that the agency wouldn't be paying up front, so I would need to wait some time for my first paycheque, and that it often took longer than expected to get international banking matters resolved.

I was utterly frustrated to realise that she was right. I had very little money left from the loan I had taken from my friend Jos. I really had no choice but to get a flat mate if I was going to be able to stay in the dirty little hovel I had managed to acquire. I put out an advert in the free local paper, but had little time to devote to vetting interested parties. Ultimately, I accepted the first woman who turned up in person and agreed to pay the amount I asked for. If I had been thinking straight, I would have realised right away that person was not someone I would have chosen to live with under any other circumstances. But given my situation, I didn't have much of a choice.

My flat-mate had grown up in the local ghetto, much like I had, but the similarities ended there. Where I spent my days and nights tirelessly working to improve my situation, she sat around primping for social outings. Her mass of bleaching creams, coloured wigs, and scanty outfits took up a large portion of the front room. She was up at all hours of the night and would frequently return loudly from a boisterous night out in the wee hours of the morning, which affected my sleep and made settling into my new work routine a challenge. I made a mental note that professionals must flat share with like-minded professionals. Much like a marriage, a successful union of flat-mates relies on compatibility in the majority of things.

The situation with my flat-mate could not last, and I realised that the flat itself was absolutely unsuitable for my arriving family. I had settled into my role at the school and started to feel confident with the town itself, so I started looking for a new place where my daughter and sister could move with me. They were expected to arrive in less than two months.

In the meantime, I began readying the dingy flat for the possibility of our needing to live there - minus the flatmate, of course. I missed my daughter immensely, so getting the house prepared for her made me happy in a way that nothing else had since my arrival. There wasn't a great deal I could do with the flat, but I began to clean as much as possible. I was like a new mother who was nesting before the birth of their baby. I freshened up the foul carpet, obtained a nice, but cheap, duvet cover and some soft, plush toys. I even sought out ethnic food shops to gather some familiar foods, to help ease their introduction to that new life. I also learnt where the libraries, parks, schools, and churches were located.

As my excitement mounted, October seemed to approach at the pace of a snail. I began calling home frequently and spending all of my extra money on phone cards. Finally, the day arrived when they would land at Heathrow and there was no way I was going to let them experience the isolation and uncertainty I had when my flight had landed. The trip to the airport felt like I was driving across the country, instead of just across town. In my anxiousness, I managed to arrive at the airport several hours early, but I didn't care. I was just thrilled to finally be reunited with my baby girl.

After their flight had landed, the arrivals area became thick with people awaiting the arrival of their loved ones from the interior. I couldn't see past the crowds and was afraid I would miss Jasmine and my sister. As I craned my neck to look above the mass of people ahead of me, I heard an all too familiar voice saying, "Excuse me, has anyone seen my mum? Where is my mum?" I flew through the crowd and towards the little angelic voice of my daughter. There she was - such a big girl, confidently walking into the arrivals area, decked out in her denim jacket and matching jeans and a dainty pink bow laced through her hair. I flung my arms open wide and she landed in them like a little angel settling onto a cloud. We hugged in a deep, long embrace and I felt complete. Suddenly, it didn't matter how much I disliked that massive city and its strange culture; my life was filled with sunshine because my daughter was back with me.

I next grabbed my sister in a strong embrace and we headed out together, to face the challenges that London had to offer. On the ride to our flat, I could see the looks of amazement and trepidation on their faces as they scanned the city outside of the cab's windows. I was reminded of my first day here and I became even more determined to ensure that their experience would be easier than mine had been. They told me all about the flight and the newness of all they'd experienced while crossing the Atlantic. I told them about my job and the town in which we would be living. The chattering continued when we got to the flat. My sister updated me on all the community news I had missed since September. We stayed up so late into the night that the cold began to creep in from the outside. Even though I had the front room cleared and set up for my sister to live in, we all snuggled in my bed together that night and fell asleep.

Neither Jasmine nor my sister cared about, or maybe didn't even realise, the poor state of the flat or the neighbourhood in which we were staying. Even though it met none of the high standards I had made them accustomed to back in Jamaica, they showed me that the only thing that mattered was that we were together again. As I drifted off to sleep that night, happier and more fulfilled than I thought possible, I began to think about the next big thing we needed to prepare for. Tobore was coming in December.

"The presence, support, and comfort of family are the best remedy for the soul."

Follow me on Twitter: @avabrown24

Chapter Twelve
READJUSTMENTS

"Readjustments can sometimes feel like a crisis on self-esteem."

———————

The adjustment of us all living together in the small flat took some time. I managed to get Jasmine registered in the neighbourhood school and helped Kem find a job nearby, which was literally a two-minute walk from our home. I was pleased to see how quickly these two girls acclimatized and it served to inspire me in the same vein. Certainly, just having had my two beloved family members by my side made London feel less like an island of banishment and more like our home. Even though I was still working long hours at the school, I took odd jobs to get the extra income we would need to be able to afford an adequately sized place that would accommodate the three of us, as well as my husband when he arrived in December.

I was excited about Tobore's arrival, but also somewhat apprehensive. I felt we were strong enough individuals to overcome all the hurt that had passed between us and mend the frayed connection. My prayers were that our relationship would work out since we would have left our major problems back in Jamaica. In fact, I believed we had already forgiven each other for all of our past transgressions and were ready to move on. Accepting the reality of his other child and suppressing my sense of utter betrayal had been hard, but knowing that he was sitting at home equally excited about coming to join me eased my pain.

As December rushed forward, I became more comfortable making the types of phone calls to just simply say, "I miss you." One morning, when I had quickly finished getting ready for work and had a few extra minutes, I ducked into one of those iconic red telephone boxes and made such a call, even though it was two a.m. in Montego Bay. I still remember the smile that was on my face as I held the phone to my ear, waiting to hear the sleepy voice of the man who had recaptured my heart. But to my surprise, a friend of his answered the phone, telling me that Tobore had gone out for a walk and had left his phone behind. Something in his tone piqued my feminine intuition and I knew I was being lied to. After all, I knew my husband well enough to know that he did not have the dreamy spirit of a poet who went for contemplative walks on the beach in the middle of the night.

As I hung up, my mind immediately went to the memory of the day before I'd left for London, when his 'baby mama' had been beating at his front door and screaming in heartbroken anguish. My fingers moved over the phone's number pad without me consciously moving them. I dialled her number. She answered on the third ring and my number must have shown on her screen because she simply said, "Babe, it's for you," as she handed Tobore the phone.

To be perfectly honest, I don't recall exactly what else transpired on the phone call after that moment. I do, however, remember how I physically felt; all of the hope I had for our relationship wafted up and out of my body, like steam rising from a boiling pot. All the dreams I'd carried inside my heart, that had buoyed me through the past months, disappeared into nothingness. Blackness started to close in around me and I nearly passed out, the phone slipped from my grasp and clanged sharply on the glass pane of the telephone box enclosure. I managed to keep myself upright; I staggered out of the phone booth and made my way to my school for the work day. I cried the entire walk.

My mind was spinning. How could Tobore have done that to me, to us, right after we had agreed to start over? How could he so blatantly disrespect all the hard work I was doing to set up our new life? All I had done to ensure that his own transition would be easier than mine had been? The night we'd spent together before I left, we had made a solemn promise to one another. Recommitting ourselves to the marriage vows we had taken so many years before. He broke that promise. I was so distraught that when I arrived at work, I didn't care what the kids did that day. I allowed most of my classes to simply do their own thing. I sat at my desk in a near comatose state; I just stared at the floor and tried not to dissolve into tears. I couldn't have been more relieved when the day finally ended.

Back at home that night, I didn't speak to anyone and I couldn't eat. I just wanted to shut the world out. In my mind I reviewed all the conversations Tobore and I had shared since my arrival in London. I searched desperately for any clues as to his true intentions, anything that I might have blinded myself to. Eventually, I called a friend back home in Jamaica. I needed to unload my misery and find some support, but the conversation only led to my learning that Tobore had gone back to his lover's bed the day after my flight left.

Even though I was disgusted at the thought of Tobore coming to join us, I continued to look for a house that would fit our family. In November, I located a two-bedroom maisonette that was tiny, but a vast improvement over our dingy little flat. There was a garden in the back and a charming corner bathroom directly after the kitchen. I never could get used to the English design of putting the toilet beside the kitchen, but until I could afford to design my own home, I would have to live with the style that was normal in that country. In fact, many things that were normal fixtures in a middle-class home in Jamaica were considered amenities accompanied by a premium price in London, including the en-suite bathroom, a power-shower (which sometimes simply meant a shower head), a garden, dedicated or merely convenient parking, double glazed panelling, and central heating.

The perception of England back in its previous colony, and a largely poor one, was that the motherland had streets paved with gold. While my expectations on arrival were not quite so luxuriant, they were certainly higher than what I had been exposed to so far. I came to realise the importance in the distinction between how things appeared when one was on holiday and how they actually were for the full-time working citizens. Despite all my petty complaints, the maisonette was the best that my budget could afford.

My sister Kem, Jasmine, and I moved in and we instantly fell in love with our new, clean place. We were cramped but cosy. In addition, despite what had transpired between Tobore and his lover, he had told me that he was still planning to join us. I began to dread what was in store for us. Were we soon to be back enduring each other's company in a broken relationship with no hope of survival?

December arrived before I knew it and I found myself in a cab on the way to the airport to pick him up. I was surprised to find that a part of me was still happy to know that he was finally arriving after all that time. Maybe Jasmine's excitement at her daddy's arrival had rubbed off on me? Jasmine and my sister joined me on the trip to the airport and, to a stranger's eyes, we made a very joyous welcoming party. The journey home was more subdued, and reflected the true feeling or lack thereof, between my husband and me. It was clear, even on that first night, that mending our broken relationship was not going to work.

Over the next six months, we made a somewhat valiant effort to rekindle our unconditional love for one another, but all our interactions were tainted with the mistrust of the past. At the time, I did try to identify exactly what our fundamental problems were, so that we could attack them head on; but looking back, I realised I was too close to the situation to be able to carry out that kind of self-assessment in a productive manner. The clarity of hindsight, supported by the years in between then and now in which I have matured, has allowed me to see what my faults were in the crumbling of our marriage.

I suffered greatly from low self-esteem, which had been further weakened by my experience with the attackers that had caused me to flee Jamaica in the first place. I had always felt inadequate next to Tobore, he being from such a strong and wealthy family compared to my own, but then I also felt somewhat unworthy of him. I was plagued by the feeling that I had failed as a wife. I blamed myself for him straying into the arms of another woman and creating another child. With the move to London, I felt that I was failing him even then. I felt that I was the one that moved him from our luxurious life into a struggle for survival in a strange country, without our families or life-long friends.

We endured a tense life under the same roof for about six months, with no progress being made towards each other. Then one night, during the last weeks of the spring term at my school, our frustrations with one another came pouring out in a massive argument. At the end, we were both physically and emotionally exhausted and I knew we could not go on like that without utterly destroying ourselves. In the silence that followed, I was the first to speak, "I will move out of the flat."

Follow me on Twitter: @avabrown24

Within a few short days, I had secured another two-bedroom flat and moved myself, my sister, and Jasmine into it. I had settled Jasmine and myself into one of the two bedrooms so that Kem could have a room to herself. However, as our move-in day progressed, Kem never showed up after she removed her things from the flat we were vacating. As the afternoon wore on and I'd had no contact with her, I began to get nervous. "Oh, god, please don't let that be Jamaica all over again," I pleaded in silent prayer. I certainly did not have the income to afford that flat by myself. I calmed myself by rerunning all the conversations we'd had in the previous days, when she had constantly assured me she would stay with us and had helped pick out something we could afford on a two-person income.

As the evening began to fall, Kem finally called. My heart sank as I listened to her telling me that she had decided at the last minute to move in with her friend instead of Jasmine and me. I felt her words as if they were a slap to my face. I reasoned with her about the rental contract that I had signed, with the agreement that she was to live with us. Her answer was only to suggest that I abandon the new flat and find another that was smaller and that I could afford without her. When I explained again that was impossible because I would lose all of the money I had deposited, she remained unmoved.

If I broke the rental agreement, I would have no money for a deposit on another place, so I went ahead and stayed in the flat with the knowledge that I had to find a flatmate, and quick! Luckily, the advert I put out in the next day's paper was answered promptly by a lovely white girl from Yorkshire named Jenna. Before we knew it, she moved in and I finally felt some relief from my financial worries. Jenna wasn't the cleanest person, but she tried. She was kind-hearted and would try to help out as much as she was able to. For example, she would wash her dishes, but she never remembered to rinse the soap off them. I would have to go back and rinse anything in the cabinets so that Jasmine and I wouldn't get sick from eating the soap residue. She never thought to clean the bathroom and I often felt like I was cleaning up after two children in my spare time. I began to picture myself as a child, doing endless chores every waking hour when not in the classroom, and I became convinced that my lot in life was to clean up after others. Still, I couldn't complain because she was always on time with her rent.

When the spring season rolled around that year, it blew Kem onto our doorstep, asking to move in with us. Jenna was still occupying the second bedroom and paying her part of the rent, so there was no room, even if I had wanted to forgive my sister so quickly. I told her that I could not make the flat-mate vacate the house, and explained that there was no room and it would be terribly inappropriate of me to cram another person in the single bedroom that Jasmine and I shared.

Not surprisingly, Kem was quite upset with me. She cried and said that she was in need, that I was her blood, that she had come to rely on me as her fortress of protection when the world was not treating her kindly. It pained me to see that, but I had no option. I had to harden my heart and realise the truth in what everyone else had always warned me of; I was a softie when it came to my sister and she preyed on me to make her life easier. Still, I could not just absolutely turn her away. I told her that I would help her find someone else who could help her out and provide a temporary, or even permanent place for her to stay.

Tobore had recently moved out of the flat we had rented together and I had helped him find a house to rent through the woman who owned the house. Even though their situation was cramped, I thought that they might be able to accommodate one more person. I made the call, and within thirty minutes, the whole situation was resolved and Kem had somewhere she could live temporarily.

That stressful situation made me reflect on the freedom that came with owning one's own home. I missed having my own place terribly. The move to London had proved regressive in so many ways. I had stepped backwards in my career and was living more like a college student than a woman who was a mother and provider. I decided that I needed to get my life together and focus on buying my own place. I knew I would have to rely on my traits of perseverance and determination to make my dream come true. I mentioned my new plan in passing conversations to some of my friends and was told to calm down because I was being too ambitious for my own good. "After all," they said. "You have only just come to Britain in the past year and so many others have been here for years and years and they still cannot buy a house." I didn't know anything about these other people, so I began planning how to make that idea work out.

"Perseverance can be the platform on which
goodness is staged."

Chapter Thirteen

WEAPON

"The most significant weapon people can use against us is our own mind."

I was shocked to find out at the end of the school year that my salary had not been divided on a twelve-month schedule and that staff provided through an agency was not considered for work during the summer holiday. I also found out that I was still considered a temporary worker, known as a 'supply teacher', provided by an employment agency; someone who they could choose not to extend on contract for the next school year. I understood why the agency had decided to hide that fact. Who in their right mind would have given up their whole life and journeyed more than forty-five hundred miles to take an unstable job that could be revoked after only a few months? I began to panic when I thought about how I was going to be able to afford our monthly rent, and I lamented that I would never be able to save up to make my dream of purchasing a home a reality.

Follow me on Twitter: @avabrown24

I was anxious to prove myself to the school in any way possible so that they would see what a good worker I was. I needed them to consider me an indispensable part of their teaching staff who should be hired on a permanent basis with a salary increase. I took on all sorts of extra duties and never said no to any requests that were made of me. That was difficult since I also needed to be taking on other jobs in my spare time for additional income so I could save up to either provide for the months in the summer when I would be unemployed or add to the savings for a down payment on a house.

Because of all the extra duties I was doing at the school, I had made a request of the deputy head teacher to please consider an increase in my salary, which was lower than that of the staff teachers. Instead of getting a response to my request, I was told by the head of the faculty that I had been assigned to run an after school club in addition to all the other things I was doing on a voluntary basis. I didn't argue, and instead called the agency to see if they had heard anything about my status at the school or whether an increase in my salary was at a negotiation stage. The answer was a resolute, "No, we haven't heard from the school at all in the past five months."

Since it appeared that nothing was going to get done without me pushing it forward, I scheduled a meeting with the head of the faculty to discuss the disproportionate level of my workload and compensation. When we met, I was ready to use the extra club assignment as a bargaining chip in my negotiations, but she quickly shot that idea down. I was told that, although clubs were technically voluntary, I wasn't employed in a position that allowed me to turn it down, and that it was being assigned to me. She ended by firmly stating, "That was the role of the Food Technology teacher." I was absolutely frustrated! Even though I didn't mind running a club for the students, it was unfair that I was expected to take it on without any consideration for my desire or time.

Follow me on Twitter: @avabrown24

Unfortunately, the head of faculty was right; I wasn't in any position to deny that assignment or bargain for something better. They had me over a barrel. I had to accept whatever situation they put me in, regardless of the blatant unfairness of my doing equal or more work than the permanent staff, while getting paid much less as a supply teacher. My work permit was tied to that school. My conversation with the head of staff had left me far too timid to fight back and potentially lose everything I had worked so hard for.

During my short time at the school, I had already seen numerous other supply teachers come and go. Since I was so busy and their tenures so short, I was never able to become friends with any of them and ask how they planned to survive the summer break with no pay. I started thinking about what other type of job I might be able to find for the six week period, but remembered that my visa had a stipulation that forbade both work for any other entity besides the agency that brought me in and recourse to public funds.

With that realisation, I gathered up my courage and went to the head teacher to ask if there was any way that the school could pay me a retainer fee for the summer holidays, to make up for the absolute lack of income I was to have during that time. I was disappointed, but not surprised, when she told me no. I called the agency again to find out if there was anything I could do to avoid the situation of financial stress that was impending, but was told that these terms had been explained to me before I'd arrived. I was in no position to argue, as I had been in such a fragile mental state when I had accepted the job. For all I knew, they had detailed every last bit of their policy and I had simply not understood it. I didn't blame myself too much; after all, I would have never imagined that anyone would have set up a system in which they expect people to stay tied to an employer who does not provide any work for a part of the year, and then to restrict the employee's ability to do anything else gainful during that off period.

Follow me on Twitter: @avabrown24

The one good thing about my job at the school was that the official workday ended at half-past two. It meant that I could dash off to pick up my daughter at the end of her school day, even if I had other after school duties to attend to later in the day. I focused on that fact and decided not to let myself get depressed about the other things that were out of my control. Before I knew it, summer was upon us, and I had not been invited to work through the summer session at the school. I knew the next six weeks were going to be tough, and I prayed that God would bring us a miracle by stretching the little bit of money I had managed to save so that we could eat and keep a roof over our heads.

The time off passed relatively quickly and I returned to work on the first day of the autumn term. Things progressed without incident and I was saving every penny that came into my hands. Before I knew it, I had saved up enough to start looking for a small house in the area that I could afford to buy. I found one and was thrilled to start the process of securing a mortgage.

As that part of my life began to come together, my life at work started to unravel. A tension had grown between the head teacher and me, it stemmed from the disagreements we'd had at the end of the spring term. I wouldn't have minded if the tension had remained unspoken, but I started to notice that the head teacher was acting on her displeasure with me. Several other employees who were much newer to the department than I was, were suddenly offered promotions and I was completely unaware of the process by which they were selected for that honour. That baffled me, especially because I had been designated as a form teacher; a teacher who performed with excellence and was given newly qualified teachers (known as NQTs) to shadow them to learn the job. I loved being a form teacher and I was quickly assigned many NQTs because I was able to form such great relationships with my students.

However, before I could use that as an argument to support my request for a similar promotion, there was an unfortunate and unfair incident that occurred, involving a boy in my class who had HIV and me falling on my sword. The boy's infection status was strictly confidential, and as far as I knew, the NQTs were not privy to that information. Because of that policy, I neither spoke to my newest NQT about the sensitivity of that information nor provided her guidance in how to handle it. By the end of her first week, I found out that she had told the entire NQT group of the boy's illness, and I was furious! I spoke to her in private about the issue, but I could not calm down over her immaturity and the injustice that had been done by it.

My disappointment and anger did not subside and it showed itself in my interactions with her. In the end, I was called up by my supervisor and reprimanded for my behaviour towards the NQT. I didn't want to make the situation worse than it was, so I didn't explain why I was so angry, as her behaviour would have cost her job and ruin her entrance into a teaching career. I took full responsibility for my behaviour towards the NQT and remained quiet on everything else. The meeting was attended by the assistant deputy head teacher, a fellow Jamaican who had immigrated many years before and who had abandoned all traces of her heritage. As the meeting ended, and I sat contrite in my chair with my head held low, she gave a single comment. Her biting advice to me was to get rid of the Jamaican attitude I carried with me, thinking that I was better than others.

That situation threw me over the edge; I no longer wanted to work under these conditions. I went home that evening and called the immigration department just to enquire how I could apply for my own visa. I knew doing so was risky, as I would certainly be flagged as a visitor with questionable intent. The immigration representative told me the steps involved, but also warned me that there were no guarantees and that my application may in fact damage my future plans related to my current status. She explained that by starting the process, I would lose the four years that had been granted in the original visa, and my stay would be valid for only one year. I didn't care at that point and just wanted out of the bind I was in with that job that felt like indentured servitude.

Starting the process required a reference from my current employer. That would be tricky as it would alert them to my wanting to leave their employment, and I was worried they wouldn't let me go, as I was basically cheap labour. I decided to tell them that I was requesting the reference to continue my studies to get a bachelor's in business administration. In the end, the deceit actually worked in my favour, without my planning it, because I found out that my original degree wasn't accredited and I had to get another degree that the British regulatory bodies would recognise.

My real plan, however, was to take the letter of recommendation to the home office to apply for my own visa. I filled out the application for the 'highly skilled' visa, and my stay time was immediately reduced to one year. When I told my friends and family, their only response was that I must be mad. They asked why I had decided to limit myself to one year when I was struggling enough with the ability to try to make a successful go of that move in four years. I, on the other hand, felt like a slave that had just been freed.

The next day, I went to the head of faculty and told her I was thinking of resigning. She sat back and looked at me with an emotionless expression on her face. She advised me in a cool voice to seriously consider my immigration status before I made any decisions. I told her that, as a matter of fact, I already had considered it and I had found a way where it wouldn't be a problem. She made no reply but merely raised her eyebrow in curiosity, her mouth turned down in a hint of displeasure. I could suddenly see my situation with clarity. I knew that the visa status was a way of holding workers, like me, as prisoners. I felt confident in my decision to get out of that place before it destroyed me.

I went home feeling rather pleased with myself, knowing I had gotten the best of my jailers. I knew it was ego, but I didn't care. I was so proud of myself for finding a way out of that restrictive mess I was in. I realised that I could use the head of my department to my benefit in that situation as well. That man had been a completely ineffective manager, who needed to justify his position by assigning pointless tasks and publicly berating the staff beneath him. He was intensely jealous of the relationships I had established with many of the pupils and teachers, where he, on the other hand, had not. The students recognised him for what he was and wouldn't warm to him.

A week before, I had handed in some reports, but he refused to accept them because he wasn't happy with the way I had structured one of the sentences. Even though I knew there was nothing grammatically wrong with the passage, and I'd double-checked it with the head of the English department, he insisted that I change the sentence. If I didn't, he threatened that would cause my report to be delayed and that I would be written up for tardiness. I was certain he was acting out of his displeasure with the recent NQT issue, of which he had limited understanding. Because of that, I refused to change the sentence just for the sake of appeasing his unnecessary demand.

When he realised that I had not cowed to him, he came rushing down the corridor where I was talking with some of my year eleven pupils. He was yelling and flailing his arms at me, reprimanding me for being disobedient, as if I was a child. I was incensed at his audacity in such a public setting and I sunk to his level, shouting back until we were engaged in a full-force shouting haggle. I stood my ground, refusing to change the grammatically correct sentence just to meet his preference. I left school that day in a huff, and listened to the advice of a colleague in my department to take the next

Follow me on Twitter: @avabrown24

day off as a sick day so that the situation could calm down. Unfortunately, my absence just made the issue worse.

When I went back to work the following day, I was immediately called into the office of the assistant head of faculty and told that I had been labelled as disobedient staff and it would be nearly impossible to live that down. I was so disheartened by the unfairness that I wanted to take the day off again, but several other teachers happened to be out so I was told that there was no way they could forgive me if I left that day. I gave in and attended to my classes. As the afternoon approached, however, I was called into a meeting with one of the school's deputy heads, who explained to me that my absence the day before proved that I was a waste of the school's funds. I tried to stand up for myself and we entered into a debacle. She wasn't being fair and I felt too hurt and mistreated. I resigned on the spot, without even considering that I had just signed the paperwork for a mortgage on my first home in the UK.

As soon as I calmed down, I realised what a tremendous mistake I had made while I was in a snit. I berated myself for once again not being able to handle conflict gracefully and mindfully. But that's who I was, a young woman who ran from conflict rather than facing it head-on and fighting the battle to the end. The day was just around the corner when Jasmine and I would complete our sale agreement and move in to the house I had just got a mortgage for. Yet, at that point, I had no idea how I was going to pay for it. My head raced with the fear of our situation. I wondered if there was any way I could call the mortgage company and cancel the sale, but everything was done, the papers were all signed and I was holding the key to unlock another burden in my life.

"Ego can ignite a satisfaction so deep within us, regardless of the consequences."

Follow me on Twitter: @avabrown24

Chapter Fourteen

PRISON

"Money is a prison for those born without it."

_____

The first month my mortgage was due came quickly and there had been very little work where I could earn money. I was unaccustomed to the employment practices of the UK and I didn't realise I could register with multiple agencies to increase my chances of finding employment. Gradually, I became more savvy and the work began to trickle in. By the beginning of November, I had worked only a total of three weeks over the previous two months. December wasn't any better, and I only managed to find work on four days out of the entire month.

Our savings were rapidly dwindling down to nothing and I asked myself continually how I could have been so stupid and egotistical to put us in that situation. The proud part of me would always retort, "How dare they treat you that way?" Certainly, I had grown up poor, but I had some dignity and I was sure that they were cheating me at that school. But, in my anger

Follow me on Twitter: @avabrown24

and haste, I had robbed myself; no one had forced me out; that was all my own doing.

The jobs I had found through the other agencies were in the teaching profession. But, instead of getting a classroom of pupils that I would teach on a daily basis, I found myself running from school to school. One day I would be assigned to a school in East London, the next day I would be in the north, and the next in the southwest. I felt dizzy and unsettled at the constant moving about, but I couldn't complain because the bills were being paid. For the second time in the UK, I lamented that I had given up stability for instability. I was immersed in the life of supply teaching and I just had to deal with it.

Of all the various schools I was assigned to during that hectic period, the one that stuck with me the most was a special needs school. The school catered to children who suffered from various disabilities, and the student population ranged from mild cases of Down's syndrome to severe cases of cerebral palsy. In my short time there, I met a young woman named Charlotte. She was a pupil in my classroom and, even though she was eighteen years old, she had the body of a twelve-year-old and had never learned how to speak. She was mentally unable to participate in the lessons, and instead, she would just sit next to the adult in the classroom and run her nose all over, smelling them and contemplating something unknown in her head.

I was terribly distraught by the experience of working in that school. The sight of the children in their wheelchairs or with assistants physically supporting them brought me to tears. I thanked God for the health of my child and realised that I was not one of those special people who had the internal strength to deal with these children on a daily basis. I tried my hardest to harden my heart and get over my own feelings at seeing their situation, but I was unable to do it. I felt like a terrible person whenever a wave of nausea would hit me after seeing some type of regurgitation as an assistant was attempting to feed a child. Many of the children had to be fed through tubes.

I remember one child in particular who looked perfectly normal among the mass of other physically challenged students. I focused my attention on her to keep from crying in the lunchroom, and I wondered why she was there. One of the assistants set a chocolate cookie on the table in front of her, and while she showed interest in it, she never made an attempt to pick it up and eat it. When I asked one of the other assistants what her ailment was, they explained to me that she had a severe stress anxiety disorder that inhibited her ability to carry out even the simplest of tasks, such as feeding herself.

The day didn't get any better after lunch time and I had to rely heavily on the assistants, especially when there was a situation involving a child soiling themselves, as I was not trained in medical hygiene care or the subtle social care that was needed to address that type of situation. I prayed that I wouldn't have to come back the next day, as I was completely unequipped, both professionally and personally, to deal with that type of student population.

The high school I was assigned to the next day was set in an immigrant area of the city and was largely composed of students that were from African nations. I learned the lesson that day that sharing a skin colour does not equate sharing a culture. The children were louder than I had ever experienced. Every conversation was carried out at the top of one's voice. I kept trying to 'shush'(quieten) them in the hope of creating the Jamaican decorum. One of the permanent teachers watched my fruitless efforts for a while and then came over to explain to me that in many cultures in Africa, talking softly in the presence of other people was considered extremely rude because it indicated that you were trying to secretly talk about the others around you; loudness was the African decorum.

Follow me on Twitter: @avabrown24

There was one boy in my classroom that was surprisingly louder than all the others. When I tried to engage him in the lesson, he instead focused on my obvious West Indian heritage and began making a slew of disparaging remarks about people from my region. I addressed him by explaining that I may be Jamaican by birth, but I was African by origin. He was pleased with my remark, announcing to the class that it was a good thing to hear that I embraced my origin, but that some in the Caribbean didn't.

I used the opportunity to explain to the class that it might be due to the fact that our fellow Africans had sold us into slavery and that's how we wound up in the Caribbean in the first place. Many people have forgotten that to this day. I was shocked by his retort. He said that all the Africans who were sold into slavery were the lowest and the weakest of their people; they weren't good enough to be worthy of staying with the better part of their race. His prejudiced attitude made me want to vomit; even more than being faced with a mentally-impaired teenager the day before who had pooped himself and managed to smear the mess all over. My heart was sick, too, because I knew that ignorant kid's views echoed what he heard at home. I wondered to myself, was there any hope for the future? That experience was not my only introduction to prejudice that day. During a science lesson that I was sent to cover for a teacher who had fallen ill, I was, at first, happy to have found a Jamaican girl among the pupils. However, one of the boys in the classroom was very focused on bullying her. Right in front of me, he announced that all Jamaicans were born with a criminal record. I could not believe what was going on in that school! I felt like so many of these children had poisoned minds at such a young age.

It was definitely not the environment I wanted to be in every day. My spirit couldn't stand to be constantly belittled like that. Little did I know that someday in the future, I would marry an African man, have a child

Follow me on Twitter: @avabrown24

with him, and look back on that experience for some clarity about our interactions.

Since my career as a supply teacher provided no permanent job, I became very frugal, saving for the ever-present possibility of there being no work on any given day. I was taking any job that was offered me, in fear of the same eventuality. One day in October 2006, I didn't receive the usual early morning call for a placement. Instead, I used the morning to attend a parent-teacher conference at my daughter's school. When I arrived, the teacher showed me a poem that Jasmine had written. The poem was entitled 'ANGER'. While the teacher focused on the exceptional cadence and advanced word usage, I focused on the message and realised that this hectic existence I was leading should not interfere with my time with my child.

I was not a neglectful mother by any stretch of the imagination. I never considered the time I spent with her as a sacrifice of my time that could otherwise be spent making income. I loved every minute we would spend in the evenings doing her homework or simply talking about her day over dinner.

"When all around you seems to be a whirlwind, just stand still and allow the calm to take effect around you. It will sort out the chaos."

Follow me on Twitter: @avabrown24

Chapter Fifteen

UNBROKEN

"Societies differ and can make or break you, so you must be mindful to stay

unbroken as those same societies will eject you if you are weakened."

The home I had purchased was a flat located on the third floor above a street-level café. On first glance from the street, it looked like an eyesore, but once I stepped inside, it was as if I had stepped into a charming cottage straight out of some fairy tale set in a hushed forest. However, I soon found out that serene calm only existed when the owner of the flat below was away from home. Turns out, the previous owner of my new flat had neglected to mention that his reason for selling was because of the nightmare neighbours that lived below.

My first encounter with reality came the day after we had moved in. When I met those neighbours in the building's entrance, they were blatantly cold towards me. I thought they might be upset at the noise created by our move-in, but my apology was met with nothing more than a hostile dismissal from their presence. I soon found out from the neighbourhood gossip that these people hated all blacks and were very vocal about their dismay that 'niggers' were coming into their building.

I handled the situation by steering clear of them whenever I saw them, and making sure that our house was very quiet so they would not have anything to complain about. However, my attempts were all for nothing. These people wanted Jasmine and me out, as soon as possible. I started receiving threatening and derogatory messages on my front door. I ignored them. I had hoped that their interest in that campaign would fade if they got no response; instead they began a more aggressive campaign. Back then, whenever I was in the building's common areas, no matter what hour, day or night, the neighbours would suddenly appear, with their pet Rottweiler in tow. They would leave just enough slack on the leash for him to run at us viscously while he snapped his jaws at us with only a centimetre or two to spare. They would even leave the dog in the stairwell, the only exit for my flat on the upper floor, so that Jasmine and I would be trapped in our home.

The situation only escalated from there and turned into an outright campaign of harassment and threatened violence against myself and my young daughter. When the situation got too dangerously close to physical violence, or when I would fear for our lives, I would call the police; if for nothing more than to document the threats in case we were found dead in our apartment the next day. Unfortunately, that whole situation fell under the definition of a civil matter, and until the people caused bodily injury to us, there was nothing concrete that could be done by the authorities.

I reverted back to my all-consuming, stressful environment. The threat of the neighbour's hatred and their snarling dog was as bad as the threat of the four gunmen I had fled from in Jamaica. I was also under massive stress at that time to continue to afford the mortgage payments. Since my work was not stable enough, I found a flatmate to move in with us and ease that financial stress. The lady who answered my advert was kinder than I could have ever hoped for. Abina had quickly become my confidant and dearest friend; she filled a place in my heart like a sister. Together, we bore out the trials with the downstairs neighbours.

Despite the fact that the troublesome neighbours would raise hell if even the smallest of noises crept out of our flat, they would routinely host all-night parties, often going on full-force until the sun started to lighten the morning sky. We simply tried to sleep through it all, but some nights were just too much; both Abina and I had work the next day. On those nights, one of us would steel our nerves and go down to politely ask to have the blaring music turned down, explaining the late hour and our need for sleep. All we ever got in return was verbal assaults or threats that they were going to get the dog on us. Invariably, we would find used needles and alcohol bottles in the stairwell the next morning. The stench of marijuana would permeate our walls and cling to everything in our upstairs flat. I worried constantly about Jasmine being exposed to the drug smoke that clouded the stairwell and wafted in through our adjoining ventilation system.

The couple that occupied the downstairs flat fought with everyone they encountered, including their party guests, and each other. The fights between the couple were epic! She was always drunk and he was always high. During their most violent blow-ups, which always happened outside of their apartment door, I would have to intervene to help protect the young woman from the beating her partner was giving her. Yet, her gratitude never extended beyond the few minutes after she had been saved from his pummelling fists.

I never saw either one of these people keeping a routine work schedule. We soon figured out that neither held a job, but lived off government subsidies for the disaffected. However, most of the social help they received was immediately translated into alcohol or drugs. The rest of their money went towards the latest technology and luxurious items I could only dream about having. It was shocking to see the material items these two could acquire while never holding down a job.

Meanwhile, Abina and I were working our butts off and struggling to make ends meet. By summer, I was really in financial trouble. Not only was I in arrears for the TV and the telephone bill, but I also had a large amount of debt on a credit card, for which I couldn't afford anything beyond the minimum payment. But things soon got worse when the bank holding my mortgage sent a certified letter stating their intent to take me to court over a complicated matter involving paid bills that were misclassified in their system and were accruing massive late fees and penalties. I would have to hire a lawyer to help me rectify the issue, which was growing more serious every day. Anyone who has dealt with a lawyer knows that not only do they cost significant money but they also require a significant amount of time to adequately understand the situation they were addressing. My free time and every extra cent I had started going towards the lawyer.

Things were getting so bad that one morning, I had to spend the majority of the single pound I had left in my purse just for postage to send some required documentation to my lawyer. When Tobore dropped Jasmine off shortly thereafter, I panicked with the thought of how I would be able to afford food for her. She would be hungry; the refrigerator was empty and I only had twenty pence in my wallet.

The phone rang and I was greeted with a less than lucrative offer from one of the employment agencies I was registered with. The consultant asked me if I was available for work. When I said yes, she became very chipper. On the other hand, I became more despondent as she talked to me; the work paid little, and out of that, she told me, I would have to pay her two hundred pounds out of each week's wages. On the face of it, the amount was paltry, but when you were living pound to pound, it adds up. I kept thinking how a full five days' fee would be two hundred pounds, which equated to one 'cost' too many or a portion of the week's groceries for us. I wound up taking the job. People who were in my situation had no other choice but to accept the terms that in the end benefited others.

Those experiences with temporary employment served to remind me of the importance of higher education. I recognised that having a solid education and firm set of degrees behind your name were critical steps towards steady employment and a more secure life. I stressed these ideas to Jasmine and supported her in every educational pursuit. She excelled at her studies naturally, but I was always there to push her further so that her life would be easier than mine was.

The next job placement I was offered was in Luton, which was about an hour away from our home by train. I struggled with the idea of the long commute and how much of my time it would take away from all of the other things that needed my attention, but an old Jamaican adage kept creeping into my head: "When a man is drowning, even a moving mosquito is an option." However, my apprehension melted away when I heard that the job was permanent.

Before the lady from the agency provided any of the details of what the work would be, I accepted. I knew that whatever the tasks were, I would work my hardest to master them. All that mattered to me at that moment was that I was finally gainfully employed. I let out a joyous shout of praise to God.

"Struggles can be medicinal."

Follow me on Twitter: @avabrown24

Chapter Sixteen

TEMPORARY BREAKDOWNS

"While trying to carve out your own destiny, you sometimes

leave dents in someone else's."

The new job afforded me a stability that I had not had since I'd first arrived in London. I was catching up on my bills and adjusting to the long commute. Things were finally starting to come together for me and I was so relieved, but that calm was only a temporary break in the storm of my life.

Shortly after I started my new job, I received a frantic call from my family back in Jamaica. The news was that my sister, Anna, had been picked up by the police and was currently sitting in a jail cell. At first, I didn't understand what I was being told. How could my thirteen-year-old sister have been in jail?

I was told that after I'd left for London, she had run away from home. I immediately felt a twinge of guilt. You see, I was the one who had made her move back into my mother's home before I left Jamaica. She had come to live with me right before I'd left, but she had cultivated a clandestine and age-inappropriate relationship with a much older boy who was my helper's relative. My only way to curb the situation, and hopefully stop her from getting pregnant or being taken advantage of anymore, was to send her back home.

Apparently, she was terribly unhappy back under my mother's thumb and she absconded in the night only a few days after I had left for London. I was shocked that no one had bothered to share that news with me until now. The excuse was that none of the family knew where she was. They had reported her disappearance to the police, but even the police didn't seem very concerned about it. The general consensus was that she was just being a rebellious teenager.

However, now that she was locked up in jail, everyone realised the seriousness of the matter. When my mum called to talk about it, I could tell from the tone of her voice that the situation was much worse than I had imagined from that first phone call. She said that the situation my sister was involved in was so scandalous that it was even being covered on the nightly national newscast.

I didn't need to hear another word. My family back home needed me and I felt partially responsible for putting her on whatever path it was that led her to that sad state. I used every last bit of credit I had to purchase a plane ticket back to Jamaica so that I could meet with the local bank and try to secure funds for her bail. I called in to take some days off of my new job, dropped Jasmine off with my sister, and went on a mission to save Anna from the treacherous situation she had gotten herself into.

When I arrived in Jamaica, I was given a rude awakening to an unforeseen consequence of my having left the country. I had taken the title for my house in Jamaica to the bank to use as collateral for a loan to make the bail. But when I started to fill out the required forms, I was informed that any money I had would be ineligible for posting bail due to my resident status in another country. I could not believe what I was hearing. There was nothing I could do for her.

With the bad news in hand, I went to visit my sister in the juvenile centre where she was being held. The sight that greeted me broke my heart. There she was, separated from me by thick black metal bars. Her eyes were wide with fear. I ached with the desire to save her, to tell her that I was there to take her away. When I told her that the law forbade me from helping her, she began to weep uncontrollably. The pain in my chest was tangible, like someone had scooped out my heart and left only a raw, gaping hole. I wanted so badly to hold her and tell her everything would be okay. But it wouldn't. That, I could not fix.

When I left, I went immediately to my mum's home. Little by little, the circumstance of what had put Anna in that predicament came to light. The information had come flowing forth from every family member that stopped by. They had found out that my sister had been living with some unsavoury people who had very bad reputations around town. Apparently, she had become intimately involved with a man who was on Jamaica's national most-wanted list of criminals. The news only got worse from there. People had told them that she was known to carry a gun and flash wads of cash around. I couldn't stop picturing the little girl I knew, play-acting as a character living in the wild, wild, West. The person they spoke of was not the Anna I knew.

That situation was nothing like a child's game of Cowboys and Indians. As I sat and listened to an almost unfathomable tale, my mind drifted. I didn't want to hear it. I needed to distract myself. I began to take stock of my surroundings. My mum's place, while still humble, seemed much nicer than it had been when I was last there. The longer I was there, the more I noticed subtle changes in their entire lifestyle. If that had been twenty years ago, I would have thought they were rolling in the dough, so to speak. From what I could tell, though, nothing else had changed.

However, the matter at hand involving Anna completely overshadowed my curiosity about that. That evening, the conversations shared with different family members, all ended in the same way; everyone lamented how embarrassing it was for our family as a whole. She had brought a great shame upon us, which flowed throughout the entire community. I was stunned to hear them speak of Anna in such a fashion. I was told that people were now openly accusing all of us of supporting and benefitting from her unsavoury exploits.

By evening's end, I finally got the full story about the situation she was involved in that led to her arrest. She had accompanied a group of boys when they went to rob a supermarket. Things got out of hand when the owners resisted and the boys ended up killing them. They had almost gotten away with it, but the group was living in a rented home and when they stopped paying the rent, the landlord sought to eject them from the property by reporting to the police that they had a stockpile of guns on the premises. When the police searched the house, they indeed found a multitude of guns and ammunition, some of which matched the evidence from the supermarket killings.

I couldn't believe what I was hearing. I felt like I must have fallen into some Hollywood thriller movie plot. How could that have been real? How could my very own sister, who was still a child, be involved in that sordid affair? Robbery? Murder? I couldn't make the information align with reality. My memory of little Anna was shattered. My guilt overwhelmed me; if I hadn't left...maybe. In the end, I had to catch my plane back to London. There was nothing I could do for Anna and my job and child were waiting for me back at our UK home.

Eventually my life in London continued as if the horrible plight that

Follow me on Twitter: @avabrown24

played out in Jamaica did not exist. I finally received word that Anna had been released and was living once more with my mum. She was on probation and needed to report to the police every day. My mum told me that she was very calm and quiet; she stayed at home and didn't even try to go out. We both expressed our relief that she must have learned her lesson and had been scared straight out of her dangerous lifestyle.

It quickly became apparent, though, that Anna wasn't merely acting out a penance to her wild ways. She was simply staying at home and sleeping a lot because she had a general sense of feeling unwell. We all equated her malaise to depression and didn't give it much thought beyond that. As the day of her trial approached, however, the family began to notice an alarming deterioration in her physical appearance. Again, we all thought it was due to the stress of the trial. Everyone believed the entire ordeal was taking its toll on her overall health. She was found innocent of the most serious charge of accessory to murder. We were then sure she would perk up and start to feel better.

We were completely mistaken, however. Over the next few days after her trial finished, her health deteriorated at an alarming rate. One of my sisters had called me in a panic, asking me to come home right away because they didn't know what to do, but knew that something was terribly wrong. They had gone to visit several doctors, but none could come up with a diagnosis.

I had just surrendered my passport to the home office for my visa to get extended. I therefore couldn't make any trips outside of the country. I felt trapped and helpless. The news that came from home was worse every day. Finally, God performed a miracle and my passport, along with Jasmine and Tobore's, arrived at my house by post. I immediately went to the travel agent and bought plane tickets for Jasmine and myself.

I spent the next days packing and getting our London lives in order during the time we would be gone. The day before we were to leave, I was exhausted and fell into a deep sleep mid-afternoon. My nap was interrupted by the jangling of the telephone and the weight of my housemate, Abina, coming to sit beside me on the bed. Her hand on my shoulder was so gentle, as she leaned in to whisper for me to wake up. Before I put the telephone receiver to my ear, I knew something was dreadfully wrong. It was my sister's voice on the other end; she told me that Anna had just died.

I couldn't believe what I was hearing. How could that be? She had just been to a new doctor and they had again found nothing wrong with her. She had been scheduled for an exploratory surgery that morning. We all believed she would have had a diagnosis soon and be starting the treatments for whatever was causing her illness.

I crumpled to the floor as the truth of what I was hearing sunk in. Even after my sister had hung up, I sat frozen on the wooden floor in my flat, unable to move or even hang up the phone. The disconnected buzzer alerted Abina to come and take the phone from my hand, but I never heard it.

When I was able to move again, I knew I had to change our tickets to fly out that night. Unfortunately, I could not simply change the flights. Instead, I would have to relinquish the old ones, apply for a refund, and purchase new ones. Since the refund would take up to eight weeks to be processed, I was stuck without the necessary funds to afford two flights. The only way I could afford to go home then was if I went by myself, leaving Jasmine with my sister, Kem.

I travelled to Jamaica on my own and met with my family to bury our little sister. The funeral was a low budget affair, and most of the cost was left to me since I was still the most successful of our family. It was also left up to me to identify her body in the morgue and to claim it for burial. While I picked through her clothing to choose something for her to spend eternity dressed in, I thought the sadness would kill me. I was also to deliver the eulogy at the funeral service. I was at a loss for words that could adequately describe the absolute tragedy of her last year of life. It was so unjust that she would not be allowed to live out her life and redeem herself in the community's eyes.

My poor mother was in so much distress; I began to fear for her health as well. Although I had grown up seeing her suffer the life of the desperately poor, that was nothing compared to the suffering she was experiencing now. The grief radiated from her; it permeated the entire family. I was again plagued with guilt for leaving my family to pursue a new life so far away. I couldn't stop wondering if Anna would still be alive had I only chosen a different life path. After the funeral, we received word from one of the doctors she had seen in the days leading up to her death that they had finally come up with a diagnosis - lupus. I also found out that she had been baptised in the church right before she'd died. She was merely 19 years old.

She was gone too soon.

"Death is a thief, it robs us of our loved ones and keeps a hold of all the person is and was."

Follow me on Twitter: @avabrown24

Chapter Seventeen
FIERCE

"Some events in life can rob you of your soul,

but our bodies function nonetheless."

———————

The death of my little sister changed my life in more ways than I could have imagined. I had become fiercely protective of my own child. I felt like I could leave nothing to chance when it came to her future wellbeing. I swore to myself that she would never find herself feeling unloved or unwanted. I wanted a kind of guarantee against her feeling the need to seek out security and intimacy from friends or lovers who could turn around and take advantage of her.

After we laid Anna to rest, the journey back to London was a hard one for me. Not only was I drowning in my sadness over that lost life, but also I was weighed down by the knowledge that I had spent my very last penny. For the first week of my return, I could think of nothing but memories of her. My heart ached with the unfairness of the situation; I cried out to God, asking why the young had to be taken.

Anna and I had shared a birthday and I kept playing back the memories of all the celebrations we had shared together on that day each year. The memories were sweet, but caused as much pain as they did comfort. Both Anna and I had been born on the 28th of February, but when my birth had been registered, the officials had made a mistake and wrote 22 February on my birth certificate. It had never caused any problem so the family just ignored it. But since my sister's death, I could no longer find joy in celebrating in her absence. As the years went by I just accepted the 22 as the day that was for me alone, burying all the happiness of the past along with my sister.

The Luton job had fallen through due to my travel back to Jamaica. I was back at square one, waiting for the phone to ring each morning with news of any temporary position. The positions were very few and far between, so I registered with as many employment agencies as possible, not caring what the industry was that they served. I was ready to take any work, as long as it brought in money.

The first job offer I received was as a contracted cleaning lady for a large firm. Since there was nothing else coming my way, I swallowed my pride and forced myself to go in with a bright spirit. The whole way in, I chided myself for thinking that job was beneath me. After all, I took our rubbish out to the bin and dusted our house every week, how different could it be? Well, the answer to that question came the minute I met my new supervisor. Apparently, the job wasn't so much general cleaning, but was specifically scrubbing public toilets for ten hours.

When the supervisor told me about the job's sole duty, she gave me a swift look up and down, and commented that I wasn't dressed for the job. I must say I was happy to hear that, thinking that she would find another duty for me to earn the day's pay, but it was not to be. She dismissed me, despite my assurances that I was willing to do whatever they needed of me regardless of my attire.

As I left the building, my eyes were already stinging from trying to hold back the flood of tears. I felt like I had reached my lowest point. I couldn't even get a job as a toilet cleaner! By the time I reached the bus stop, the tears were running freely down my face. I couldn't get on the bus while I was blubbering like that, so I ducked under the bus shelter to get out of the rain and called my friend Jade for moral support. She comforted me and we prayed that God would see me through that rough time. We prayed that he would lead me down the right path that would provide work for me and an income for my family.

Over the next several weeks, work opportunities continued to be scanty, so I began looking for alternative means to afford the basics of life, such as food and utilities. When I looked into the possibility of getting help from social services, however, I found that my immigration status inhibited me from receiving government-funded assistance. As I look back on those times, I cannot imagine how we survived, but we did. It was only by some miracle that there was always food in the refrigerator and light that came on when we flipped the switch. We must have had an angel following us around all of those days.

During that time, I worked very hard to conceal my emotional distress from my daughter. I wanted to spare her the burden of worry and my continued anxiety over our financial matters. She was only a child and needed to be focused on her studies and her friends. When I sunk so deeply into depression that I was having difficulty functioning in daily life, I took antidepressants to help lift me out of the blackness that was clouding my entire outlook on life. But the doctor's visits and medication added more strain on our nearly non-existent budget.

When I had finally reached the end of my wits and there was nothing left in my control, I lifted my voice in prayer, crying out to God to help us out of the hole I had dug us into in London. The next day, I got a call from the agency that had originally offered me the teaching job in far-away Luton. I had lost out on the position due to the situation with Anna and my unexpected travel. I couldn't believe my luck when the agency representative told me that the position was open again and it was still for employment on a permanent basis. There was no hesitation on my part that time. I took the job immediately and praised God for His mercy.

The distance I would be commuting back and forth each day necessitated childcare for Jasmine; for the hours she would be out of school and I would be travelling on the train. God was again merciful in that situation and I found a Jamaican lady named Afua, who had lived in the UK for some time but had outstayed her visa so she couldn't obtain employment otherwise. Unfortunately, the arrangement didn't work out for long.

After the first two weeks, she seemed to have lost enthusiasm for the job and started showing up later and later each day. Abina had a job that was closer to our home, so on the days she could stay longer than me, she waited for the lady to show up and take charge of Jasmine, who needed to be escorted to her school. Finally, the morning came when Afua never showed up. I was on the train, on my way to Luton, when Abina called to tell me that Afua had called to say she wasn't coming in at all that day.

I didn't know what to do and I was in a panic. I was half-way to Luton already and there was no way I could get back home to Jasmine before Abina needed to be at work. Abina could hear the distress in my voice and she told me that she would call in late for work and escort Jasmine to school. I was so grateful, she was an angel sent by God. But I was still left with the problem of finding reliable care for Jasmine during my work days. Unfortunately, the challenge proved insurmountable and I had to resign from my position in Luton shortly after.

Meanwhile, the contentious relationship with my downstairs neighbours was still going on full force and escalating by the day. The week after I had given up my permanent position in Luton, I had one of my most frightening encounters with them. I had decorated the stairwell on my landing as an extended area of our home. Besides the several plants I had cultivated to give a fresh feel to the atmosphere, I had placed a picture of my dream car, a Ferrari, on the wall to serve as a motivator for me to keep up with the struggle of making a success out of my endeavours in that place. I had also put up a bright light so that we could see up the stairs when we came in at night.

The landing was a private area and was accessible only by a locked door, for which only Abina and I had the keys. When I arrived home late one night after running some errands, I found that there was no light in the stairwell leading up to my flat. It was pitch dark and I became very afraid, thinking of the neighbour's vicious dog. Maybe he was resting in the stairwell and would attack if I surprised him in the dark. I started up the stairs on tiptoe and was flooded with relief when I neared the landing without incident. However, I started to notice something coarse crunching beneath my feet.

I reached the door and fumbled to get my key in the lock in the darkness. When the door opened, I was able to see by the light on the landing that I was treading on smashed remains of the light bulb. The sight on the landing itself was even more sinister, though. The Ferrari picture had been obviously moved, the window that opened into my home was smashed, and all of my plants and pots were gone.

I was certain it was the neighbours and I could not handle the harassment any longer. I thought of sinking to their level and calling on some friends of mine who lived in the roughest area of Brixton. I imagined these tough guys coming around to scare them into behaving. But that was a silly wish, and I knew I had to overcome the challenge that these people represented on my own.

I was now back to full-time job hunting and accepting any temporary position that came my way from the various agencies. The jobs I took ranged from a call centre representative to ironing and babysitting.

I knew one way out of the mess was to get more education for myself, so I took any savings I could scrape and enrolled in courses at a local college. The coursework was exciting and I loved having something to stimulate my mind again. In fact, some of my fondest memories were made when Jasmine and I would spend our evenings together doing homework at the small dining room table in our little flat. I was determined to make our lives better and I instilled the importance of education in my daughter so that she would never find herself in such a fix.

"Being a mother shouldn't just apply to your biological child, but should transcend to each child you come into contact with."

Chapter Eighteen
PENALTY

"Someone else's errors can be the penalty of the innocent."

———————

I was terribly distraught about having to quit my job because of my child's day care needs and I was very angry with Afua for being so unreliable. In my head, I blamed her for my dissatisfaction with my life, but I soon made a complete turn-around and started sending up prayers of thanks for her poor work ethic. She seemingly saved me from a disastrous situation that was brewing at the school in Luton where I used to work that I had been completely unaware of.

I found out through the temporary staffing grapevine that the principal of the school was into all sorts of trouble and was let go, along with most of the newly employed teachers (of which I would have been one), only a few weeks after my start date. That mass exodus gave everyone involved a bad reputation for being part of whatever shenanigans the administration had been up to, even if they were only on the periphery or not involved at all.

Follow me on Twitter: @avabrown24

I realised that Afua's irresponsibility was really a blessing in disguise. God was looking out for me, after all. All of my efforts to re-enter a teaching career could have been destroyed and we would have been in an even worse position. Moreover, I had even been considering moving to Luton to be closer to the school, but would have wasted all the expense and effort and been left with no job. I had already put our flat on the market and that, at least, remained a good decision because regardless of my job situation, we would be out from under the burden of a mortgage I could not afford.

I had to make a quick trip back to Jamaica to sort out some bits and pieces regarding our citizenship and residency status. I needed to apply for a new birth certificate, as there was some new movement in the Jamaican government system that necessitated re-issuance of old birth certificates. I took my old white one and went down to Spanish Town, where the official office was.

I had met a man from that area over the Internet many years before, and we had kept up a genial online friendship - nothing romantic, just friends. His name was Alfie, and our online communications were sufficient enough for me to feel comfortable staying at his place even though we had never before met in person. Through our communications I had discovered that my family knew him very well and he had a good relationship with my mum. I was still under the impression that Jamaica remained the trustworthy place that I had grown up in; I was blissfully unaware of the ways its society had become depleted morally. Luckily, God was again watching over me and I was safe in Alfie's house.

On the second morning of my arrival, I woke early and left for the office of the registrar of births and deaths . My plan was to be first in line so that I could get my new birth certificate and be able to spend the rest of my time visiting family. Man, was I in for a big surprise! I was called forward by one of the first workers to open a window for service, and was greeted by a lovely lady who looked over my plain white paper certificate and directed me to enter the inner offices. I was so proud of my posh new British accent and the immaculate way I was dressed, thinking how it really was paying off in a professional setting and earning me better treatment.

I was taken into a secluded office and, to my surprise, met by the same woman but then with a very stern look on her face. She informed me that I was in very serious trouble for trying to pass off a false document. I was totally confused, what did she mean by false document? I explained that I had that birth certificate from the time I was a teenager, when my parents had applied for an update regarding my father's name being listed on the certificate. She asked exactly where I had gotten the document I was trying to pass off. I told her that my parents had given it to me. She gave a slight smirk of disbelief and I realised that there was a serious problem at hand.

I had never questioned the authenticity of that document. I had even used it to secure my visa to enter the UK and never had any trouble. The lady informed me in a very official tone that I was in possession of a false birth certificate and whipped out a large book filled with others that looked exactly like mine. She flipped from page to page, pointing at the signature line on each, and told me that the signature was falsified. I was in total shock. I again explained that my parents had obtained the certificate and given it to me when I was still a minor. I then asked how it could be such an obvious forgery, as she was suggesting, since I had used it to get my passport, my travel certificates, and my degrees...everything in my life that required an official governance approval.

Instead of answering me, she told me she had to call in the police. She said that was an offence that necessitated a criminal charge. I couldn't believe what I was hearing, the police? Was the woman mad? I had just come to get a new copy of my birth certificate, and now I was being threatened with handcuffs and a criminal charge. It was as if I had entered a nightmare. I had a flashback to the terrible juvenile detention facility where my sister had been held, and I knew that the Jamaican jails for adults were much, much worse. A wave of panic rose up in me. The lady told me to stay calm; she had already called the authorities. I was locked in the little room until they arrived, and those minutes were tortuous. I fretted over that confusing situation and how I had come to be in the midst of it. Surely, I thought it was all a mistake or that I would simply wake up safe in my bed and breathe a sigh of relief that it was all just a bad dream.

Finally, a group of men in uniform entered the room. They stated in official, barking tones that they were a special force from the fraud squad and were there to collect me on the charge of fraud. I couldn't even move to stand up from my seat. That was my first time being in such proximity to lawmen that were looking at me as a target. They firmly gripped my upper arms and helped me to my feet, escorting me directly out of the building and into the police car waiting outside. I was driven down to the fraud squad office, which was located in downtown Kingston.

I didn't utter a word for the entire drive, even though they kept throwing questions at me about how I had managed to get into the UK with a false document. All I could think about was being jailed and stuck in Jamaica awaiting a trial, unable to get back to my daughter, who would be thinking her mother had abandoned her; she would not understand what was happening. I began thinking that I was actually getting a more brusque treatment than anyone else because of my British status.

I was taken into an office and a guard was placed outside, while I waited for whatever my fate was to be. It was nearing noon, and I was hungry. The guard on duty checked in and said he would send someone to fetch some food for me. Finally, I was visited by the interrogators. They asked all the same questions that had been fired at me during the morning hours and repeated the same charges that were levied against me. I could only reiterate that I had nothing to do with it, that I was telling the truth about how I had come in possession of the document that had never before been questioned by any other governing body. But they weren't interested.

I was allowed one phone call, and I called my mum to ask her to come down to the station to help explain the situation - better yet, I said, please have my dad come. After all, he was much closer, since he still lived in Kingston. My mum said that she would come, but it would take some time, as she would be travelling from St. Elizabeth. She also said that there was no way my dad would be coming. Apparently, he was too afraid to enter the police station and become entangled in that mess.

I found out later that my dad said he didn't feel any need to be involved, because he had only agreed to make his status official on my birth certificate by changing my last name to his own because I had wanted it for so long as a child. If I had known back then what the price of that small token of ownership would be, I would have opted to keep my mum's maiden name and would have happily maintained my outsider status.

My mum made the three-hour journey by bus, and when she arrived, she helped the police to coerce my dad to come in as well. I remember those phone calls vividly; the officers assured him they weren't going to arrest him because I was the one in custody. They finally convinced him to come in by telling him all he needed to do was give a statement so theycould determine what to do with me. I was sure my mum cursing him to within an inch of his life also helped. I almost fell over with relief when he finally made the twenty-minute trip from his house to the station. I realised that I may actually be released so that I could be allowed to go back to London to be with my daughter.

My mum and dad were interviewed in separate rooms to see if they would corroborate my story. I was petrified about what might be going on. Would they provide any new information? Would I be hauled off to jail? I was not in the room when my father finally gave his official statement and the truth came out. He had admitted that when he went to change my name on the birth certificate, he didn't go into the registrar's office. Instead, he gave my original certificate to one of his brothers who lived nearby and who knew someone that could get a '*bandulu*' (fraudulent) one for much less hassle and much less money. The bottom-line was that he had produced a fraudulent document that I had been carrying around and showing off to all the governmental agencies since then.

The whole ordeal of my parents' interrogation took only about one hour, but it felt like an eternity to me. When the officers came back to the office where I was being held, they produced the written statements that my parents had given and told me to sign off on them. I was shaking with relief and my signature was a wobbly mess. The officer who took the papers from me said that I was one very lucky lady to have the opportunity to get out of there.

I wasn't sure what he meant, but it became clear when he explained that I now had to pay one hundred thousand dollars, Jamaican, to get free. It was all done under the table, as they say in Jamaica. I was furious! But I kept my outward calm, knowing that no misbehaviour would be tolerated in that situation, no matter how justified. I hadn't done anything wrong, but here I had to pay for a crime that my dad had committed and admitted to. As I gave up the money for my freedom, I steamed inside, thinking that if my dad had only claimed me from the time of my birth, it would never have happened.

I was finally allowed to leave the police station a free woman, but my day with the authorities was not over. I had to go back to the registrar's office, along with my dad, to get the situation completely cleared up. He was required to sign some official forms so that the name change could be officially approved.

Follow me on Twitter: @avabrown24

I was still fuming from the unfairness of it all and demanded to see the head of the office, who came out and was delighted to hear that I had gotten it all cleared up. My joy did not equal hers, though, and I demanded to know why I was punished for something that could have been just as easily proved by a phone call from their offices? And I wanted to know why I was the one arrested when the people who had made my certificate without my knowledge were the wrongdoers? She listened to my rant and apologised, explaining that the office had to follow protocol, adding that there were many others out there just like me who were innocent participants in others' crimes. She even said that she was thinking of how the office could provide amnesty for these cases.

I was granted an expedited new birth certificate, and when I got it in my hands, I couldn't wait to hop on the next plane out of Jamaica. I returned safely to London, held my baby tight, and told her how much I love her. As I explained the situation that had nearly kept me away from her forever, I was reminded of how quickly our ordered lives could spiral out of control. A deep-seated dislike towards my father blossomed that day and I gained a greater respect for my mum.

I arrived home to an offer on the flat and praised God for his mercy. I had even managed to make a small profit on the sale, which provided some security while I tried to figure out our next move. I was still convinced that purchasing a home was better than renting, so I looked for a house that was more in our budget, and found one in Mitcham. While I waited for the sale to be approved, Jasmine and I had to move in with Tobore and his flat-mates. We wound up staying for about six weeks, and the experience of Tobore and I living under the same roof again was strange, but not unpleasant.

The house they were in at the time had ample space and Jasmine and I had our own room. In a way, it felt like our old life towards the end of our relationship with us residing in separate rooms, but getting along cordially in the common areas. I suppose our being back in a familial-type living situation stirred something in Jasmine's mind too. She had begun to recall our life in Jamaica, when we had lived in our dream home before that fateful night of the attack. She even started asking questions about what had happened to make us leave, which led to more pointed questions about strange men with guns and her other flashes of memory about that night. I could not muster the courage within myself to revisit that painful memory, but I didn't know what else to do. If I had been in a more stable situation myself, I would have sought out intervention from a professional who deals with traumatic events, but I didn't.

We finally obtained the new house and were able to move in. I was so relieved to have a safe place away from the drug addled neighbours and their vicious dog. In that home, we even had our own front door, with no communal space. Our new neighbours turned out to be absolutely lovely and we settled in nicely. We even had a lovely garden space, where Jasmine could play and I could find some peace while tilling the soil by hand and planting flowers. I didn't mind that there was only a tiny bathroom and rather flimsy tub; the freedom I felt there was invaluable. I felt like my life was finally progressing, like I had begun to grow roots in that country and had found somewhere that I would no longer feel like a stranger.

I realised that having a house of my own was something that gave me a sense of security like nothing else did. Maybe it was because I grew up with my mum not having one for herself, or maybe it was the constant moving around that I did as a child. I always felt unsettled, but when I had a house, I felt like I was safe on my own, like I didn't need a man to provide for me.

My professional life was going steadily, and I had work daily. However, there was a strong governmental push at the time for teachers to have their Qualified Teachers Status, known in short as QTS. I sought to get the QTS certification, but I was lacking math as a subject for my education degrees. In Jamaica, accounting was considered a math subject in college, and during my time in high school, our main math teacher had suffered from diabetes and was constantly on sick leave, so I graduated without that subject. I did get some math lessons, but they were few and far between. In addition, I wasn't the brightest student in the class, so I always presented a challenge to the teacher, who chose to focus on the smarter students in her attempt to get her lessons caught up for the times she was off. The whole situation had made me hate math.

But that had become a problem. I couldn't get the QTS because of my missing math credits. I also didn't want to own up to anyone that I was so severely lacking in that subject. I was still expected to teach it. Sometimes, when I had to cover for a math lesson, I would sit and stare at the textbooks, terrified that the students would start asking me for detailed explanations. I couldn't tell a logarithm from an exponential, and the thought of having to discuss algebra frightened the life out of me.

I was so far behind in my math skills that no amount of studying would catch me up in time to achieve the necessary QTS. I conceded defeat and started looking for a way out of the teaching profession. I thought of the irony in the end of my teaching career. Originally, it was me who didn't like the field and thought it was beneath me, but in the end, I was not good enough to stay in it. That's not to say I was a bad teacher. I was actually very good in all the other subjects, and I genuinely cared for my students.

When the reality finally hit that I was no longer allowed to teach, I grieved as if I had lost something as important as my husband or my sister. It hurt just as much to be rejected by a system as it had to be rejected by a loved one. I had given so much of my life to that career, and I experienced a real heartbreak when it was taken away from me. Here I was, in London, a single mother with a new house, having to close another chapter of my life.

Follow me on Twitter: @avabrown24

What could possibly lie ahead?

"Heartbreaks are not always caused by people or intimate love gone wrong; they can come in unexpected forms, and I have had my fair share of all types."

Chapter Nineteen
PERMANENCE

"Sometimes, just swimming into the waves is all you can do,

letting the tide carry you to the destined place."

———————

It was coming up to Easter 2007, and I was at my wits' end trying to find a job through the agency. My opportunities for teaching had dwindled to nothing without my achieving the QTS, but more worrisome was the fact that summer was nearly upon us and the pool of job seekers would soon be flooded with fellow teachers who were unemployed between terms. I was back to taking any job offered so that I could ensure enough money came in to pay the mortgage.

I realised that a high-stress and unstable lifestyle was not sustainable long-term. So, I began to work towards completing my master's degree in business administration. My daily life was so full of my activities chasing a paycheque that I had no social life to speak of. The thought of seeking out and finding a life partner hadn't even crossed my mind. Besides, if I was to be honest, I'd have to admit that I still considered Tobore to be the missing partner that completed our little family, so in some ways, I didn't feel like I was missing anything.

I still was dealing with the persistent issues of having to keep my schedule flexible enough to be available for my child and to be ready for any situation that might have arisen with childcare. Every parent has had to deal with these issues, but they were even more of a burden when you were assigned as temporary staff. The administration was much less forgiving when hiccups arose in the daily schedule. I began to feel like I was giving my own child the same instability that had marred my childhood, and that was the one thing I had promised myself I would never do.

I threw myself into the work of finding a stable, permanent job. Soon, I had applied for so many jobs that I couldn't even remember what I had applied for. When people called, I was completely confused about whether the job was temporary or permanent, what the job itself was, and how I should present myself to make the best impression. I was a mess, and finally I felt the burden of it all crushing my spirit.

I had managed to buy a small car in the previous year; there had been no getting around it, the available jobs were so much more widely scattered than feasible by the bus routes. One afternoon, I got into the car and drove to some nearby woods where I hiked out into the field and sat down on the grass and cried. In my grief, I turned my face to the heavens and asked God to answer all of the blasphemous questions that had hung in the back of my mind for so long. Why was He punishing me? What had I done wrong that had attracted His wrath? Why did He give everyone else a smooth path in life, while He made me fight for every step along mine? Why did He stand by and allow me to be knocked back five steps for every one step I took forward?

No answers came booming down from the skies. I felt so alone and broken. I couldn't let my precious child see the utter distress I was feeling,

Follow me on Twitter: @avabrown24

so I pulled myself together and put on a calm and cheerful face to greet her at the end of her school day. I even took her on a quick jaunt to the park so that she could play and, for at least a while, feel the carefree spirit that I had never experienced.

In a way, being outside of the house was also an escape for me. For a short while, I could clear my mind of the dreaded letters that were coming with bills I have no idea how I would pay. When we returned home that day, a pile of letters were waiting, just as I had feared. I took a deep breath and sorted through them. It was one after another with big red writing, signalling an overdue account and calling for immediate action. But one envelope in particular caught my eye. It looked like regular, non-threatening business mail. I selected that one to open and discarded the others in a heap on the table.

As I began to open it, I remembered all of the job applications I had put in and started to remind myself that it was probably just a run-of-the-mill rejection letter. To my surprise, it was a letter from a well-known supermarket chain inviting me to interview for their on-the-job graduate management programme! I didn't recognise the location where the programme was going to be held; some place called Erith that was southwest of London. That was no matter to me, I didn't care how far it was, I would drive there every day, if need be.

It looked like God was looking out for me after all. In my excitement, I went and purchased a cheap, but nice, power suit. On the day of the interview, I arrived at the site to find a slew of other applicants, all anxious and dressed professionally. We were a diverse group, each of us representing a different nationality and age. They put us all in a waiting room and we sat in awkward silence for a few moments. It seemed that no one was willing to break the ice, so I took it upon myself to ease the tension in the room by engaging each person in a group conversation. Soon, we were getting a sense of where each of us came from and our current situations.

It was there that I met a young man, near my age, named Tre. He was of German and Cameroonian descent, and I was instantly attracted to him. His demeanour was so classy, and he had an amazing sense of style. His dark suit was cut perfectly to fit his extremely tall and sinewy body frame, and the colour complimented his dark skin. I was smitten. We were called in for the interviews in turn, and the process was gruesome. At the end, though, I found out that I was among those selected to return to attend the second round of interviews. I overheard Tre getting the same news and my heart leapt when I realised I would get the chance to see him again.

I had kept our chatty conversations going through that same waiting process and by the end of the second interview; Tre and I had exchanged numbers. I was given the promise of a dinner date as well. But I did not get any news that day of an invite for the third interview session. I thought maybe they weren't letting people know directly that time and went home with a light heart from my flirting with Tre.

When Tre and I met for dinner, however, I found out that he had received word shortly after the second interview about the third round. I went home and rummaged through all of the mail for a second and third time, hoping to find an envelope that I must have overlooked before, but there was nothing. My heart sank. I really thought I had done a good job in the second interview and it was the most promising career lead I'd had in a long time.

The next day, I resigned myself to the fact that I was going to be rejected from the programme and I got myself ready to visit yet another employment agency to see what jobs might be coming up. As I was stepping out of the door, my phone rang. It was the supermarket administration, and they were inviting me back for the third round of interviews. I was thrilled and determined to knock their socks off when they spoke to me next. The interview was to be held the next day at one of their stores that happened to be located very close to where I lived. I sent up a silent prayer of thanks to God. I couldn't believe I might land a job within a stone's throw of my home; that I might be able to stop the crazy commuting schedule that had me travelling all over London, from pillar to post.

The third interview was even more intensive than the first two; I felt like I was on trial. It was the business world I was re-entering, and it was so different from the teaching system that I had been immersed in since my arrival. The interview consisted of cognitive skill tests as well as physical skill tests. I was given pallets to pull and pack; it was hard and heavy work. I couldn't imagine that type of manual labour would be part of the role they were expecting me to fill, especially after all the administrative interview questions in the first two rounds. They had me count items on the shelves, work the cash register, and help with the end-of-day accounting and deposit of money into the safe. Basically, I had a go at every duty that any employee would perform in the store on a daily basis.

One of the hardest parts for me, however, was seeing all of the cash being counted at the end of the day; I was so envious. There I was, only barely making ends meet while working my butt off and I couldn't imagine having that kind of income. It was a torturous test for my psyche, and I battled to not fall prey to my downtrodden emotions.

When the interview ended, I was sent home with no idea of where I stood or when they might contact me next. The pessimistic side of me thought that they hadn't given me an answer straightaway because I must have failed in one of the important tasks; maybe I hadn't packed enough on the shelves or maybe I hadn't been fast enough on the tills? I began to lament that I was again back at square one. My nerves were frayed and I went directly to my friend's house and cried my eyes out to her. She comforted me and reminded me of God's unfailing love, which I was still doubting. She left me alone to think, and I wrote a prayer to the Lord:

Dear God, why have you given up on me? What sins have I committed that are so unforgivable? Why, regardless of how hard I try, does nothing seem to work out for me? Why don't you just take me in your protective arms and prevent me from going through all of this pain, suffering, and shame in front of my friends, my foes, and my child? Was running away from Jamaica not enough punishment? Was being held at gunpoint not a hard enough experience to endure? What more shall I be required to go through, to give up, to be worthy in your eyes? God, please release my blessings. I am in need of a miracle, right at this point in my life. My mortgage is due, and after I pay it, Jasmine and I will have no money left. My bank account is empty, the bills are piling up, and I have this beautiful and innocent child that I have to shelter and feed. Lord, remember that my family, especially my mum, still depends on me. Lord, please help me.

I left the prayer at my friend's house and headed to my home to face my mounting debts and the sadness that was threatening to take me over completely. I made dinner for Jasmine, tucked her into bed, and laid myself down to sleep. A week passed and I heard nothing from the supermarket, so I started reaching out to people around town for stints doing cleaning work. After two weeks of that, I couldn't take it anymore. The dust and cleaning solutions would cause such severe allergies that I would have asthma attacks. But, there was nothing else and I had to make money somehow.

As I finished my most recent cleaning job in Shirley, I decided to treat myself to a pint of lager. Jasmine was staying with a friend and I had the evening to myself. I pulled my car up and parked at a nearby pub garden that my friend said she would meet me at. Right then, my mobile phone began to ring. The ringing of a phone had long since lost its appeal to me, as it was almost always a debt collector on the other end of the line. I was certainly in no mood to fend one of them off.

As the ringing continued, I began to worry that it was family back home calling, but that, too, turned me away from answering. More often than not, a call from Jamaica was only made to ask for money, any contribution I could make to cover school fees, medical expenses, or clothing. The requests seemed never-ending, especially since they thought I was living a rich life across the pond, no matter what I told them to the contrary. I thought of how my cupboards at home were empty. The money I had made that week from cleaning was barely enough to buy groceries that would last for only a few days and how the car petrol was low. I reached over, switched the phone off, and headed inside to forget for just a moment that my life was so pathetic.

The alcohol did just the trick. It took away all my pain and eased the nagging worries that plagued my mind. I rarely ever drank, so I became quite tipsy rather quickly. When it was time to drive home, I didn't even care that I was still feeling so light-headed. As a matter of fact, a part of me wished that the journey home would end with me just being taken away by the angels, spirited away to a place where there was no hunger, no embarrassment, and no weight of responsibility on my shoulders. The life I lead in London, hand to mouth, was slowly killing me.

When I finally reached home and parked the car in my driveway, I decided I was still numb enough from the alcohol to hear whatever stressful or bad news was left on my voicemail. I was shocked to hear a voice identifying itself as a caller from the supermarket chain letting me know that I had successfully passed the final interview and offering me the management job at the very store I had tested in on the last day. I was struck dumb; I couldn't believe the news I was hearing. I didn't even realise that tears were streaming down my face, unbidden. I must have sat in that car for more than thirty minutes, just crying and staring out into the darkness. Eventually I was able to move. I dropped forward onto my knees in that small space in front of the driver's seat and I sent up a heartfelt prayer of thanksgiving and worship.

When I gathered myself together, I made my way inside and had a dinner of baked beans and eggs on toast and I saved a portion for Jasmine, in case she was hungry when she got home. I called the friend whom Jasmine was visiting, to tell her that I was on my way to pick up my daughter. She instantly noticed the uplifted tone of my voice, but assumed it was due to my having found a man. No, I chuckled at her; there was no Mr. Right that was causing my euphoric state. I had found a permanent job, which was much better. Before I started driving, I made a call to Tre, to see if he too had gotten the job offer. He hadn't and my reward turned bittersweet.

The salary they offered was great, especially considering the pittance I had been working for, and the thought that it would arrive on a consistent schedule was almost too hard to believe. It had been more than four years since I had made a steady monthly salary. The job was to start with a one-week training session that was scheduled at a location rather far away from my home. I was going to have to find someone to look after Jasmine. I began to panic, thinking that childcare issues might again foil my chances of attaining stability in the workforce.

I finally decided to reach out to my sister, Kem, and ask her to stay with me again. Considering our difficult times in the past, she wasn't my first choice, but I couldn't think of anyone else who I would trust with Jasmine's care. In the time since we had lived together in that filthy little flat back when she had first arrived, she had birthed a daughter. Coming to stay with us now included her child, and I knew that ultimately represented a greater financial burden for me. Even though Kem was currently unemployed and spent her days watching her own child, she insisted that

I pay her for taking care of Jasmine and include the cost of food for both of them, plus free board in the house. She knew I was in a bind and not in any position to deny her demands.

With Kem and her daughter settled in to watch over Jasmine, I left for the week of training. I had begun to feel a little bit comfortable about my situation. For all the mistrust I'd had for Kem regarding our relationship, I did not fear that she would fail to take care of my child. I thought that situation might even work out in the long term, with her being home for Jasmine while I worked at the store near my home. Unfortunately, I discovered rather quickly that I didn't like the job at all. Yet, there wasn't much I could do about it. I needed the job desperately, and I would just have to suck it up.

The people who visited the store and the people who worked under my supervision were so rude and there was nothing to be done about it. Every interaction had to end with me putting my tail between my legs and letting the other person feel like they had bested me. The job also included all of the physical duties that we had run through in that on-site interview. Apparently, there was nothing a store manager didn't have to do, from picking up trash in the car park, to cleaning up any mess in the aisles. My workday didn't end after the store closed, either. In the after-hours, I was expected to fully wash the floors and lift heavy boxes for stocking. I realised my managerial job was really nothing more than a glorified cleaner/ stocker.

I did have the responsibility of tallying up the sales at the end of the day and depositing the money in the safe, but I also had to work the registers and ring people up throughout the day. Rather soon after starting that job, I was transferred to another store that was a bit further away, and told that store was to be my 'mother store'. That meant it was the store where I was to stay for the duration of my tenure with the company. The hours remained long, and I found myself going to work before Jasmine had awoken in the mornings and coming home after she had gone to bed. I was hardly seeing her at all, and it was taking a toll on me. Kem told me that she was also pining for me, and that she wasn't happy.

Over the next few months, I dated Tre, but for some reason, things never turned serious with him. I soon found out that it was due to his womanizing ways. He had nine children with six different mothers. On top of that, he was legally married to one of them. He tried to explain to me that his wife was back in Germany and he needed women to comfort him in her absence. He told me he had women here, there, and everywhere and that I could be one of them. That offer did not appeal to me. He was far too carefree for my liking.

We managed to remain friends, even though deep down I was mad that he hadn't been the man I was hoping he was. He always made me feel special. When we walked down the road, girls would lap him up. It gave me a nice inner feeling that I was the one he had chosen to be with that night, and I would laugh privately in the knowledge that if they knew all his secrets like I did, they would probably turn him away too. The proverbial last straw in our relationship was broken one night when he made the crucial error of leaving his mobile phone at my place. One of his many women called and when I answered it, she warned me off her man! Oh dear, if only she knew that she didn't have a thing to worry about. I quickly assured her that I had no interest in taking him and I counselled her to think the same.

The job was beginning to take a toll on me, physically and emotionally. I found out that the other managers in that job had been there for years, yet they were still classified as deputy managers. It was blamed on company politics, and I was advised that the only way up was to keep your head down and your mouth shut. Kissing ass never hurt either. The way to help ensure a pay raise or promotion was to put in even more hours without any complaint. Asking for vacation time or sick leave would drop you back to the bottom of the pool. I felt trapped. To me, the more work you put in, the more they took advantage of you. I realised rather quickly, too, that I had significantly more real-work experience in the business world than the majority of the managers. That fact did not gain me any friends among the management staff, though, and I was viewed by many as a threat. I found out that all of the other managers, except the manager who was supervising my programme, were former cashiers. They weren't happy that I came in and started at the top, while they had to work their asses off to get there.

The hostility manifested in our workplace. When new processes were introduced or I found an old one that I was unclear on, I could never count on help from my colleagues who had an intimate understanding of the supermarket's inner workings due to their long history with the company. I whipped out my sales personality, hoping to charm my way into getting people to come to my aid. That only ever worked with the cashiers and never with the managers. In many ways, the experience of working with these people was like being back in grade school. They would sabotage one another, making the tills short at the end of the day or offering to help and then leaving things half done. Really, they would do anything they could to make each other look bad.

The challenges in the job extended beyond the management and cashier staff and went up to the executive level. The regulations that guided our workdays were proof of that. There was an unwritten rule that no one was to leave the premises during their lunch hour. Even the cashiers would quietly grumble that it was time they needed to go pay bills, make a doctor's visit, or deal with issues involving their children. It was apparent to all, however, that the reason for that practice was to keep the whole staff available for dealing with urgent matters as they arose, regardless of the fact that those urgent matters were usually the result of chronic understaffing.

At one point, I was even instructed on how to keep cashiers on shift who were trying to leave, regardless of them having completed their workday hours. And no consideration was given to the urgent need involving children that might have been calling them away. No cashier could leave their post until they were tallied up and cashed out by their manager. In my role as manager, I was told to simply ignore the cashiers' bell, which signalled their need for my services. I was told to busy myself with any mundane activity so that the cashier would have to stay on duty for as long as possible.

Leaving one's post before being cashed out was grounds for immediate sacking; the cashiers had no choice but to stay until I made my way over to tend to them. The thought of doing that to someone else, especially another parent whose child was waiting at home hungry or to be picked up from childcare or school, put my stomach in knots. I couldn't bring myself to do it. I marvelled at the way other managers could simply ignore young mothers waiting at their registers and crying softly, torn between the needs of their awaiting children and the need to hold onto their job.

One of our star workers, a young man named Elton, a single father, was a perfect example of that. Like all parents, he had childcare issues. But, instead of being honoured for his stringent work ethic, he was routinely exploited for the good of the company. If he reported a potential upcoming conflict in his schedule, such as a parent-teacher conference that was scheduled before his shift that day that may make him slightly late, Elton's schedule would be restructured to completely obliterate that time off so that he would have to show up earlier than scheduled, miss his child's conference, and ensure that he would not miss one minute of work.

Follow me on Twitter: @avabrown24

My refusal to play the corporate games earned me the mocking title of 'softie manager' and scored me no points with my bosses. There was a rumour floating around that the company had already blackballed me from any type of promotion. I found myself once again stuck in a dead end job and lacking momentum in my new career field. Was that to be my fate forever?

"The unknown is wrapped in cycles of belief and dare to."

Chapter Twenty

REPUTATIONS

"Reputations can attach themselves to us and become a

permanent part of our person."

———————

Things remained difficult at the supermarket, but I maintained my gratitude for the job and the opportunities it promised for a long-term career in administration. But the longer I was there, the more I became aware of their inner workings; or lack thereof. I became disillusioned with the managers who were supposed to be mentoring us as trainees. Things really started to disintegrate for me over a three-week period. I struggled with making a simple request for allowed time off work to meet in-person with my bank to rearrange my mortgage. I followed the company's policy for making such a request, yet each time I asked my direct supervisor, Sam, for an hour off during a single day of work, I received the clipped response, "Not today."

The deadline that had been set by my bank for completing the necessary paperwork was rapidly approaching. I was getting very anxious about how to resolve this conundrum and finally decided to take one of the days in lieu owed to me, instead of pestering my supervisor anymore. Asking for lieu time presented its own challenges, particularly because that time was routinely denied under some vague explanation that involved the inaccurate scheme in which we were never allowed to report the overtime hours we worked.

I knew that my daily overtime, like everyone else's, had not gone unnoticed by my colleagues and my manager, and I prayed that Sam would be fair when considering my request. I needed to prepare myself before approaching him. I first carefully checked the corporate schedule and that of my local store to find a date when my absence would be least disruptive. The upcoming Friday looked perfect. Moreover, I decided to not simply take the day off, but instead request to exchange my rotation with that of another trainee manager, Emmanuel. That way, the other staff would not have to cover the duties of an absent trainee manager.

I showed up on Monday prepared to present my idea to Sam, but found that he had taken a day in lieu. I was not surprised to find that he had not made any attempt to cover himself, and I felt good about myself for having enough respect for my colleagues to avoid the uproarious situation that these always led to. As the day wore on, the staff came on a few small situations in which we needed the advice of Sam. I volunteered to make the call, thinking that I could be clever and use the call to also discuss my rotation exchange idea with Sam. However, as soon as I brought up the rotation exchange, Sam cut me off by saying, "There's never much to be done in the store, so don't worry about it." My heart sank when he hung up. I knew that statement didn't reflect the truth of our working conditions; there were tons to do, and the staff and I were living proof, as we were all scrambling to take over Sam's responsibilities in his absence. I knew I could never act so irresponsibly towards my coworkers.

Follow me on Twitter: @avabrown24

On Tuesday, I again showed up ready to present my reasoned ideas for rotation exchange to Sam, but again I found out that he had just called in to take yet another day in lieu. I checked Emmanuel's schedule and found out that he wasn't scheduled to be in again until the next day, so I would have to finalise my whole plan with both Sam and Emmanuel first thing the next morning. When I reported for work that Wednesday, the first person I met was Sam. We exchanged our normal friendly hellos at the canteen door and made our way inside to get ready for the day.

I had planned to lock my purse up in my employee locker and pop into Sam's office for a quick chat before either of us got overwhelmed with the daily routine. But, as soon as we walked into the welfare area, a stocker named Kumar came up to us and started telling me that the employees from welfare had just been discussing the on-going problems with everyone getting their requests for days in lieu approved. I felt a flicker of excitement, thinking to myself what perfect timing it was, since Sam was still standing right next to me. Kumar went on to explain that another employee, Michelle, had suggested that a good way for the staff to get the lieu time owed to them was for them to accurately record all the hours we worked in a single day. She had even gone as far as to question the legality of the current practice of inaccurate recording the company had.

I could sense Sam's growing agitation. He had stayed silent so far, but it was time for him to stop the blasphemous talk once and for all. "We cannot do that. The District Manager will go ballistic about it." I was surprised at his strong tone of voice and tried to lighten the situation by telling Sam that I found it hard to believe the company's administration would not want to at least hear the suggestion of something that would ensure we were within the boundaries of the law. Sam simply shrugged and said that such topics of discussion were not for the day's start. He turned on his heel and beckoned me to follow.

Follow me on Twitter: @avabrown24

As we walked, I figured at that point there was nothing ventured but for me to put my request to him at that time. I was relieved and a bit shocked when he merely sighed and gave me verbal approval for my time in lieu that Friday, as well as for my exchange of rotation with Emmanuel. We even chitchatted a bit after that, before I headed to the warehouse to start my workday in earnest.

A little over one hour had passed before I finished my tasks. As I began to make my way to the main store, I was delighted to see Emmanuel and I waved to catch his attention. Before I could speak, though, he started yelling angrily at me, saying that someone had just told him that I had changed my shift with him without asking. I rushed to clarify the misunderstanding, telling him that I had only gotten permission from Sam if we could exchange shifts. I explained I had been waiting for him to come into work that day so that I could talk to him about it.

Emmanuel said that Sam had just told him the exchange was already complete. He was understandably angry with me, thinking that I had disrupted his schedule without any forewarning or consideration for his opinion on the matter. I couldn't get a word in edgewise and before I knew it, he was pointing a finger at me and saying that since I had taken it upon myself to mess with his life; I would have to come in on Friday night after closing to pick up the store keys for opening on Saturday. I was a bit flustered at that point and stammered that I couldn't come in that late on Friday night because my child would already be in bed, and besides, I wasn't scheduled to open the store on Saturday morning - Sam was. I asked if he could just give Sam the keys when their shift together ended on Friday night. But Emmanuel just glared at me and stormed off.

I went to see Sam straight away to get that messy situation resolved, but he was busy with the cleaning contractor and unavailable for a discussion right then. Emmanuel was refusing to even look at me and I realised that the situation, though unintentional, had been unfair on him. I needed to resolve it and take care of myself without involving him. I peeked back into Sam's office, but he was still with the contractor. He knew what I was seeking him out for, and when he saw me, he simply pointed to the stack of rotation sheets for me to take and fill out. I changed Emmanuel's shift back to its original schedule and marked Friday as a lieu day for myself.

Not long after, Sam came storming out of his office, waving the rotation sheets in the air and yelling at me, "Come with me right now!" I was shocked at his red-faced anger and said, "One moment, please, let me wrap things up." He barked out, "I said come with me right now. What I have to say is more important than what you are doing." He was bearing down on me, and I had a flash of the men who had attacked me that night, waving their guns and coming at me with a similar cold look in their eyes.

My first instinct was to cower, but within seconds, I found my voice to stand up for myself. I steadied my tone and said, "Please calm down and please don't talk to me like that. We shouldn't yell at each other in the workplace." That set him off. He shot forward and screamed in my face, "For fuck's sake! Come with me now!" I steeled myself and stayed standing upright, staring directly into his eyes. I told him that I wasn't going anywhere with him until he calmed down and apologised for cursing at me.

He must have been dumbstruck by my unexpected refusal to cower to him because he stood motionless with his mouth hanging open. I took advantage of the moment and reminded him I had never been rude or disrespectful towards him and that I didn't appreciate his rudeness or his undermining approach. Not surprisingly, the ruckus had attracted the attention of all the nearby staff, who started edging away. Sam began to realise that all eyes were now on him. He took a deep breath and stepped back from me, quietly saying a quick "Sorry."

Follow me on Twitter: @avabrown24

That was it? I thought. That whispered utterance was absolutely unacceptable as an apology. Before I knew it, I was telling him that he knew my name and that he needed to apologise to me properly. He set his lips in a hard line and gestured for me to follow him into the welfare area, where we would have some more privacy. Instead of getting the apology I was expecting, however, he turned on me and said firmly that it was his privilege as my manager to speak to me however he saw fit, and asked how I dare embarrass him in front of his other staff.

It was fortuitous that he had led us to the spot right in front of one of the corkboards with random company news, announcements, and policies tacked onto them. I immediately noticed one of the company's policy sheets and grabbed it down off the board, pointing to the paragraph that specifically addressed that exact situation. I reminded him that way of addressing me was considered harassment. He went back into his silent mode and stared hard at me. As the moment of silence stretched on, I turned on my heel, gathered my belongings, and left the store.

As soon as I arrived at my home, I called our District Manager, who was Sam's direct boss. He wasn't in, so I left a message telling him that I needed to speak with him urgently regarding an inappropriate and explosive situation at the store. He called back shortly and I was able to tell him about what had just transpired. He agreed that Sam was out of bounds and that an employee should not be spoken to like that under any circumstances. He told me that he would start working on the situation.

About an hour later, the District Manager rang back and asked if I felt I could work with Sam again. I replied that I could work with him again, thinking that time heals all wounds and sometime in the future we would likely cross paths, as our careers were parallel in that company. To my surprise, though, the District Manger responded by telling me that he needed me to go back to working under Sam within the hour. I nearly started crying when I explained to him that I didn't feel comfortable going back into the situation so quickly after what had just happened. My breathing calmed down when he said that he understood my apprehension and asked if I felt that I could finish out that day's shift in another store instead.

When I agreed to his alternative plan, he said he would arrange something in the next hour. In the meantime, though, he wanted me to just drop by my home store and have a quick chat with Sam. "It will be good for the relations of the store," he explained. I reiterated that I didn't feel comfortable talking to Sam right away and said that I was happy to go, just on another day. I was shaken to my core, though, by his response. He said, "OK, Ava, you have left me with no choice but to start a formal investigation."

For the second time that day, I found myself stammering out an explanation to defend myself against an unfair attack. Sam had been so angry and so disrespectful. Having to interact with me right now because his boss was ordering it was unlikely to ease his anger. I didn't make any headway though, and the District Manager told me he would have to figure out what to do from here that fit within company policy.

When he hung up, I rang my home store straight away. Sam answered, and as soon as I identified myself to him, he said that he was actually angry with me for four things that day, but I had not let him talk to me about them before I had chosen to leave the store in a huff. I had not expected that, and I could not imagine what these four things could be. After all, that day was still young and I hadn't even been at work that long before our situation exploded, and he hadn't seemed bothered by anything during our first morning chitchat session.

He began to tick them off, one by one. First, I was in the wrong for calling him to ask work-related questions on his days off. Second, I had been in the wrong when I had left a message for Emmanuel about wanting to talk on Wednesday when he came in (apparently, Emmanuel said my tone was abrasive). Third, I was in the wrong about an ordering mix-up, which actually had nothing to do with me and I knew for a fact was his screw up. And, finally, that I was in the wrong for modifying the rotation on the scheduling sheets that he had pointed me to.

I immediately tried to defend myself, reminding Sam that he had told me to call him at home with work-related questions. It was a common practice among all the staff, as sometimes, important items couldn't be found when he was gone and we needed him to tell us where to locate them in his absence. My temper began to boil at the unfairness of it all. I justified my role in the situation involving Emmanuel, explaining that my intent was to protect my coworkers by having someone cover me when I was out so as not to be a burden.

I asked if he had listened to the message I left on Emmanuel's phone, and if he agreed with the assessment that I was rude. He said he didn't need to listen to anything, he already had the word of my coworker and that was all the information he needed. He then brought up the conversation in which I told Emmanuel I would not be able to pick up the keys on Friday night. When I started to speak, though, Sam cut me off and said that it didn't matter what my excuse was, I needed to make allowance for doing anything that anyone told me to, even another trainee manager. He ended the conversation by telling me not to waste my breath on explaining any of my actions or defending myself, he had already made a judgment on me and the case was closed.

I could not believe that, in the end, I was the one who was going to be put at fault for the entire situation. I felt utterly used and disrespected. There was nothing more for me to do but wait to hear back from the District Manager and learn my fate. When the call finally came, I was surprised to find out that I wasn't the one being transferred; it was Sam who had been reassigned to another store. There was a new manager by the name of Adelaide and I was to report to her the next day.

When I showed up and introduced myself, it was evident that Adelaide had been briefed about me. The way she looked at me made me feel like there was a sign above my head that read 'troublemaker'. The stress of the situation the day before still had me on edge. My asthma was acting up but I felt there was no way that I could take a sick day with the previous day's events still so fresh in everyone's mind. I spent the morning wheezing and gasping for air as I pulled around the pallets of newly delivered vegetables and completed the stocking of the shelves. Adelaide noticed my struggles and inquired in a tight voice if I was ok. I told her that I wasn't feeling very well but she just gave a short "hmm," rolled her eyes, and went on with her business.

The other workers were more solicitous in their concerns for me, coming over to help me with the unpacking. One colleague even went to Adelaide and told her that my audible struggles to breathe were making him scared for my life, and he thought maybe I should go home early. That only earned him a loud rebuke in which she snapped at him and told him to stop being an "interfering git." She then called me over and told me in a low voice that she was onto me, she knew all about the tactics that staff would come up with to get out of putting in a good day's work and she wasn't about to put up with any of it.

By that time, my breathing had become so ragged and I was getting so little oxygen that I passed out. I could hear someone calling for an ambulance and felt myself being carried out to the car park into the fresh air. The ambulance turned up in no time and whisked me away to a nearby hospital. I found out later that as soon as the ambulance was called, Adelaide had started rushing around to act as though she had been

Follow me on Twitter: @avabrown24

concerned and that she had told as many staff as would listen that she had only leaned in to tell me to go home for the rest of the day but that I had turned her down and insisted on staying to work.

In the meantime, the hospital staff gave me a nebulizer, which immediately eased the constriction in my lungs. I was physically and emotionally exhausted by the time I was discharged to go home, with strict instructions for bed rest. The doctor had told me stress was the most likely trigger of my severe attack; he gave me a sick note to take a three-day break from work. In my time off over those next few days, I wrote a letter to the Regional Director, outlining what had really happened over the past week and that morning with Adelaide. My hope was to somehow correct the injustice of the whole affair and regain my esteemed standing with the company.

Since I had witnesses who could attest to the truth in the matter, my complaint garnered a formal acknowledgment that Adelaide's behaviour had been inappropriate. I was disappointed that there was to be no consequence for Adelaide's actions, but when I returned, I found a new policy pinned to the corkboard that said any employee who was in physical distress should be dismissed to go home or to a doctor's office immediately. At least I was assured that the company hoped to avoid that situation happening again to any other employee.

I also found out when I returned to work that I was being immediately transferred to another store. The new store was farther away from home, but I was relieved as I felt like my reputation was tainted at the present location ; now I would be given a chance to start afresh. However, I quickly came to realise that the spots on my professional persona extended company-wide. After one week at the new store, I still had not been entrusted with the duties involving cashing out or taking the cashiers' money to the safe. That was one of the key responsibilities of any mid or senior level manager, but my duties were kept to no more than those of a cashier. When I wasn't at the till, I was put on C-checking duty, which was where an entry level employee would walk up and down the chillers and check each stocked item to ensure that the sell-by date hadn't passed. It was that duty that made my demotion the most obvious.

Still, I didn't make any complaints and did everything I was told. My tactic for restoring my reputation was to be the perfect yes-man. However, after a month of that strategy, nothing had changed. I finally mustered up the courage to ask my manager if the job title I had been transferred under was different from the one I'd had at the last store, but he said that I was still a trainee manager. I wasn't sure how to respond to him, so I left the conversation and waited until I got home that evening to place a call to ask him about the details of my upcoming schedule in compliance with my trainee managerial status. He was very congenial and said that I was set to start taking over cashing-out financial duties soon. He told me that anytime someone was transferred, it was company policy that they learnt the store's tills and stocking duties before they moved on to the administrative stuff. I had worked with plenty of transfer employees before, though, and knew that wasn't the truth. I was a special case.

"Exit strategies can creep upon us so secretly."

Follow me on Twitter: @avabrown24

Chapter Twenty One

THE CRUMBLE

"Removing one brick from a stack can send walls crumbling down. Quickly escaping isn't always possible, so we sometimes get crushed."

———————

At long last, I was given the cashing out and closing up responsibilities befitting my trainee manager status. I breathed a sigh of relief and thought for sure I had finally redeemed myself in the eyes of the upper management. That day, I was so proud when the money from the day's sales balanced with the money in the safe and I held my head high as I prepped to lock up the store. I gathered my personal items together and went to reach for the store keys that I had expected to find in my pocket, only to realise with a thrill of panic that I had not retrieved them from the manager's office before he had left earlier that evening. I ran to the office, hoping against all odds that he had somehow forgotten to lock his office door and I could sneak in and retrieve them without anyone being the wiser to my mistake, but there was no such luck that night.

Follow me on Twitter: @avabrown24

I stood and pulled at the locked door for a full minute, even though I knew the door was locked tight. "Why? Why? Why?" I screamed in my head. My conscience taunted me with the answer, "You messed up! You are no good! They should have never trusted you!" I turned and fell back into the door and banged on it with my fist in frustration. "Damn!" I yelled out loud. The only way out of that mess would be to call the district manager, who had never forgiven me for my refusal to speak to Sam the afternoon of our frightening confrontation. Now I was going to prove him right in thinking I was a waste of the company's resources.

I tried to steel myself for the phone call to him, and his last words to me echoed in my head, "This Company isn't for the weak hearted. We speak bluntly and we expect our employees to accept their lot without complaint." I knew that time I would be in for a particularly awful berating, and I just didn't think I had the fortitude to handle it. I started to cry but fought back the tears of self-pity. I paced the room and took deep calming breaths. Finally, the panic and utter dismay started to dissipate and I remembered that another manager had mentioned being in possession of an extra set of store keys due to a mix-up earlier in the week. I nearly collapsed with relief and felt the full weight of my anxiety lifted when she answered her phone and agreed to come down right away and bring me the keys.

I went home that night with a cry to God for his mercy, but also with a plea in my heart for the tenuous situation I had found myself in to somehow be resolved. I knew that I could not survive under that type of stressful working environment for the rest of my life, especially when my efforts were leading nowhere and I was killing myself to merely get back in the good graces of the 'bigwigs' (bosses) in the company.

That night, after I put Jasmine to bed and settled myself in, I took the time to reflect on my situation and to try and figure out a plan to get out of it. Writing in my diary had always helped me to organise my thoughts and gain clarity on anything troublesome that I was facing, and that night, I was in need of such clarity.

April 2008
Dear diary,

Life here in London has been the most challenging I have experienced since my time at teachers' college back in 1993-1996.

At this particular moment, a number of factors are challenging me: my finances (I owe over seven thousand pounds on credit cards!), my job (I hate it!), and the way I am belittled and pushed around on a daily basis (I am the most qualified person in that stupid store, but I am treated like the biggest underdog!) Why is that, Lord?

I am disgusted by the people I work with. They are vipers, hypocrites, and ass-lickers. I am surrounded by the lowest of the low.

I am in the middle of doing a re-mortgage on my house, and that alone makes me have to hang in there and just take all the crap I am subjected to every day. I have no other source of income, so either I put up with everything that is sucking the life out of my soul and pay the bills, or I fight to save myself and lose my livelihood. Then the bank will reclaim the house and I will lose everything that I sacrificed in this fucking country.

If it was me alone, I might even consider giving up right now, but I have to keep a roof over Jasmine's head. God, and now my sister and my niece are living here, too. Her help is invaluable, but the extra mouths to feed and board have exhausted all my resources.

So, really, I have no choice but to go back to work. And even though every morning starts with a panic attack and ends with another sleepless night as I toss and turn with the anxiety of what is to come, I enter that damn store's doors. If I do fall asleep, my dreams are all nightmares about what will happen if my alarm somehow fails and I oversleep past the 6am opening time. Certainly, I would be fired. I know I am at my breaking point because I have started reliving my attack experience every time the alarm goes off, my mind tricking me into thinking it is the shot of a gun aimed right at my head.

I know that I am not eating well; the stress has just killed my appetite. No one needs to tell me that I am just going through the motions at work. I hate the lifting, the cleaning of the floor, and the packing of the shelves. My hands are so calloused that I am afraid to shake anybody's hand when I meet them.

My life has reached a stage where every time I compare it with what I left back in Jamaica, I cry. I really want to go back home, but Jasmine doesn't. She is ever so close to her dad and it would kill me to leave her here in London while I went back to Jamaica. I see no way for me to be able to go home. I just have to hang in there and put my desires beneath hers. I wish that there was some way both of us could be happy, but it's not possible at the moment. This is the harsh reality of motherhood; sometimes you have to sacrifice your own happiness for that of your child. Maybe my time to be happy will come when she grows up? Right now, though, she is all I have and it would kill me to lose her.

To make matters worse, her uncle is moving here, so she has one less tie back to Jamaica and she will now want to go back even less for the holidays, which are the times I look forward to like a drowning man looks for a lifeline. As far as Jasmine is concerned, London is home.

I hate so many things about being in this dreary country. The cost of survival is far too high. I have to take every hour of work offered, even late at night, even when my daughter is home sick. It kills me to come home at

1am and find her homework left open on the kitchen table with a note to me asking for some clarification of something she doesn't understand, and knowing all I can do is write her a note back before I have to leave at 5am. This is what our interactions have deteriorated to, notes written in the wee hours of the morning.

Tonight was an early night for me. I got home and was in bed right before midnight. I don't know if it's the exhaustion or my realizing the pathetic state of my life that is making me cry right now. It seems my prayers asking God why my life has turned out like this has only been met with a stone-cold silence.

I am sick of struggling! I want to be able to enter the grocery store and buy meat without having to sacrifice other items on my list. I want to not feel like an outsider anymore. I want to go home. Or find a way out of this constant cycle of working to near death and breathing a great sigh of relief every time a bill is paid. Please God, hear my cry! Please help me!

I went to bed and hoped God had heard my cries that night.

When I went to work the next day, I found that the new rotation had been posted. The last day for me having the safe responsibilities would be the day before inventory day; I was scheduled to have the day off. I asked the manager about the discrepancy, but instead of switching my day off for another day, he asked me to come in on that day, even though I was not scheduled to be in the office. I had become so downtrodden that I simply agreed and went about my regular work duties.

That whole day, my heart bothered me. I needed a day off that week, as I had promised to take Jasmine out for the Easter holidays. I could not break another promise to her, as I was constantly making up broken promises to her. I went back to see the manager and asked him if we could please find a way to reorganise the schedule so that I wouldn't have to work an extra day that week. He told me not to worry and assured me I would get a day off as requested, but it would be the day after the inventory was completed. It was the best I was going to get, so I rescheduled everything with Jasmine and finished the week without a complaint.

The night after the inventory was completed. I received a call from the district manager, who asked if I could come in for a one-on-one meeting the following day. I explained that my rotation had been changed to provide for the day off that I'd had to miss to accommodate the inventory schedule. I also told him that I had rescheduled all the arrangements with my daughter to fit with the store's needs, and now those were set for the following day. I still remember the sneer in his voice when he said to me, "And you were very crafty in setting those plans to ensure that you had that day off. Well, it's not going to work." He told me I had better get busy changing my personal schedule around because it was not a request, but an order that I meet with the Senior Manager of Operations that next morning. He ended the call by telling me not to worry too much, the meeting would be brief.

Something in his voice put me on guard. An uneasy feeling grew inside of me. I began to wonder, had I done something terribly wrong at work that day? I wracked my brain for every movement I had made that day, every word I had spoken, but nothing stood out. Maybe he had found out about the key incident? I felt a sick feeling churning in my stomach and I realised I was afraid of that man. I was shaking so badly that I feared I would be ineffective in the meeting the next day. I called on my friend Shoa and asked her to accompany me to the meeting for moral support; she immediately agreed.

When Jasmine awoke the next morning, I explained that we would have to move some things around and get a later start to our fun day than we had planned. She was disappointed once again, and I could see in her eyes that she didn't trust me to come through with my promise to spend the day with her. I promised her that as soon as that one meeting was done, we would have the whole day together. When Shoa and I were walking out, though, I received a call telling me that the Senior Manager of Operations was running late and the meeting had been rescheduled for a few hours later in the day. It was just going to be too little time to leave the house to do anything and just enough time to make me have to break the promise I had just made to Jasmine.

When Shoa and I arrived at the office, the receptionist took one look at us and told me that I didn't need to bring any legal representation into the meeting. I explained that was just my friend and the lady directed Shoa to a seat in the waiting area and me into an inner office. As soon as I sat down in front of the District Manager and the Senior Manager of Operations, they handed me a letter and instructed me to go over its contents.

Even before I began to read, my heart sank. I was fired.

The two men were stiff and formal with me, simply dismissing me from the room. There were no false attempts at easing the pain of my being sacked. No one said to me, 'Good job' or 'you did try, but the fit just wasn't right'. I emerged into the waiting area in a daze and mumbled something to Shoa about being sacked. She immediately took over for where my spirit had shut down. She asked the two men who were hovering nearby what was the reason for that. To both of our surprise, they answered her directly, but only said that because I hadn't worked there a full year yet, they were not obligated to provide any explanation. I felt the world unravel around me. The last glimpse I had of the District Manager as Shoa took me gently by the arm to lead me out to the car park was of him slightly smirking. It was if he was saying to me, 'Well, you got your day off'.

Over the next few days, I began to realise the extent of planning that had gone into my sacking. Apparently, my sacking came as no surprise to everyone else; they knew it was coming on that very day. I was the only one who was blindsided. I began to wonder how stupid I could have really been. How did I not see what was going on around me? However, I still could not get any concrete answers as to why I had been sacked. The most I got was one of the cashiers suggesting that it was almost my one year anniversary with the company. After that point sacking gets a lot trickier from a legal standpoint. And that in management's opinion, I was going to be the manager that went against the fabric of what they stood for. I was being punished for being too nice to the staff; my consideration and Christianity were stumbling blocks and I was too gentle with the female staff workers who were mothers. In fact, I was always saddened and bringing up the issue of having women on the cash registers when their children were left at school outside of regular school hours just because we didn't do a rotation with sufficient staff to cover the daily shifts. I got fed up at seeing grown women cry and my hands being tied, so in a sense, I really didn't fit into the culture of that organisation.

Even though my life had just taken the proverbial leap off the edge of a cliff, my dependents and family remained just as strongly reliant on me. I didn't know whether to cry or laugh when I received a letter from a friend back in Jamaica a few days after my sacking, asking me to give her an update on how I was coming along in collecting money to cover her university tuition and fees. I knew in my heart that I could do nothing for her and it pained me to think about how that would be yet another person I loved who I would be letting down. I would have rather just crumpled up the letter, thrown my phone into the river, and pretended the request had never existed, but I couldn't do that. I sat down and put pen to paper:

Follow me on Twitter: @avabrown24

My dearest Cassie,

I write to you this morning in one of the lowest states I have ever found myself in; my life just seems to be a series of low points. I am beginning to wonder if I have personality disorder or if there is something wrong with me that attracts this kind of oppression. I am depressed beyond anything I have ever felt before; I don't even have the words to properly express what I am going through. When I am not numb, I am having a panic attack, and I feel like I am very near not being able to cope. Just the hustle of trying to stay on top of the most basic bills makes me miserable. Being on my own and with no one to help emotionally or financially is killing me.

Simply put, I am tired of life. I sit here typing and crying...and thinking how very tired I am of fighting this unwinnable battle that is my life. I want out of this rat race. If it weren't for Jasmine, I would probably be searching for a way to exit this life entirely, but I cannot pass my sorrow or burden on to her. I love her more than life itself. I have to hang on for her. But all she sees of me is the depression, which makes me impatient, short-tempered, insecure, and frustrated to distraction.

It was very hard for me to sit down and write this to you. I hate having to admit how much my life has regressed. I am so unhappy here in London and I want desperately to return to my native Jamaica. However, Jasmine is now going on ten and she doesn't want to leave; London is almost all she knows and her dad lives here. All the jobs I have found here have been jobs of circumstance and nothing I would have chosen. The hours have prevented me from even being a mum properly.

I just received word that my mortgage has gone up due to the credit crunch. I had no idea how to pay it now that I am out of the job at the grocery store, but now to think that it is even higher than I expected, I really don't see how this will work out. I finally made an appointment to see a psychologist and she agreed that I need to be under some attentive care, but where will I find the money to cover such an additional expense? I am nearing a breakdown...

"How low can one get tossed before they just sink into nothingness?"

Chapter Twenty Two

WEAKNESS

"I think men become who we want them to be. They curve into the man that we expect them to be, and when we are no longer there, they become who they really are."

———————

The day I lost my job, my house seemed lonelier than it had ever felt before. I sat alone in my room and cried. As I cradled my pillow for comfort, I remembered how so many times before; Tobore would have been the one snuggling next to me in bed. He would have been the one holding me while I wept into his shoulder, assuring me that however bleak the situation was, he would help see me through it. It broke my heart even more to think that I had lost that companionship, to know that I was really on my own against the world now.

Just days before, I had contemplated requesting that Tobore sign off his part of our house in Jamaica, so that it would be under my name solely. That would allow me to cut off my last tie to the one person who should have been my partner for life. Now, here I was with the weight of the world pressing even harder on my shoulders. I tried in vain to pull myself out of the emotional black hole that was consuming me, but even sleep proved to be another luxury denied me. I started using sleeping pills, but the few hours of pharmaceutically induced unconsciousness never left me feeling refreshed.

Before the sacking, I had been looking for other jobs; I had even had a few interviews (which I had secretly attended so as not to jeopardise my already tenuous position). My efforts had been rather weak and unsuccessful though, largely because of the extensive time demands from the store, and my distraction with all the other pressures in my personal life. Now I was living in a constant state of needling anxiety and on the verge of completely losing my ability to function in even the simplest of daily tasks. When I sat down to take stock of my situation and come up with a productive plan, I would start to feel the walls closing in on me and the air becoming thick and hard to breathe in. There was nothing that I wanted more than to run outside and escape everything that was constraining me.

I knew I couldn't go on like that, so I asked my general practitioner for a referral to a psychologist. Having a stranger to talk to seemed more effective at that time than leaning on my friends alone. They had their own issues, and I also didn't know who could handle the terrors in my past that I was still carrying around. I did consider calling on Tobore at that time, to make him my confidante; after all, we were on friendly terms with one another and he already knew all of my past. Our wedding anniversary was coming up and he had even called to ask if he could take me out for a private dinner that night. I had agreed because I was fairly certain that we would have no expectations of one another.

We had built a comfortable, platonic relationship and it benefited Jasmine as much as it did Tobore and me. Gone were the days of angry glares across the table, and screaming matches over the smallest of offences. We were able to do things together, as a family in peace, like taking trips to animal parks and sharing holiday dinners. Tobore and I still supported each other financially, too. If he was ever in a bind, he knew he could come to me to borrow cash and I knew I could count on him for the same. Unfortunately, neither of us had much to spare at any one time since coming to the UK.

I found out that the wait to get a psychologist appointment was months, so I decided to reach out to Tobore for some emotional support. Over the next weeks and months, I felt us really connecting in a meaningful way and thought maybe it was because we were building a friendship without the distraction of romantic involvement. We had even had several conversations where I shared with him my desire to find a man to share that physical side of life with, discussing my hopes for the occasional man I found attractive or with whom things could turn intimate. Little did I know that was piercing his heart.

Tobore's silent torment finally came to my attention when something began to develop between him and a single parent from Jasmine's school. He began acting very strange and unnecessarily hostile around me, so I confronted him about it; I was not expecting what he told me next. HHe said that he still loved me with the same depth as when we'd conceived our daughter, and told me that he couldn't ever love anyone else like that. He even told me that I was the only person he would ever consider having another child with, and expressed the deepest regret for how far we had strayed from one another and all the things that had happened in the years we had been apart.

My heart melted. I began to think that somehow, after all we had gone through as a couple, we were both still subconsciously involved, and had been all along. Maybe, I wondered, nothing had worked out with other people because neither of us had ever really wanted to move on. We hadn't been intimate in a very long time, and in a way, the thought of it scared me. I had come to love and treasure our friendship and I wasn't completely sure how I felt about abandoning that to enter into the tumult that we had left behind when we'd left each other's bed. The one thing I was sure of, though, was at that time in my life, I could not emotionally or mentally handle one more complication. I feared that chance at reconciliation might have to be delayed.

I had started submitting applications for work again, but nothing was panning out. One afternoon, after a particularly dismal interview, I was driving home and feeling so low that I was thinking how much better life would be if someone would just run a light so that I could be met by angels who would carry me off to heaven. It was an insane thought, I knew, so I called Tobore and immediately started crying so hard that I could barely talk. He told me to pull off the road and compose myself, then to head straight home. He would be there shortly. I did so, taking only a few minutes to get my emotions under control and reaching the house only about five minutes later. As soon as I arrived, I sat down to wait for Tobore. While waiting, Kem and I fell into a conversation about my low mood. She offered to make me something to eat, but I declined because Tobore would be arriving at any moment and I wasn't hungry.

Before I knew it, two hours had elapsed. Tobore finally arrived, but he seemed in such a normal mood that I figured he had just been waylaid by something unimportant. He took me for a drive and we talked. He listened to all of my complaints and fears and gave all the right bolstering responses. By the time he dropped me off at home, I felt ready to go on with my life's battle. I was even able to make a few more appointments for potential job leads, one of which told me to come in right away. I grabbed my purse and was heading out the door when a call came from Jasmine's school. They needed me to bring her asthma medication because she was in the nurse's office with some worrying symptoms.

I cursed my luck. If I went, I would miss the meeting with the employment agency, but my child's health was much too important to be put second to anything else. I decided to call Tobore and ask him to help out once more today. Because he had just been so solicitous towards me, I was a bit surprised by his reticence to help out with that small situation, but there really was no time to dilly-dally. I told him that I would take care of it myself and not to worry.

I jumped in my car and drove to the school to drop off the medication. I called the employment agency and asked if I could be a few minutes late, but was told that their schedule wouldn't accommodate the delay. So, I drove home. Kem told me that Tobore had been at the house just a few minutes before I came back, but he had left when she'd told him I had already gone to make the delivery. Something in her voice made me nervous and I asked her what she was holding back. She told me that he had come to the front door alone, but that she had seen someone else waiting for him in the car; a woman.

I rolled my eyes dismissively and told her that it was probably just some friend that needed a favour that day like I did. Her silence let me know that I was being a fool. She told me that it was clearly something else. The woman was very young and dressed like she was ready for a hot date, looking bored and very at-home in the front passenger seat, with her feet propped up on the dashboard. She didn't need to say anything more about what she had seen; my heart recognised the truth of the matter.

I called Tobore to ask him about who the girl was that he was spending his day off with. He immediately went on the defensive and said it was none of my business. I told him that since he had just professed his undying love to me and opened the door to our reconciliation, it was most certainly my business. His tone turned very gruff and harsh, and he said that I was jumping to conclusions in my head about what he wanted of me. He said that our friendship was the end of whatever would be between us and that was where our relationship was and that was where it ended. I felt tricked and utterly betrayed. In an instant, all the trust and love that I felt for him disappeared with a finality that would affect the rest of our lives.

I knew that we would still have to interact with each other as Jasmine's parents, but I closed my heart to him beyond anything else. A week later, as I was continuing my job hunt around town, I got a call from Kem saying that Jasmine had been sent home from school with worsening symptoms and she needed to get to a doctor right away. I was half way across town and knew I couldn't get back home through traffic within the next hour. I moved my heart into professional mode, thinking that I would call Tobore as Jasmine's father to come and assist with his child getting to the hospital, since it was again his day off. He agreed and drove straight to my home, but quickly announced to Kem that he thought she looked fine. In his opinion, she didn't need a doctor. He said that there was nothing wrong with her that a nap wouldn't fix.

I found out later that he really was just anxious to get back to his girlfriend and had gone home grousing to a mutual friend that a visit to the doctor would have taken hours out of his day, just to possibly find out that she had a typical virus or something else common in kids. Back at home, though, Jasmine rapidly grew worse and Kem became so frightened that she had me call another friend, who came over and immediately drove Jasmine to the closest hospital. Jasmine's state on arrival was so alarming that she was admitted and prepped for surgery to address an acute appendicitis.

The news shook me to my core. My baby was so sick that she needed to be cut open? My shock quickly switched to a seething anger towards Tobore. How dare he have been so flippant about our child's health? The doctor had told me on the phone that appendicitis could be deadly if left untreated; she could have died if we had ignored her symptoms. If I had known then the real reason Tobore had left (to cavort with his new paramour) I don't know what I would have done. I rushed to the hospital and found Tobore there at her bedside. My anger with him had only grown during the drive and I flew into a rage at the sight of him. I literally chased him out of the room, screaming all sorts of accusations that he may have caused her death with his ignorant attitude.

I settled into the chair next to Jasmine's bed and refused to leave her for the night, even though the nurses advised me that visiting hours had ended. At around three am, a nurse came around to check in. I told her that Jasmine had kept telling me that her IV was hurting her, saying, "Mummy, it isn't comfy," while trying to pull on it. I asked the nurse to check it, and it was a good thing I did, because she discovered that the cannula had not been placed correctly. She said that they would try to replace it right away, but I stopped her and asked why she needed it. She said it was all part of the precaution to have her ready if they found out that she had appendicitis and they needed to operate on her.

I was confused, from what I had understood, Jasmine had already been diagnosed. I asked the nurse to clarify everything and she said that they really didn't know what was wrong with my baby. They just suspected appendicitis, but the tests had all been inconclusive. I did not know very much about medicine or diseases, such as appendicitis, but I was appalled that they were getting my daughter ready for surgery without really knowing what was wrong with her or what they needed to do. Surgery was so invasive and such a physical trauma. I didn't want her subjected to it on a suspicion. I demanded that they do more testing and get a better handle on what was really wrong. In the end, the nurse called the doctor and they acquiesced to me, and before noon, all of Jasmine's symptoms had resolved and she was released from the hospital; the test results came back and ruled out appendicitis.

Over the next few weeks, Tobore's visits were very infrequent. Jasmine noticed and started complaining that he was neglecting her, so I doubled my efforts to keep them in contact in other ways. They would still get together on the weekends, only now he would just drop in for the minute it took to collect her and her things before they sped off in the car. Each time she came back from these visits, she would tell me about a girl that would stay with them for the whole weekend. I could tell that she was jealous of the attention he would shower on that woman, seeing it as time stolen away from her. Tobore was blind to that, though. Jasmine was demoted to the back seat of the car on journeys, even though it was an unspoken rule that she would never sit in the back of either of our cars. But the front seat was now occupied by Tobore's latest woman.

It all came to a head a short time later, when, one afternoon, I found Jasmine crying in the bedroom. She said that her daddy never paid attention to her anymore. It broke my heart to see her suffering like that, so I called Tobore to ask him to talk to her and to get his act together for her sake. He immediately flew into me; he told me that his personal life and his relationship with his daughter were none of my business. But, as every mother knew, anything that affected your child immediately became your business. I gave him a stern lecture and he agreed to speak to her about it.

I was afraid that Jasmine would get on the phone with Tobore and crumble into a frail little girl that gave up fighting for herself. I was filled with pride when she got on the phone and told him everything she had just told me. She asked him when she could see him next and they settled for Wednesday, his next day off. I drove her to his house on the appointed day, but asked her to first wait in the car while I had a quick talk with him. My intent was to stress to him the seriousness of the situation and that he couldn't merely dismiss her distress. However, what happened next would again change my life forever.

"Being totally broken and fragile can scare you forever, if you let it."

Chapter Twenty Three

LETTING GO

"Letting go is sometimes hard, but a necessity in an effort to grow."

———————

Tobore answered the door and silently invited me inside with a wave of his hand. We started talking about the situation, and he immediately became furious, yelling that I had no right to control his life. The personal attack took me off guard, but I got some clarity when he told me he thought my problem was that I didn't want him and didn't want him to be with anyone else either. The conversation became an all-out argument in each other's faces and screaming at the top of our lungs. He was angrier than I had ever seen him before.

His eyes had turned bloodshot red, and before I knew it, he lunged forward and grabbed me by the throat, squeezing so hard I choked for breath. I managed to bite his other hand so hard that he dropped his grasp on me. Before I could recover my wits, he had pushed me into the kitchen and we were both striking at each other. I saw his fist coming hard at me, and I grabbed a knife from the counter. I didn't know what I was planning to do with it, but it didn't matter because he had already shoved me into the passage and slapped me across the face. I had dropped the knife in the melee and, in defence, kicked him hard in the leg. I sensed a hot wetness on my face and reached up to touch it, only to realise I was gushing blood from somewhere. I was filled with terror and looked at Tobore, only to see that he was bleeding too.

For some reason, that realisation set a fire in me. I reared back to fly at him with all my force, but he had grabbed a broom and used it to strike me across the face. The pain was tremendous and nothing like I had ever felt before. I was sure he had broken my nose and I found myself flat on the floor. He was standing over me, screaming and cursing that I had rejected him and that it was his time to take out his revenge on me, once and for all. I will never forget the coldness in his voice when he said he had been waiting for that moment before we'd left Jamaica. He said I had brought it on myself because I had cheated on him and made him look like a fool.

I was in total shock. A strange silence fell between us and he finally grabbed me and pulled me up roughly, turning and shutting himself in a side room. I didn't know what to do. The whole scene felt like I had just experienced a nightmare and was merely waking from it. I started to come to my senses quickly, and remembered that Jasmine was still sitting outside, waiting in the car. I grabbed at a curtain on the front window and wiped the blood from my face, thinking that I could simply walk out and pretend that nothing had happened. I didn't realise that I was covered in blood. As soon as Jasmine saw me, her eyes widened in shock and she started crying.

I tried to calm her down and told her that I was going to be ok, but that I needed to call the police. She begged me not to, saying that she didn't want her dad to get into trouble. What was I to do? She was in hysterics at the thought of losing him. I started the car up and drove home. I finally got

Jasmine to calm down by saying that adults, especially parents, sometimes have disagreements and it was nothing for her to worry about. I began to try to figure out how to handle the situation. I decided to call Tobore's newest female friend, who had been spending a lot of time at his house. I had heard that she was a mother also, and I thought that maybe I could explain to her what I'd tried to explain to Tobore about Jasmine being upset with him for not spending enough quality time with her. My irrational hope was that she would pass on the message I had originally intended to get across before our altercation.

I meant to only ask her to try to help Tobore understand how Jasmine was feeling and ask that she help him be a bit more sensible and conscious of his daughter's feelings. I ignorantly assumed that, as a female and a mother, she would be my ally and would understand that girls were far more wanting of their dad's attention. After all, I was still legally married to him and I also hoped she would respect that. I immediately found out how foolish I was being. As soon as I said hello and introduced myself, she laid into me. "Ey dutty gal, a long time me a wait pon you fi call me! Why the fuck you nuh left him alone and divorce him so him can be free to love who him want? Why the fuck you nuh get it that you and him over? Why you keep calling him to come round to your fucking yard? You nuh get it you a wife pon paper, but mi a him baby mother! Fuck off, gal; I am pregnant with his son. The one you could never give him."

I couldn't even speak. Instead, I just hung up the phone. Her words hurt me more than any of the blows that Tobore had rained down on me earlier that day. Clearly, she had been fed the idea that I was the one holding onto him, when in fact it was he who was holding on to me. Mainly because divorce would have ruined his chances to get his citizenship in the UK. The pregnancy also pierced me and I understood why it did, to some extent. During one of our last civil conversations just a few weeks before,

Tobore and I had decided that if we were still estranged and not with anyone else by the time I turned 35, we would come together and have a baby so that Jasmine would have a full sibling.

The conversation with that woman was not over yet, though. She must have used my phone number off the caller ID to start sending me abusive text messages, threatening my life and calling me all sorts of despicable names. I began to put two and two together, remembering her from an earlier time with Tobore and how he had vehemently denied having any interest in her, saying that she was just some 'ghetto gal' from his work. I should have just turned off my phone, but I was so incensed at the whole situation that I fell into a text battle with a person I didn't even know. I had no one to blame but myself for that event. Even though my intentions for contacting her had been good, I had opened the floodgates to set us on this hateful path.

I went outside to talk to my friend Norma on the phone and calm down. She tried to encourage me to delete the hateful texts, but I felt that I needed to keep them as evidence if things deteriorated further. The intensity of the situation exhausted me. I collapsed into a heap on the ground and buried my head in my hands. Just then, I heard a car stop and heavy footsteps come up the walkway. I lifted my head only slightly to see who was visiting me at that inopportune time and was confused to see three sets of shining black shoes. I lifted my head slowly up the legs of three sturdy police officers, their hands firmly on their truncheons. I instantly knew that they were here for me. Tobore must have called them to report me after I had left his house.

One of the officers calmly asked if I was Ava Brown and I told them yes. They beckoned me to get up off the ground and said that they needed me to come with them. I wasn't about to object. I cursed myself for not having called the police first and instead giving in to my young daughter's wishes

Follow me on Twitter: @avabrown24

of not wanting to cause Tobore any more trouble than we already had in our lives as immigrants. I told the men that I would come quietly and they allowed me to first tell my sister that I would be out so that she could watch my daughter. If Jasmine asked where I was going, my plan was to tell her that I was just going out for a walk to clear my head.

However, Jasmine was the one who met me at the door, and I saw the extreme anguish on her face as she noticed the police standing in the background. Before anything else could happen, Jasmine began screaming and flailing, her heart tormented. She banged her head hard on the wall and fell. The police came rushing to help with the situation and when they persuaded her to take deep breaths, she calmed down to a miserable crying state. They tried to explain to her that they just wanted to take her mum somewhere quiet for a while so that we could have a talk, but my child was far too intelligent and she knew better. In the end, I left with them, sitting like a scolded child in the back of the police car. Luckily, they spared me the handcuffs because I was being cooperative. My whole being was in shock, I couldn't even feel my heart beating and thought that maybe I had died and my spirit was just somehow locked inside my body. I spoke up to make sure of the reality of the situation. I asked if I could use my phone to make a call. That was when they gave me the official word that I was under arrest; they then confiscated my phone and they read me my rights.

We arrived at a police station in Norwood, drove up a back entrance and straight to where the cells were. I had remained silent for the entire drive, but my mind was working overtime. I kept asking myself how someone who had once loved me so intensely, someone who had shared so many momentous events in my life, someone who relied on me as much as I did on him could have done that to me. I was crying copiously and could hardly understand what was being said to me when the booking process had begun. I finally heard the charge against me; Tobore had reported that

Follow me on Twitter: @avabrown24

I had come to his house and instigated a physical attack. I finally found my voice and tried to tell the police that they had it all wrong, but they were quite dismissive at that stage and said that they were just doing their jobs.

I realised that I had no advocate in that police station, so I decided that my best tactic was just to stay quiet. My God, I was shaking with fear! In no time, I was being led further into the building. Someone removed my belt and took off all of my jewellery. A body search was then performed by a female officer, and in the background, I could hear another officer making account of my possessions. Finally, I was given one phone call, which I used to call home and talk to Jasmine to reassure her that I would be fine and home soon.

After the call, I was taken to be fingerprinted, to give a DNA sample (by mouth swab), and to have my mug shot taken. Everything they did was so invasive, on a physical and a spiritual level. I knew I was experiencing what it was like to lose my freedom, and I flashed back to how awful the experience must have been for my little sister in those weeks before her death. The jail staff asked if I needed anything and I requested to see a doctor and a solicitor. I still had open wounds from the earlier altercation with Tobore and I was afraid of infection or scarring if they were not attended to. They said that it was all in the process and ushered me down to a cell.

When I heard the heavy metal lock clank into place, I felt lower than I ever had in my entire life. The whole situation was surreal, almost as if I was suddenly in a TV show. Again, I started to think that maybe I was simply experiencing a very lucid stress nightmare on the eve before I was to confront Tobore about spending more one-on-one time with our daughter. Maybe I had fallen out of bed and was lying on the hard floor of my house; that must be the uncomfortable feeling under my back. But, no, it was really the hard bed in the cold cell I was occupying. I had to face the reality that I was in jail, placed there under the false accusations made by my husband. It was clear that he was at war with me, and I was losing the battle.

I started reflecting on our relationship from a more realistic perspective. One in which my heart was closed off and deadened to him. I realised how many mistakes I had made with him, especially in trusting him again after the first time he'd had a child with another woman and I had still allowed him to move to London with us. How foolish I had been to think that we could ever make anything out of the deteriorated shell of a marriage we had. I was shocked at how much he had changed as a person from the man I believed he was in those blissful first years we'd spent as a young couple while I was in teaching college. How could that loving young man be the same person who'd just sent the police to arrest me by using a blatant lie?

Even more troubling was the thought of how that man, who had changed so drastically, could still be a loving and cautious father with Jasmine. Did he not think at all about how his false accusation against me would affect her emotional well-being and her livelihood? I remembered the status of my citizenship right then, and my body went numb again. How would an arrest affect that? And, if my application were negatively affected, both his and Jasmine's would be in jeopardy as well. How could he have not thought about that?

I suppose he had reached a point where he just didn't care about any of it anymore. Something must have given him enough confidence in his own chances to feel like he could get citizenship without me. I realised that, finally, he must really see the end for us. There was no going back from that event, our lives, even as parents of a shared child were separated from one another from that moment on.

I didn't know what else to do. I was absolutely powerless to the forces shaping my life around me at that time. I closed my eyes and asked God to just give me the courage and strength to get out of the entire mess that my life had become since coming to London. I asked God to work a miracle so that I would somehow get released before the night fell. That way, I could be home before Jasmine fell asleep and I could ease her fears. I lay there crying for who knows how long. I cried until my eyes hurt and there were no more tears to come out of them. Each time the jailers passed by for a routine inspection, I would ask if my doctor or lawyer had arrived to see me yet. Each time, they told me no.

On the fourth pass, they asked if I wanted anything to eat. I had been so consumed with distress that the thought of food had never crossed my mind, even though I hadn't eaten since eight o'clock that morning and it was now late afternoon. I merely mumbled that I wasn't hungry. There was a toilet in the cell, and although I wanted to pee, I just couldn't make myself use it, as the cell was open for all to see. I had been in the cell for around four hours when the doctor finally arrived. He made some sort of joke about the delay being caused by 'London's Sunday service'. I could only suppose that was his attempt to lighten my heavy mood, but it didn't work. His visit afforded me some freedom since I was taken out of my cell for the examination and treatment.

I stupidly thought that that was my chance to finally be absolved of the false accusations. Certainly, the doctor would see that I was beaten up and call for my release. Instead, he simply went over me from head to toe, taking blood samples from the still open gashes on my lip and in my mouth, and made a report that confirmed that I had been badly beaten up. I remember him even noting the slap marks on my face, where the impact of Tobore's hand had broken the blood vessels under my skin. It made no difference. After he left I was taken promptly back to my cell.

I began to have all kinds of panicked thoughts. What if I was never released? What if prison was my new home? What if social services took Jasmine away because I was an unfit mother locked up in jail? The lady with whom I had made hurried arrangements to watch her because Kem had had to leave couldn't stay there overnight. What would happen to my child then? Would she just be left at home alone? I just stared at the walls of the cell and no answers came to my fearful questions. The ceiling and walls were covered with the names of all who 'WUZ ERE', scratched into the plaster by countless hands. I had no interest in proudly claiming my residence in any jail.

Soon, though, I received word that my appointed lawyer had arrived and I was escorted to the room where he and I were allowed to talk. I told him the truth of what had happened at Tobore's, leaving out no detail; not even the ones that made me look bad. He made only non-committal responses to all of my statements. Afterwards, I was taken to meet with another set of police officers in yet another room, where they had tape recording equipment; there they made an official record of my statement.

The lawyer had accompanied me to make my statement, and I was glad he did, because it was clear from the first moment that the police thought I was lying. They tried to convince the lawyer that I was guilty, but he stood his ground defending me and continued to ask for proof of the accusations against me. After an interminable back-and-forth, the policewoman agreed with the lawyer and said that the information just wasn't strong enough to prove that Tobore was telling the truth in his accusation against me. Instead of being released immediately, I was placed back into my cell while they processed all the paperwork and made records in their database of the event, my statements, and all of my very personal information. I was finally released, with the knowledge that my fingerprints and DNA would be on file for six years before they would be deleted. I couldn't believe it; I was in the police database, all thanks to my husband.

Follow me on Twitter: @avabrown24

As I gathered my belongings, the last policewoman who had been present for the debate with my lawyer came over and gave me a pep talk. She told me that I was lucky to be going home and reminded me that I needed to put everything with Tobore behind me and just focus on my child. She had a warm, almost motherly tone of voice when she told me to leave that man out of my life, and that he didn't mean me any good and I would be fighting a losing battle with him. She even told me that I had the right to go downstairs and make a report against him, based on the evidence of my bodily harm that was clear for all to see. But, without saying anything, we both knew that would only have stirred the hornet's nest. Besides, I was still struggling with the immense guilt of the damage I would cause to him by doing so. Even though he had just done the same horrible thing to me, I could not find it within myself to do it back to him.

At that point, I knew that I needed to go home to be with my child. I had no money, it was late, and I still needed to find a way home. I wasn't about to dawdle at the station. What if they changed their minds and tried to re-arrest me? I had run outside to the street and frantically waved down a cab. On my way to the house, I called my friend, who was still sitting for Jasmine, to ask if she had money on her. She said yes and I breathed a sigh of relief, something was finally going my way. When I got home, all I could do was grab a hold of Jasmine and hug her so tight, like I was never going to let her go. We were both crying and clinging to each other for quite some time.

My friend who had come to watch Jasmine told me that after I had been picked up by the police, Tobore's brother had arrived and said that he was there to pick Jasmine up to stay with her father. Since I had told her the situation (and Jasmine had already told her of her own fright after seeing my substantial physical injuries), she knew better than to believe his ruse. There was no way she was going to give Jasmine to anyone in my absence.

Follow me on Twitter: @avabrown24

I thanked her profusely and she headed home to her own waiting family. Jasmine fell asleep quickly; she was so exhausted after the stress of the day. I tossed and turned with fitful nightmares about the police coming back to get me again.

Our lives were never the same after that day. It was just another cruel reminder in my life that everything you know can be taken away in a moment; how your life's path can be changed drastically without your intent or input. The woman who was currently carrying Tobore's third child had started a campaign of hate against me - emails, letters, and phone calls. I was being constantly bombarded. But my experience with the police after being arrested on false charges had frightened me so much that I did not trust them to help me with any situation. I was so traumatised by all of the events, I was unable to focus on the fact that I wasn't working and had no money coming in.

My friends in London had rallied around me and Jasmine during that time and provided what little comfort and money they could to help us. Since Jasmine's birthday was coming up, my friend Norma invited us to her house for a celebration. Jasmine agreed to the plan right away because she had decided on her own that she didn't want to see her father anymore. I finally felt free to file for divorce; there was nothing left tying us together. As soon as I was legally classified as a single mother, I qualified for social assistance and it provided a positive change in my life that I had never anticipated.

The first thing I needed to do was get myself back together emotionally, and truthfully, that was one of the hardest things I had ever done. The experience of being arrested and locked up had affected my self-esteem in ways that I would have never imagined. I felt like society had labelled me as a criminal and I lost all confidence in who I was. I no longer saw myself as an independent, tenacious woman, but as a shameful blot on society. It went against everything at my core. I knew that if I was to survive and be an effective mother for Jasmine, I would have to get back to who I was before that unfair event took place.

Accepting that Tobore was not the man I'd thought he was proved to be just as hard. I relied heavily on my faith during that time, and had begun to see God's hand in many of the events of the past years. In a way, He had continually shown me that Tobore was not the relationship for me; for either of us, but I had been too strong-headed to recognise it. Serving the divorce papers to Tobore was yet another challenge. He had moved residence and I could not get anyone to divulge his location. All I found out was that he had moved in with the woman carrying his child, and her family.

I finally discovered his whereabouts when one of my friends saw the two of them shopping at a grocery store near my house. I was shocked to find out that they lived relatively close to Jasmine and me, yet he had never once reached out to her since that fateful day. I was more heartbroken to learn that he was doing very well, both personally and financially. My friend said that he and the woman were laughing and joking like young lovers strolling through the store, with a whole trolley full of items. Meanwhile, Jasmine and I were wondering where our next meal was going to come from, since I had no money, we were hungry, and our cupboards were empty.

I went back to the same traumatised and fearful state that I had fallen into after the attack in Jamaica that had precipitated our move to London. Every time I heard a police car, I became nervous and agitated, thinking that Tobore was again exerting his revenge on me. Kem and her daughter were still living with us, but she was so displeased with the situation of me being jobless and so anxious, she had decided to return to Jamaica. Instead of being relieved that I would have two less people to be responsible for, I was heartbroken that I would be losing what little in-house support I had.

Our situation became more challenging over the next several weeks. Tobore finally reached out to start seeing Jasmine again, but he refused to let her go to his home or to see her inside of mine. Instead, he proposed that I should bring her to meet him on the street in a neutral area where he would park his car and they could spend a few minutes talking. I felt like that was far too disrespectful to our daughter and I turned down his offer. I told him that we needed to find a more suitable environment rather than a car on the side of the road for them to rebuild their father-daughter relationship. He responded by sending a letter through his solicitor that demanded visitation with Jasmine under any condition, and accusing me of unlawful denial of contact with his child.

Besides that stress, I had started falling behind on my mortgage payments and I was then at risk of losing our home. Something had to change in our lives and soon. I had a long, serious talk with Jasmine about our situation. I suggested that we might be in a better position if we were to quit London and go back to Jamaica for a while. Even though it broke my heart, I told her she had the option of staying in London with her dad, if she really wanted to. My sweet girl spared not one moment in declining the offer and saying that she wanted to come along with me, no matter where we went.

I started planning for our move home. I put our house on the market, but quickly realised that we would fare better finding renters. I had to admit that there was a huge relief in preparing to go back to Jamaica. I had wanted out of London for a long time, but I had always consulted Tobore on it before. His response was always to dissuade me. He would tell me that I would mess up our immigration status and ruin everything I had worked so hard for already. Now, without him, the decision was completely up to me. I knew that my situation had become so dire at the moment, that if I stayed in London, I would lose my house and my sanity.

As the day neared for us to return back to our homeland, I assaulted myself with blame. I blamed myself for the mess that had led all of us up to that moment in time. I blamed myself for bringing Tobore to London. I blamed myself for the deterioration of Jasmine and Tobore's relationship. And I blamed myself for all the hardships that we had endured as immigrants in a harsh new country. I had convinced myself that I was a complete failure in all aspects of my life; as a wife, as a mother, and as a career woman. It was in a fog of self-hate and depression that I booked our flights back to Jamaica. I would take my child back home to the land of her ancestors in the hopes of re-joining the well-worn path that they had forged from the slave ships to independence. After all, we were both born of their spirit of tenacity and resilience, and our paths still had many steps to go.

"Life and revenge can be a very messy affair."

Chapter Twenty Four

HOME AT LAST

"Reputations can attach themselves to us and

become a permanent part of our person."

We landed in Jamaica and man it was far too hot. I couldn't believe how much I felt the striking difference in the weather. Mind you, I had a terrible cold from the constant dampness in Britain and could barely breathe. The extreme heat only made that worse. The flight back had been horrible. They were mostly Jamaicans on board the flight. Sadly those Jamaicans lived up to the stereotype; they really behaved like hooligans on the plane. They fought with the flight attendants and held parties at the back of the aircraft. The pilot had to announce they were closing the bar. The main attendant said it was the worse flight she had seen in her 12 years. We had indeed lived up to the expectation that of hooligans and aggressors. The flight was terrible for other reasons too; the food was awful; the service was under catered; and the toilets didn't work. I felt like the airline had given us the worst flight possible for our trip. The captain announced that if the behaviour continued he had no choice but to ask for police presence and that arrests were to be made when we landed at the Norman Manly Airport.

As a Jamaican, I felt deeply embarrassed that we had lived up to the expectations the whites had of us; how unfortunate that the good get categorised with the bad. I felt embarrassed for my daughter who had to endure such raucous behaviour by our own nationals.

It was a good thing she didn't see her mum participating in any such brawls. We landed and the crew gave no indication of what was to happen next.

It was a long wait on the tarmac before we were allowed to disembark. I lodged a complaint to the main flight attendant that although I felt overall most of the passengers behaved terribly; what they had forgotten was the fact that there were well behaving passengers on board the aircraft too. They should have treated us with the respect we deserved. I complained about the fact that I witnessed one of her attendants push another passenger, though she denied this happening. She had mistakenly thought the woman was speaking to her when in fact she was speaking to a fellow passenger. Both women were apparently 'ghetto yardies' and were having a conversation. The attendant had obviously felt a derogatory statement made was meant for her as the woman had pointed in the attendant's direction to the other woman across the isle. What transpired was that the accosted passenger, among the party clientele on the plane, had been sitting on one of the emergency exits. She had been somewhat tipsy as the rest of her party who were consuming all sorts of alcohol that must, I thought, have been bought duty free. The group was having a conversation and the manager of the flight was within earshot of the remark as she stood there helping another passenger.

The misunderstanding must have been born out of emotions running high as the attendants were already feeling a bit uncomfortable, from the unruliness of the flight, the heavy drinking and fragile tempers. On confronting the 'yardie' girl she tried to make it very clear she wasn't talking to her but the flight manager rushed towards her and tried to pull her off the emergency exit, where she was still seated. Now granted, she shouldn't be sitting there in the first place, but she had sat there all along and it had not been a problem. She had sat there for more than five hours. Now that there was a problem, the attendant was pulling rank. The girl told her not to touch her and the attendant quickly went and got the head of the flight and once again, the white man pulled rank.

Eventually that all settled down and we exited the plane. There were no police thankfully, because we would have been delayed even further, and I wasn't in the mood as I was frying enough now. But what happened next was worse than being on an unruly flight. Immigration was good but the baggage clearance could not have been more of a horror. The carousel looked like a bombsite, there was utter confusion; getting our bags was going to be a battle. I stood there looking at the chaos and I realised that it was a vivid image of the country I call home. A representation of what I had left Britain to come home to; utter confusion. To be honest, it was also representational of my life and where I was personally. As a matter of fact, it was where I had been for a long time; 'confused.' I stood there taking in the scene; trying to manoeuvre my mind and my life out of the mess when Jasmine saw that I had gone into my own world. Her gentle nudge in the side snapped me back from my dazed state. The child was my rock; she was always there to bring me back to reality in the sweetest way.

I took Jasmine across to a seat to stay with the laptop and the other items we had on hand, while I went to war to try to find our items of baggage. Mark you, it wasn't an easy road, but I managed to axe out our bags and we headed to customs. I didn't have anything much to declare;

after all I brought back only the items I needed most but clearly couldn't afford in Jamaica. I had cereals and nuts, mainly and that 'real' mayonnaise, as that I knew I couldn't afford to buy here. And I had the envied foil paper; those items were luxuries for me. I paid merely £1, for each; a true bargain I said to myself. There was the Wii video game for Aida, my goddaughter and the wedding party clothing etc. I was given to deliver as a favour for a friend. Hell, I wasn't going to pay for other peoples' stuff. When the customs officer asked what I had to declare and I said nothing. He said he wanted to open our cases; I invited him to. I was a little scared and nervous then, as I wasn't certain if I would be held for the wedding items and the Wii game. I had already decided I would leave them for the owners to clear if they became a problem. Mark you, at Gatwick Airport, back in Britain, I took out the last £200 from my bank account to help pay Jasmine's school fee when we arrived back in Jamaica. I only had 99 pence left in that account, so I knew I wasn't going to be able to spend any money. He asked me what my status was in Jamaica. I told him I was a returnee and went to London for a holiday and only brought back food to eat. I invited him to look as he was starting to get on my last set of nerves. Many people were getting on my nerves I noticed lately, life's stresses. Presumably, it was because I was so alone and struggling and sometimes I got worn out. But I knew I had to keep going as I had a long way yet to go. I could not fail my daughter, so I kept going. He stamped our papers and told us to have a good day.

As we both settled back into Jamaica my life seemed so overwhelming. There were school fees to pay, rent to pay and the general getting on with life. The house was empty of all vegetables and fruit. Of course, if I could have taken them back from London I would have; they were far cheaper and seemingly better quality there. I remember when I went for Christmas the first time to visit my aunt, I had eaten so many vegetables; it was as if I had never seen them before. That was due to the lack of affordability in Jamaica. Prices for fruit and vegetables tended to be very expensive. On my return they were out of my price range completely. Vegetables I was accustomed to in the UK like asparagus, only came in cans and the price tag would send you running. I could not afford lettuce, sprouts, strawberries, apples or even grapes. I rarely bought vegetables in any variety. I stuck to items such as oranges, tangerines which most of the time came from my mum in the country; cane, coconut or grapes occasionally. On the rare occasion, I might have bought plums, pears, or apples. But these items were far too expensive to purchase regularly and I had only bought kiwis once since I returned. Three for the price of £2 British pounds, which was $240 Jamaican dollars; a luxury. But I must add the Lord was good to us, somehow Jasmine's lunch box always had some fruit in it. I wished I could have gotten that girl to eat raisins as a snack. The child wasn't fussy but her eating habits drove me up the wall sometimes, I wished she had grown up like I did. I knew hunger and appreciated anything I was able to get to eat.

Before leaving the UK I had shipped several larger items of value. When the delivery arrived they had once again forgotten my barrel. My barrel was missing when we visited the wharf and it contained expensive items, including a glass basin, which were worth close to £1000 British. In my wait, I met the nicest old man, his name was Mr. Spencer and you would have loved him to be your dad. He worked at the wharf. He worked very hard and I learned he had recently had a stroke. In my mind he shouldn't have still been working; but times were hard. He touched my heart; I guess sometimes I was just far too soft. Anyway, he promised to get the barrel to his office and then we could take it home from there.

I was hopeful that my friend, Pete would lend me his truck to pick up the barrel but I wasn't sure anymore. When I rang him to ask for his help, he suggested he called me back. He had told me his daughter had some school help project to attend, where she would be handing out 'back to school supplies' to less unfortunate kids. That was a brilliant idea and I agreed to speak with him later. I thought he said he would drop it off by at half passed eleven in the morning. But instead, he did not show until after three o'clock and then didn't even spend ten good minutes before leaving again. Earlier on in the day, he rang to tell me that someone was at the gate to pick up the cardboard boxes we needed to discard from our unpacking. I thought he was arranging for a friend to come round to help me, but to my surprise it was his friend Cam, a handcart man and another man. Our things were still in boxes and cluttered. I had wondered what the neighbours thought of us because it was a gated community. To me, it felt like it was them versus us. I didn't like it much. But the guys made a disastrous mess outside with the boxes and I hated the sight. The neighbours possibly had never seen anything like that ever before.

When the job was complete, Pete's friend told me he rang a guy who told him it would cost about $4000 to collect the rubbish but he had originally thought it would be about half that price. But having seen the load, he felt $2500 was adequate. I needed help from a friend and Pete had sent hired help who were looking to get as much money from me as they could. I felt ripped off, so ripped off I wanted to cry. I wondered why everyone that heard my voice and my adopted British accent thought I had money; or because I lived in a gated area, I must have been loaded wish cash! If only they knew how I was completely broke and struggling. I told myself that was the last time I would ever be ripped off. From then on, I would choose who I asked for help, no more friends of friends.

Pete did come round later that day with May, a lovely girl and he spent about 10 minutes chatting. He was looking to be an overseer, as usual. I was so angry; he didn't even bother to ask what he could do to help. In the end, I felt so betrayed. He told me I should get a carpenter to come and finish off whatever else I needed to do. There he went again, more money to spend! I guess everyone thought I was loaded. I listened and told myself not to ask for any more help. In the end, to my dismay, I did have to ask him if he could help me set up my computer desk and entertainment centre. He said yes; although, he didn't have any time frame on it. At that point, he said he needed to drop his daughter off and would update me later. I was far too annoyed to even respond. Pete left and I stood there fuming. He was one guy I didn't understand. Did he not know how to do it; or did he just not know how to say that he didn't; or was he just plain stupid? Then there was the other option of him just simply thinking; "Ava, can afford it. Let her pay someone to do whatever was needed." Whichever it was, I didn't know and that frustrated me even more.

As the Jamaican heat bashed us in, I went to bed most nights confused with my thoughts. The nights were so hot I couldn't clear my mind. Even though I had grown up here; I could not understand how people could live in that hot hell. I was also having difficulty breathing; I had a terrible stuffed nose due to the heat. We slept on the floor; on the sponged mattress we had all of eight inches worth at a total cost of $7500. In Jamaica, everything was thousands of dollars; nothing was ever simple and inexpensive. Perhaps it was just me? Everyone else seemed to look at me when I exclaimed how expensive everything was. Jasmine and I slept on the floor on the mattress and we kept turning the air conditioning on and off trying to keep the room cool enough to sleep. I wished I could have kept it on all night, but I was too aware of the cost to run the thing. After all, that was in fact Jamaica; if you owed money to the utility company they disconnected you. In England we were able to keep playing the game of; "I will pay bit by bit" and wait until the final due notice to pay. I wasn't going take that risk there in Jamaica; moreover, the landlady informed me that the utility was in her name and if it got disconnected she would not be happy. She basically told me to pay on time whether I had the money or not.

One the Sunday, I woke up at half past six because I couldn't sleep; it was far too hot. I tidied up the kitchen and tried as best as I could to get some semblance to the living room; it was slowly coming together. It was Sunday morning and we hurried to get showered and dressed because I was adamant that we were going to church. All indicators were saying not to go, but I insisted; just as we would have gone to do any other thing that needed doing. We went and it was such a blessing. I wore my Nigerian outfit and I felt so regal, Jasmine wore her Ghanaian dress kente cloth with a white crotched cardigan. We found the Baptist Church that adjoined her school; but I missed my friend Angel. It wasn't the same without her hopping by to say good morning or sending us something nice to eat. She loved us with her sweet cooking. She was always sending Jasmine something especially nice to eat or drink - like her guava juice - so thick, it filled you up - and every sip tasted amazing.

The pastor had spoken about being prepared for when our time comes. As I sat there in the congregation, I felt anxious with all the other emotions of being unsettled. I tried to keep calm. When the ushers came by to collect the offering, I put $1000 in the bowl but initially I felt apprehension. I asked myself how was it so easy to have paid $2500 to get cardboard boxes removed but I hesitated to give back to the Lord who blessed me through all my trials. As the service continued in front of me there was an elderly man who seemed to have collapsed. I initially thought, had he died; perhaps it was the heat? He was whisked away by the elders and no sooner than five minutes later he was being rushed to the hospital. It was a poignant reminder of the pastor's sermon.

Later that evening as I was writing my thoughts, I had to pause because my daughter came in and asked me what I was doing. It was obvious that I was typing. I was doing about 60 words per hour; so I asked her; "Can't you see, I am typing." She pointed out to me that I had been snapping all week. I was aware of this but thought I had it under control. I was so stressed and I thought I'd like to go down the road of oblivion and pretend everything would all be okay, sooner rather than later. I wanted to believe I had faith in God, not as much as I would have liked, but enough faith. I felt I could get away with hoping that God would take care of the rent and all the lost bits would have fallen into place. My days were filled with nothing but despair.

The next day, I woke up and called to check if the rent on my London flat had been paid into my account and found that wasn't done. I was furious because once again the estate agents hadn't set up the mandate, although that had been in place since July. I rang the estate agents and their attitude was so disgusting, they basically said they didn't care. In the meantime, I was an ocean away and at their mercy to follow through with their responsibilities; and I desperately needed the money. All the other issues aside, Jamaica was in the middle of a major hurricane; Hurricane Gustav. Can you imagine, I didn't just come home to Jamaica; I had chosen to come back during a hurricane! It would have been difficult enough to find a job there when the economy was stable, but can you imagine how difficult it was going to be while there was a major hurricane? Well, I remained hopeful. Through all of that, I was still hopeful.

"When life knocks you down, don't stay down
- crawl your way out."

Follow me on Twitter: @avabrown24

Chapter Twenty Five

LANDLADY DRAMA

"Money is the root of all evil they say, yet it adds
such comfort to life ,one cannot ignore its power."

The landlady whom we were renting from was quite a piece of work. When I took the place, in her eyes I had no job and could not afford the rent. Fair enough. Generally, she said, she only rented to companies and I had arrived in Jamaica on my own. I had not worked since April of that year. She was more than correct; I was jobless in every sense of the word. My friend Pete had been able to arrange to get the house rented for me through strings he pulled. His company took the cash out of his salary and I paid it back to him. So the rent appeared to be paid monthly by a company. I thanked God for him in that case, he had served a purpose after all!

The landlady had been given a cheque for $120,000 for the August rent.

Because I had taken the house on the 10 August and she was insistent on collecting on the first day of each month, she needed to pro rate that first month. I was waiting for her to refund me the pro rate money. The woman had no respect for anyone's time. She had you wait on her and then did not show up; she didn't even have the decency to call to tell you she couldn't come. I had left many messages requesting the money. She kept telling me she would send it via her nephew. Needless to say I never saw him.

I was still waiting for the money when one night she stood me up, again. She had told me she would meet me at seven that evening. We got to the house on time, Jasmine and I. I rang her and she told me she needed to call me back, but she didn't. I rang her again and she told me she would call back, again she didn't. We waited for her until after eight o'clock. My god, she didn't even care. We went back to our apartment when she rang to say she was now in Cherry Gardens and could I come to collect the money there. She said she had been decking a house. I wonder who the hell she thought she was, not only didn't she have any regard for time, she wanted me to kiss her kitty. I was having none of that. Yes, I was renting her house but I had two of my own; one in London and one here in Jamaica. I wasn't renting because I was someone who didn't know what it was like to own their own place. Anyway, she didn't bother to show again and I wasn't going to chase her.

I went for an interview on the following Wednesday, with a company called GeofoTech, when Jasmine rang to tell me that our power company, had disconnected the light in the communal areas. Damn, I thought, how could out landlady do that? The utilities were in her name. She came across so diligent with things like that. She apparently had not paid her bill. So now we had no washer and dryer; not that I could afford to use them. She made us buy tokens from her to wash and dry our clothes. Our dirty clothes were piling up. That day, I knocked on the neighbour's door and she told me that having the utilities shut off wasn't normal. I took solace in that and I went back indoors. About twenty minutes later the neighbour rang the door to tell me the landlady had told her that she was going to fix it and the lights would be back on soon.

At about half past eight that night, the landlady came round with her brother and she went into my kitchen and started eating my guineps fruit. I found that incredibly distasteful, but said nothing. Her brother tried to look at the cooker to see if he could hook it up because I had been waiting on that as well. It appeared that all that time the place was wired for 110amps; and there I was with a 220 cooker from London. Never mind that, it was set up for gas and electric, so I could have used the gas, but the lease agreement insisted that you used electric! So, since I moved in, I had not been able to cook a single meal. My last option was to cook some tikka masala rice in the microwave. And I attempted to cook rice and chicken in my vegetable steamer; but that took hours. They left and she never mentioned my money at all. I was so thrown I couldn't speak. I rang her and left a message asking her to send me the cheque, because I knew she had only forgotten to leave me the money seeing she was so busy. The next morning she rang asking me who to write the cheque to; I told her me. She then turned up with it later that day. Thank God for that.

My sister Sheena came to stay with me for a bit; while there, she drove me mad. I was surprised she was still so naive and had to ask myself if that was how I would have been if I had lived with my mum all this time. She was as unexposed as I had been. I was glad she was there. I was glad Jasmine was very exposed to an international lifestyle; but more so that she was a sensible and relatively clever child.

Despite the hurricane, I went to Mandeville to meet up with my mum. She insisted on taking me to see her pastor, because she was worried about the path my life had been taking. She wanted me to see a spiritual man. I was scared, but trusted my mum. Thankfully, on arrival, it was nothing like I had envisioned and it was in fact, a true pastor and a church. We were in Mandeville, en-route to Kingston, mum going back to Santa Cruz. Before we parted, I asked my mum for some lotion. You see, security had taken all my hand creams out of my handbag since our visit to Ireland in May. I hadn't bothered putting more back in my hand luggage, as I had planned to visit London soon and would have lost those to security too. The other part of that was I had been plain busy trying to sort every other thing out to replace them. I asked for a bit of lotion and my mum whipped out a black roll-on bottle, which looked like roll-on deodorant. Jasmine and my eyes met in shock; and we retorted; "No mama, we said lotion." "Hold your horses," she said, "its lotion." My mum had taken out the marble like section of the roll-on bottle and poured lotion into the bottle. I couldn't help myself. I had to laugh. My god, she was resourceful. It went a long way to explain to me how they survived their living conditions. Although, it killed me each time to see where they lived, they seem to be content with it. Even then, the lotion had a lovely smell; one that I would have taken even if it were in a roll-on bottle any day.

We headed to the Mandeville market because I desperately wanted a cow's head. At the mouth of the market there were police officers threatening to close the market hall down. In spite of that everyone went about their shopping. But there were no cow's head to be found because the butcher had already left; I was so disappointed. I really would have thought that I was pregnant had I been sexually active; how I craved that cow's head! In the end, we purchased all sorts of fruit and vegetables; pumpkin, Jasmine's favourite; and spring onions; Callaoo, yams; cucumbers; and bumpy bananas. They saved my life one day when we came to a Tollgate and realised all the shops were closed. We would have starved if we hadn't resorted to the bumpy bananas we had packed. Anyway, that was all I could

Follow me on Twitter: @avabrown24

afford because our funds were running low.

Being a mum was still at the forefront of my life regardless of the turmoil. Reading stories to Jasmine was very important especially with trying to keep her sane and in a routine, as much as I could in our current situation. One night, at about half past nine and I had read Jasmine a story and tucked her into bed, when I realised that God knew why he gave me only one child; perhaps with more than one I wouldn't have been able to cope! She took so much of my time but was such a blessing. She was in year six at school and I didn't remember having so many books growing up. Of course, I didn't have the money to buy them so I didn't have them. The number of books per day so far was roughly 15; I felt so sorry for her. The kids piled their books into pulley trolleys on wheels, similar to the ones taken to the supermarket in London by the older women, who filled them with their food shopping. I personally didn't like it, but it seemed to be the in thing in Jamaica at the time. It almost looked like a sin; it was painful seeing those little kids pulling what almost looked like suitcases for travel to school full of their required books.

Jasmine had a male teacher for the first time that year and it had not gone down so well. Coupled with the fact that teachers in Jamaica tended not to be like those in the UK; where there were positive words spoken to the pupils consistently. I had to tell her to understand the differences in methods etc. She gave me one prime example where a pupil didn't know something and the teacher told her she should have known that by then. We knew in the UK it would have been said in a more positive way even though it meant the same thing. I felt as if I was back in school because there it seemed when your child was in school, you were too and full time. There was much more parental involvement needed in Jamaica versus the UK for sure. We were still facing lots of adjustments, but were spending much more time together; it was lovely, and Jasmine seemed to be coping.

Follow me on Twitter: @avabrown24

She had been hard on herself; she got 88% in math and that wasn't good enough! I prayed for her to be able to handle all the adjustments, although to be fair, she was doing well; perhaps better than I was. She had met a girl, also in year six, who had lived in Clapham Junction; that was refreshing for Jasmine. She needed to make friends; it was necessary.

I had also met another parent, one from Texas, who had taken her two sons and moved to Jamaica. I felt blessed when I found out that the woman didn't even have a car and she had to travel with the kids in a taxi for miles. Luckily, she was moving closer to me and I offered to help her settle in, while I was trying to do the same thing myself. When she told me her story I realised again that in many ways I was truly blessed. At that point her kid's school fees had not paid, she wanted to pay via credit card and that wasn't possible. I said a prayer for her. In the end, she revealed that her move to Jamaica was for self-preservation, she needed to or else she would have gone mad! I knew about the need to escape. That night after I placed Jasmine into bed I wrote an email to a few of my friends I left behind in the UK.

Hi guys...life is really settling in and I have two interviews next week... took the adventurous bus ride to downtown Kingston...Welcome to jam rock I guess, it was an interesting ride. I have to point at everything as despite my efforts everything seems to cost me more...and they claim I have an accent. All aside, I am coping and I am enjoying Jamaica. God has been truly good to us. Jasmine had a blessed week. She ended with a 95% average and we are truly glad.

We are happier than we have been in a few years. I feel God's promise that I will get a job in the near future. Despite missing you all, I know you are just a phone call away and we are accessible to each other.

Once again, thanks for helping to keep me sane during my most testing

Follow me on Twitter: @avabrown24

times...I love you all so much and appreciate you all.

Here is my home number; 6314827 area code 1876; please do not give it anyone!

Guys, I am knackered and am going to go now. I need to sleep. BTW we have also found a church...it's at Jasmine's school...so that is perfect for us. We fellowshipped there last Sunday...hope to go again this Sunday.

Miss you all. Love you all. Sept 5th

Love Ava and Jasmine

September 7, today was a very sad and melancholy day, I felt so ill as if I were pregnant; if I didn't know better I would have thought I was. Of course I wasn't. It had been ages since I was last with a man. Still I was in and out of bed all day with a bad stomach. Jasmine had come home from school the day before with rashes in the palms of her hands. I didn't take it too seriously at first, but when she took hours to complete her homework, I became concerned. That night, I decided her rash wasn't getting any better and I took her to Andrew's Memorial Hospital. They told me she had scabies. That explained the itching I had been having since last week. I thought it was because I had changed brands of my feminine pads. The change was for no other reason but cost, as I couldn't afford my preferred brand anymore. But, I too seemed to have scabies; in my vaginal area of all places (of course, it was never tested and how I contracted it was uncertain). As long as the night was, I couldn't sleep. Jasmine was itching. I was itching. It wasn't a lovely feeling. Goodness, I itched until that area was sore. I was relieved that there wasn't anyone going there.

As the days went by, and the scabies died down, we tried to go back to some form of normality. I was so exhausted. Every day, Jasmine had homework I needed to be involved with; so much so, I didn't even watch the news anymore. It was almost as if I was back in school. I had to admit that half the time I didn't have a clue with some of what she was learning. Thank God for math sessions online, they were most helpful.

I had to talk to Mr. Jackson, Jasmine's teacher, about how they spoke to the kids in the classroom. He tried to tell me that I babied Jasmine too much. He told me I needed to let her grow up, and to give her space. If only he knew the life she had led.

I had many interviews, yet no job offers, and I was getting terribly frustrated. I had one more that day; all the way into Spanish Town. I hoped it would be the one to change my life, and my time in Jamaica. I realised I needed to pay for the valuation report on my marital home in Anchovy. That was going to cost me all of $36000, which I would have to find all by myself - some sort of loan hopefully. I could take the cost out of the sale whenever that happened. I asked God to help me.

I sat reading the elements of my book as they were penned in my journals; I felt like a total failure. Far too often I had reflected on Jasmine. I knew she only had me to rely on and that's why I had to choose to live. If it hadn't been for her, I would have ended the pain. I had fought for that child since she was still in my womb. All those times while I was pregnant and Colette, Tobore's sister had treated me like a dog. I drove past my friend Jen's old house where I had sat on the steps while pregnant with Jasmine. Back then I lived at Jen's because Colette, Tobore's sister, had decided I couldn't stay at her house. I recalled how cold and indifferent she was. That was after I found out I was pregnant and had moved from Christiania back into Kingston and Tobore had thought I could stay with in the house they both shared, which h turned out to be one huge misconception of his.

It seemed that my having nowhere to live was part and parcel of who I was becoming. Tobore had been living in Havendale, just a few roads down from where I was living with Jasmine in my womb. As I drove through that neighbourhood I had to wonder if God was taking me back to face those gremlins. While Tobore and Colette were warm and safe in their big house, I had to seek refuge with a friend, Jen and share a room with her child, Dani. Jen was good to me, I thanked God for that; she took me in while I was pregnant with Jasmine.

It seemed that Tobore's family wanted to fight me for possession of Jasmine. Audriana, Colette's daughter rang to ask Jasmine when she could come by their house. Jasmine told them to ask me. Colette rang back to tell Jasmine that she was old enough to decide for herself who she wanted to see and when. She asked Jasmine to have me call her; but if this was in an effort cause a confrontation, I wasn't interested to say the least. It was their way of telling me that they refused to ask my permission. They had decided to see Jasmine as an adult who could decide what to do on her own.

Jasmine got to the point where she didn't want to call them or talk to them at all. That was due to the fact that when they called, they drilled her and asked her the same questions over and over for which they already knew the answers. She found it hypocritical. She had seen and heard enough. I was sorry she had to deal with this and yes in some respect; I helped to cause her that pain. But she needed to just be a child and not be put in the middle. Sadly, I thought coming home would have helped us both, but there we were with all sorts of predators prowling around.

Jasmine was in school, but of course Colette wouldn't give me the opportunity to explain that to her. I am certain she thought I was simply keeping Jasmine from them. She was too bitter and had too much hatred for me where Jasmine was concerned. I was certain they sat there crucifying me for keeping her away, not realising that there were other reasons. Would they have ever cared to ask what my reasons ever were? Of course not, so then why would I bother or care about them. She was the same child they nearly drove me to abort. They had treated me like such shit. I had gone for the abortion and while I was sitting in the GPS chair stirrups, something in my mind screamed; "No!" That may have been the single best decision I had ever made in my life so far.

I took some time out of my writing. Although cathartic, it was becoming a challenge. I was depressed and alone, reminding myself of hardships I've suffered.

Here is a diary entry from that time:

> *I haven't written in a while due to many factors. I have been really down-trodden; but more so, wondering what's going on in my life. I decided to stop applying for jobs because I have applied and sent my CV to more than 300 places in Jamaica. Okay, that may be exaggerated, but it's quite a lot, and so far, nothing has happened.*
>
> *I had just settled in to lying low and trying to figure out what was happening, when unexpectedly, my sister Babs came to see us and it was so refreshing. I loved every minute of her visit. In that moment, I realised how much living in the UK took me away from having my family's company and laughter, regardless of how hard times were. In spite of everything, I was thankful to be home where there was laughter.*

Follow me on Twitter: @avabrown24

Chapter Twenty Six

HEADING BACK TO LONDON

"Removing one brick from a stack can send walls

crumbling down quickly, escaping isn't always possible,

so we sometimes get rushed."

———————

Before I knew it, it was December and it was Christmas; a period I had always hated ever since I was a child. We were heading back to the UK and I had all sorts of emotions in my stomach. But we still maintained a home there and there were things that needed tending to. It had been a long time since I had written anything in my diary, but I wanted to get some of my thoughts down.

We had been back in Jamaica for a while, but nothing seemed to be happening for me in relation to jobs. It's rough, but through it all, I have managed to find myself and meet some wonderful people along the way. I

Follow me on Twitter: @avabrown24

call them my gems: Angie, and more importantly, Jegs and Auds. I will talk about them later. It's rough, but we are surviving. As I am writing now we are in South Bermondsey in south-east London. We travelled to London to take care of some necessities. It was a trip that I had such apprehension and fright to undertake. But it was here, in London, I got my first taste of Iylana Vanzant from her amazing book – 'Yesterday I Cried' – given to me by my friend Jegs, helped me prepare my mind. 'Yesterday I Cried' is about authentic power that has influenced me ever since reading it. And here I am, in a box room with a single bed, hardly able to hold Jasmine and myself. But hey, I will roll with the punches.

 Love Ava. x

We had come back to the UK to apply for my citizenship. On arrival we were met at the Gatwick Airport by Rafel; my new pursuit. I paid all of £51 for a taxi from the airport to my friend Hanna's house. I was meant to stay with my friend Temi, however as usual, she had a fight with her hubby and as a result we were displaced. She said we could no longer stay with her because her hubby would not have us. To be frank, I wasn't certain if it was fact or fiction, but I knew we had just landed and had nowhere to stay.

 I turned up at Hanna's door and God was good enough that although there was no one there, the front door to the apartment building was open. We disembarked in the parking lot and hoped she was home. Luck would have it that although they weren't in the door was accidentally left open. Then again, nothing happened per coincidence. I climbed the stairs and left my four suitcases there at her front door. I knew they had no space; they lived there with their three kids. God, I felt helpless. But I knew they wouldn't turn me back. With that faith in our friendship, I went to visit my old house, which was a five-minute walk away.

 I was so hurt by the condition of my front garden; the tenants had just left it to the waves of the weather. It was filthy. And even though the garbage truck had come, they didn't pick up their rubbish because it wasn't properly packed. I knocked or rather rang the doorbell but no one answered. I went to our neighbour, my dearest Ross; he was in and so delighted to see us. It was good, at least someone was happy to see us. I begged him a phone call and we called Tobore to tell him Jasmine was in London. But he seemingly already knew we would be there, that's another mystery. I chatted some more with Ross. I told him how I felt seeing my place hadn't been poorly kept. We caught up a little more and then I went downstairs to see my back garden. That really was sad because the tenants had scrapped up my strawberry patch, every plant in the back garden and thrown them out in the winter or autumn rubbish.

Finally, someone opened the conservatory door to my flat and inquired as to who I was. That must be the tenant I thought; and I was right. It was Len; he opened what was the terrible velvet curtain, which I had kept in the shed and peered out. He was about to throw us out when I explained who we were. When I went inside the house I could not believe my eyes, the house was in shambles. So messy and seemingly many more people lived there than I remembered renting the house to. I felt turmoil in my mind, but I tried to compose myself. The trouble was I had lived there so I knew what it should have looked like. I had to restrain myself and reflected on the mortgage they were paying and that I couldn't afford to lose them at that moment. I wasn't working and things were rough with me. I looked at the damp that I came to see, and talked with him about the house in general.

Before I left, I collected the post that had been accumulating there during the past months since my departure. My creditors were all after me; I knew I was in trouble. When I left the UK to go back to Jamaica I couldn't afford to pay even half of my bills. I had lost my job and didn't know any way out. I had simply hid my face in the sand. I had ignored the onslaught of past due bills. I had never been in such a position so I didn't know what to do. Anyway, once again I reminded myself of the purpose of my trip and I thanked him and promised to get the insurance company involved with the damp.

We left and tried to find the library. To my surprise our library in Pollards Hill was being refurbished; something that apparently started since our leaving, so how could we have known? We left and went to the Mitcham Library a short distance away, after which I went back to Hanna's flat and sat there until Jasmine was ready for her GP visit. You see, she needed asthma pumps and I knew I needed to stock up on them because I couldn't afford them otherwise in Jamaica. Rafel and I arranged to meet later that day and I took Jasmine to the GP before dropping her off with my friend, Joy.

Joy was taking Jasmine out shopping to keep her busy and not let her feel displaced. However, Joy called to say Jasmine had a headache and she needed to bring her back to me. Once Joy had dropped Jasmine off and I tended to her headache, we were off to my friend Shoa's home. Shoa had always been good to me and she had been a source of strength ever since we first landed in London; almost seven years before. Shoa agreed to take Jasmine for that night, while I met up with Rafel.

At midday the next day, I picked Jasmine up from Shoa's home. She and Lexi were having a birthday sleepover that night and so I needed to get Jasmine.

I didn't know where we were going to sleep that night, but there was too much to do before I had that worry. I rushed to Croydon to get my bank statements from my vault so I would have them with me when I went to submit my citizenship application at the registry office. That chore took longer than I expected. I was late in picking up Jasmine for her eye appointment. In a fluster, I called Shoa and asked her to book me a taxi for midday because I was on the number 60 bus, coming in that way and I would not have to wait on one.

When I got to Shoa's the taxi hadn't arrived yet and we had already missed one eye appointment scheduled the day we landed. I called the office to say I was running late but needed them to see us that day. I was told to not be more than five minutes late. We were already ten minutes late. Eventually, we got there and she was seen. Luckily, it was the nice people we had dealt with before. She got her eyes tested and was given a new prescription. I was hoping she didn't need other glasses; but I knew she had become used to her specs and she also wanted to choose a new style. She ended up choosing a green pair and once again, I paid for it all myself. I had paid for the first and now the second pair and her dad had not contributed a penny.

I returned Jasmine to Shoa because she said it was okay for her to stay over for the sleep over. I was happy; that was one less thing for me to worry about. I now needed to find out where I could sleep that night. The entire trip had been a struggle but I was handling it, better than I thought I would. Somehow, I had gained some strength from somewhere. I ended up sleeping at a guesthouse and that was another thing to handle. It felt so strange. I was so close to my own home but I couldn't walk to the front door and put a key in it. It was not my house to live in; it was merely rented property.

Life had many cycles then and I think I had been through all of them. I went to pick Jasmine up from Shoa's but we didn't have anywhere to go immediately. We were to go back to Hanna's house but she hadn't yet come home from church. So I lounged around at Shoa's waiting. I felt ultimately out of place; but I had learned to respond rather than react. We eventually headed to Hanna's place and she was there. Later that day, after stopping in at my friend, Temi's we went to meet Rafel's family or so I thought.

Follow me on Twitter: @avabrown24

Afterwards, we attempted to look for a room. I was very aware that Jasmine and I needed to find some place to stay. Hanna's place was too cramped. She had been so hospitable to us, but our welcome was overstayed. I looked for a place all that Sunday but to no avail; so we had to stay with Hanna. The next day, I woke up ready to apply for my citizenship. I was almost late for my appointment. I had caught the number118 bus but doing London by train and bus was proving a bit difficult for me. I wasn't use to it. It was just getting the better of my pulse; the adverse fact that the temperatures were so low; it being December I couldn't feel my feet at some points of my journey.

I got to Morden where the number 118 bus terminated. I was late so I ran to a black cab that was sitting parked. I was certain I was going to be taken but he said he wasn't working. I wasn't sure if it was fact or fiction, but I didn't bother debating it, I had no time to spare today. I ran towards the mini cab station and to my luck there was not a single cab in house. The operator sensed my agitation and I told him my dilemma. He wasn't certain what time he would have a cab but said that I could take the number 93 bus. I went to the bus stop and was mad, but I noticed I was containing myself. Another time I would have just burst. While I waited at the bus stop I sent Jasmine to tell the cab operator that I was there and if a cab came he was to send it to us directly. Before Jasmine even got to the door a cab driver turned up; I praised God and went with him. The drive was only about five minutes literally, but it was so bitterly cold it would have been a very difficult walk.

We got there and I apologised profusely to the registry people, but they were pleasant and my fears were unfounded. I learnt a lesson, not to work myself up for no reason. I was seen, but told that the forms I used had been revised and she was certain the home office wouldn't take them. She made me pay in advance and told me to return with the new forms signed

Follow me on Twitter: @avabrown24

up by my referees. I was pissed off, but told myself that God was in control.

Next, I had a meeting with my divorce solicitor, so I rushed there and managed to sign the affidavit for my divorce and decree nisi to come through. I really wanted to be free from Tobore. While at the solicitor, he called and asked where we could meet; he wanted to see Jasmine. I told him to meet us at the library in Pollards Hill because I didn't want him to get wind that we had no stable place to stay. After I hung up the phone, the solicitor told me I needed to visit another independent solicitor's office to get the affidavit witnessed; I got nervous. Was there no one in her office who could bear witness? So, I went to another office, down the street, on the corner, and as you would have guessed, there was no solicitor in house. I ran further up the road and thankfully found one in. I got the document signed.

I was so overcome with mixed emotions. Part of me wanted out; and part of me wasn't ready yet. But I quickly reminded myself of the jail and the room I was put in and who it was that put me there. So, I snapped out of it pretty quickly. Back at my solicitor's office, we wrapped up our meeting with the financial agreement. We decided I was going to go after his pension and I told the solicitor I wanted it immediately. I didn't want to wait until he was old before seeing any of that money. I was thinking I needed that money right there and then, afterall I was broke and needed to care for his child. She also said we would go after 60% of the Jamaica house; and that he should maintain me until I remarried. I could just see his face turning pink when he heard that! He was going to be mad; but I didn't care. I felt like that was revenge and I wanted it badly.

I left the solicitors office and called him to tell him to meet me instead at the HSBC Bank at Mitcham. I felt riled up to see him. After all, I had just signed my revenge on him. I felt good. As we arrived at Mitcham we crossed the road and I let Jasmine post a letter. I saw him waiting with 'her' in their new CRV. Seeing them together, I didn't know what I felt. I can't explain it; it was very strange.

He hadn't seen us and called to ask where at the HSBC he was to meet us. I told him we were waiting in the back for him. He took ages to arrive. As we waited fear sank in and I wondered if he was bringing the police with him. I had nightmares that he would try and take away my child. I would ask myself sometimes, if I was being fair; but she was all I had. He came and I felt nothing; no hatred, no contempt, nothing. He knelt at Jasmine's feet as she sat on a chair in the bank telling her how happy he was to see her. She said to him. "Dad, if Agnes is there, I don't want to go to your house." He told her she didn't have to see Agnes. He told her that he didn't know what the plan was for that afternoon. I told him, much to his surprise, that he could have her from then, which was one in the afternoon to six o'clock. Yes, I was certain that I shocked him. I knew that was the last thing he expected to hear from me. I didn't want to be predictable to him anymore.

They left and I went to sort out my business at the Department of Social Services. They had written to me so many times and I had missed my six-month review with them because I was back in Jamaica. That wasn't good, as that was my only source of income; that was how we were able to live. But before that, I needed to go to the library to use their computers; I had to find someplace to live. I logged onto Gum Tree and finally found a place to rent all the way in Bermondsey. It was a small box room the size of my closet in Jamaica and that wasn't an exaggeration. It was £79 a night but quickly went up because I had Jasmine, which meant two people. Oh, how I have had to pay my way with that child of mine, but I loved her so unconditionally that I wouldn't have had it any other way. I went to the place and paid the deposit. I was shocked when I asked to use the toilet and was told I could wash my hands in the kitchen sink. I decided I wasn't going to do any cooking there. How I would survive was another thing totally. I left without the keys and unsure if I could trust those people. But I left in good faith, they were Koreans, she gave me a receipt for my deposit and told me I could pick up the keys on the Wednesday. The room was the smallest I had ever lived in, but I had no choice I needed to be out of Hanna's place.

> *"Lack can bring such desperation that even*
> *your body will give way."*

Chapter Twenty Seven

DISPLACED IN LONDON IN DECEMBER

"Living in a country where there is government help can be the best buffer one can have in desperation."

———————

I finally went to get my review done at the Department of Social Services. I was so nervous; the last thing you wanted to do in London was to get in trouble with the state. I was told I couldn't just walk in; I had to ring her and she had given me an appointment for Tuesday. I agreed because I needed to get that resolved. I needed to pay Jasmine's school fee for January and I had no other means. Her dad had already decided he wasn't going to give us any more money than he already was. I had decided too that I would not ask him for more.

I knew somehow I would cope. I felt I was doing the best I knew how.

Kem had come through for me the one last time.

Follow me on Twitter: @avabrown24

I needed her and I was on my way to her with Jasmine. Along the way, I managed to fit in a hairdressers' appointment, which was such a success. They did my hair beautifully; I felt proud. We left for Luton and Kem's home. I was a bit hesitant on the train because I didn't trust men around my child. Especially men I did not think had the correct values. But I reassured myself that I had taught her well and Jasmine was sensible enough to know when someone was trying to take advantage of her. I called Kem from the train and asked if she had food in the house. She snapped at me and I almost turned back. But I had to remind myself I had nowhere to go; I needed someone to leave Jasmine with.

We got to Luton and it felt like the coldest day that had ever been. We took the number 10 bus and Kem and Beatrice met us. It was a happy moment.

I had never been so happy to see Kem in my entire life. I wasn't sure if it was that I missed her that much or was it seeing Beatrice or was it just that I was really feeling stuck? I realised I really missed them terribly. Kem was family and she loved Jasmine deeply and I loved Beatrice. We ran to each other and hugged.

I kissed them and we just held each other; all four of us. We hurried ourselves to her place. We sat and chatted and caught up. After sometime, I ate a quick meal of spaghetti and left for the station to meet up with Rafel. I walked to the bus stop and saw a cab waiting and asked if he could take me. He said no because he was booked by someone else. The lady who called the cab arrived and decided I could share the ride with her, the long and short of it was she knew my sister and ended up paying my way to the train station. How funny life can be and how small the world was? I met Rafel at the station and we went on to London to enjoy that evening together.

I ended up sleeping in a guesthouse again as I dreaded going back to the cramped space at Hanna's. I needed some of my own sense of independence and privacy. The next day I went to the pharmacy to collect a prescription. I also picked up Jasmine's glasses; green they were indeed and nice. She would get them when she got back from my sister's. I picked up my keys from the girl for the rental and took along my stuff from Hanna's place. Rafel came with me; he had proven to be such a supportive help for me since I have been here. If only I felt for him the way he felt about me; we could have made heaven come to earth. Alas, I didn't.

I felt displaced in the room, but just had to deal with it; I had made my bed. That evening, after I was settled in the room, the Korean girl came and told me that I had broken the door. I thought how could I? We came in and shut the door carefully and nothing broke. For about 30 minutes we were locked in the house. It was more than a fire hazard and completely unacceptable. I told her that she should call the landlord to get it fixed. She said we should all put in together to pay for it because the landlord was so far away. That said to me she was cunning and perhaps not to be trusted. Then she suggested we could walk through the living room of one of the other tenants - a Japanese guy who lived there – and try the door from outside. The door opened, of course and that was the end of that. Was she trying to make a quick buck from me, or what? I didn't know and I didn't care.

I needed to get food; I went to the corner shop and bought some supplies; fruit and vegetables and drinks and necessities to prepare meals. I had planned to spend only £20 but that didn't work out. I couldn't stand the thought of using the utensils they supplied, remembering I had been told to wash my hands in the kitchen sink after using the bathroom. So I also bought plates and cups along with spoons. I had told Rafel I wanted to be alone that night so I took the bus back alone. I wasn't certain of how I would manage with all of six carrier bags by myself but I did. I just wanted to exhale a sigh of relief when I arrived. I unpacked the bags and organised myself. I had a bath and slept like a baby. I wasn't in the mood to talk to anyone; I wanted to be alone and sleep and it did me good.

I woke up the next morning and knew I needed to get Jasmine from Kem. My life was like that, one task after another, but that was life. It came with ups and downs and I had to roll with it. I was supposed to meet Kem at the station, but after waiting for a while I decided to go to get a duvet from the Primark, which was nearby and was my favourite store. It was too cold in the boxed room and the heat came on for only two hours a night. In the middle of winter that was harsh. I also needed to sleep with one of the windows open because I didn't do well with carpets on the floors due to allergies. I met up with Kem and wished we were staying with them. I needed a sense of family, but every time I got to that point I reminded myself I needed to make my own family. We said our goodbyes and I took Jasmine to see our room. She seemed disappointed, but tried not to show it. I did the best I could in the situation, gave her a hug and reminded her it was temporary.

The London trip was something else. We ended up spending Christmas with my friend Emma, her daughter and their friends. These were people we didn't know, but it felt like we were all one family.They were such lovely people; we couldn't help but notice that. However, that highlighted even more the fact that I was alone. I really didn't have any true family of my own accept Jasmine. Granted, had I been back in Jamaica, I would have certainly been welcomed into my mum's humble abode.

Jasmine had seen her dad only twice while we were in London. Can you imagine that after all that time away he couldn't have made more time for her? He didn't even as much as give her £5 to use as spending money. Instead, he took her shopping for perfume for his girlfriend. The child had taken him into a Clarkes' Store with the hope of getting some school shoes; he quickly told her he had no money. Right after that he went and spent £80 on perfume for his secret obsession. She reported asking for a bear as they passed the Build-A-Bear store; she was presumptuous enough to ask for a £15 bear; of course she didn't get that either.

Nonetheless, we endured our trip and hung in there the best way we knew how. Once again, I felt as though I was starting over and was really stuck. That was a feeling I got a lot in my life and it seems I could not escape it. I began thinking that perhaps there was something I was simply not doing right. I spent most of my time alone in the small box room in Bermondsey. I didn't feel that was a good place for Jasmine to be. She only stayed there when we needed to take care of matters involving the doctors and the opticians. These were luxuries we couldn't afford in Jamaica; otherwise I sent her off to visit friends. All in all, our tasks were accomplished to some extent.

While staying in London, I didn't have a clean place to wash my clothes, or cook while renting the box room. I found myself waking to piles of dirty clothes, hoping that whichever friend I was to stop by at that day would be kind enough to let me wash my things there. Sometimes I was lucky, sometimes not. The last few days, nearer the end of my trip, I went to stay at my friend Ajua's house. She opened her arms and received me. The feeling of being neglected was gone. Jasmine and I stayed with her. She gave up her warm cosy bed to accommodate us. Her house was our house and she didn't make us feel in the way. I remembered when I went to move out of the box room, my friend Tim was a Godsend. He borrowed an old van from his boss and helped me move.

When I arrived at Ajua's house, she didn't exclaim why I had brought so many bags to her house. Instead, she was gentle and decent about it. I was certain in her heart she must have felt fear and confusion, but given her nature she just reassured me it was okay. She helped me to unpack and was such a sweetheart. We were like one happy family.

Follow me on Twitter: @avabrown24

I remember on New Year's Eve; Jasmine and I were walking back to Ajua's house and although I didn't have much money, we stopped at an off licence liquor store and bought her a nice bottle of wine. It was costly; but I thought Ajua deserved it. New Year's Eve caught us lonely souls; no party invites and no one to take us out. But I knew we would be on our way back to Jamaica in less than ten hours. So we drank some wine and toasted the New Year. After that I packed. I had all of four cases filled once more, the reason being I had offered to take back wedding clothes for a friend of Ajua's; it was the least I could do for her accommodating us. That felt like I was giving something back to her. The morning came quickly. I had not gone to bed until about half past three and the cab was coming for us at half past five, so I had very little time to even take a nap.

I was uncertain if I really wanted to go back to Jamaica. At least there in Jamaica I had a lovely, large, warm house waiting for me. That fact was comforting irrespective of what else was going on at home and I took comfort in that. I didn't want to be in London anymore. Well, not that I didn't want to, I felt entirely displaced. There I was, somewhere I used to feel safe and secure, at least where shelter was concerned. That entire trip I felt totally displaced and didn't like the feeling. The displacement wasn't just about me; it was more about my child. I didn't like having her feel uncomfortable.

I picked my thoughts up and continued readying myself. I quickly showered, trying not to wake up, Ajua's mate; that was almost impossible because it was a small flat. I got dressed and I made the dangerous choice of wearing flip flops, forgetting that it was four degrees outside. I was already packed and the one pair of boots I had were unfit to wear, so I left them to go into the trash. I had packed a suitcase with some clothes I intended to leave in London. Maybe the hardest part of leaving Ajua was leaving behind dirty clothes and asking if she would wash them for us. She didn't object, but within me, I felt sad.

I woke Jasmine and she got dressed. We were organised and ready to leave. Ajua helped me with the cases down the stairs. We were so loud; we must have woken up all their neighbours. I was not happy about that, but could not do anything about it. I had to rationalise within myself that it was okay.

The cab came soon after that and I was absolutely livid. The taxi driver told me it would cost me much more than I had bargained to go to Gatwick and my money was tight. I put on my regular brave face and asked him to explain why. After much haggling he called his operation room and said he was ready to leave. I had to come to terms with it and agree to the rate. Now be mindful; I was already spending double seeing it was New Year's Day. But the driver turned out to be a lovely person and we chatted all the way to the airport. He even told me I could have checked in the previous night for my flight, little did I know.

I arrived at Gatwick and needed £1 to pay for the trolleys. By that time, I was solid broke. Recession had reached me on New Year's Day. With not even a penny from her dad; Jasmine could not be of any help to me. The cab driver graciously paid for my trolleys and I thanked him for his kindness. He didn't even ask for it back with my payment to him. Pushing the trolleys was difficult but like always, we managed. The lines at the airport were crazy. I had not imagined there would be so many people there at that time in the morning. All I could think was that they must have slept there; such was my thought process. Our luggage and hampers were offloaded from the trolleys within minutes and we had ample time to scout around. James, Rafel's friend, was in the North Terminal because his mum was leaving for Nigeria that same day. We went over to pay our regards, then came back to 'lay,' as we say in Jamaica, until it was time to board.

While there in the airport we stopped at a WH Smith and I picked up the book of the moment to read on the plane, Dreams of my Father by President Barack Obama. I used up the last of my UK credit card allowance, but I needed to read something to inspire me. Jasmine got herself some books and I also got a stamp. I needed to post a letter to the Educational Welfare Officer regarding withdrawing Jasmine from the school registers there in London. And I needed to ensure I posted that letter from within London. Also, I wanted to post off a travel card to Emma; she was my sister, at least in that moment, better than my blood.

Jasmine and I walked the stores in search of bargains. Knowing full well we really didn't have any money to spend. But it was the traditional thing to do in airports wasn't it? I had to remind myself I really didn't have the money so I quickly put a stop to that. I did have £5 in my wallet that I felt I could part with, so I bought a Girls Aloud CD. We went to sit in the airport chairs in the waiting area; the flight took ages to board; or was it simply because we had checked in early? Even after boarding the flight, there were still people checking in. It was going to be a long day.

"Sometimes just letting your hair out and breathe can be the best therapy ever recommended."

Chapter Twenty Eight

HOME SWEET HOME; ST ANDREW, JAMAICA

"Home regardless of the state of play, is the only place

where I ever feel at peace."

———————

Angel picked us up at the airport. I was glad to see my car after three weeks of standing in the cold at the various bus and train stops. The sight of my own car was so delightful. I almost jumped out of my body to tell Angel that I wanted to drive as she pulled up beside the curb. But as though she had read my mind; she told me I needed to drive. Phew! What a relief I thought. I got behind the steering wheel and once again felt like I was somebody. London had all but stripped me of my sense of importance and the security of the things I had built. I felt almost the same way I did when I had gone to Britain the first time; striped of all my pride, hard work and dignity. Well, there I was gaining some of my independence back.

In some ways it was ironic, you see, I had gone to a land I thought was better. But no matter what the situation, I should not have felt that way. Now I was back in the land that was my own; one that many people see as not better. And there I felt much more relief than in the place I had called home for more than six years. As we drove away I felt that I was leaving all that baggage behind. But then I was now even more confused. How could coming home to Jamaica bring such relief? But I did know why...the comfort of my own bed and the ability to cook for myself. I loved my food. When you looked at me you could tell I lived near my kitchen. Having the ability to move around a house, instead of being confided to a single room not larger than my closet there in Jamaica, was pure heaven.

We stopped at Angel's for a quick dinner of stewed peas with pigs tail and rice and oh, that was exactly what we needed. Angel updated us about what was going on in Jamaica as we gulped the good food down. Soon after that I raided her pantry. You see Angel ran a home, an old Jewish home, which housed three Jewish people and the remaining rooms were let to university students. She had food; always. And she was always so generous to us, we felt blessed having her in our lives.

As I arrived home the joy of pressing that remote buzzer as we approached our gate was exhilarating. I drove into the parking lot and sat in the car, appreciating the fact that I had a beautiful place to live in, even though at times in my life, affording it was a mantle in itself. At that moment, I had even forgotten it was only rented, but it was home and mine. I quickly unloaded all our stuff and headed for bed. Oh, how I missed my kingsize bed. Jasmine and I hugged in our bed for a long time and the next thing I knew we fell asleep.

I was gradually able to get back into the rhythm of things. I needed to sort out Jasmine's uniforms and school things and get unpacked. I had brought back something for almost everyone, my mom, my stepdad, my brothers and sisters, my sister's kids, a neighbour in my mom's village, the head teacher at Jasmine's school, her teacher, another two teachers and two parents Angie and Jem, Angel of course, Auds, her kids, Jegs and her kids. I was blessed to have been able to touch the lives of so many people, although I went to London and came back with little or no money. Thank God for Primark. In Jamaica it's just expected of you; when you travel you are to come back bearing gifts for everyone. Unfair though it may have seemed, it was a part of our culture and you felt empty and worthless coming back empty handed.

I thought to myself the next time I travel, I was going to break that spell because I really put myself out on a limb each time I did that. I was again worried about pleasing everyone else apart from myself. I hardly purchased anything for myself just a few pairs of shoes and a bag. Not that I needed them; but to be frank I felt better buying something for me. I guess it spoke to the void inside me that I still struggled with all the time. I had a weakness for handbags, clothes and shoes; irrespective of how many of those items I bought, I still felt the void. I realised that the items I was hoarding wouldn't help. But I wasn't ready to come out of denial then and for the moment it felt good. I wanted to stay in that bubble. It was one I had come to feel safe in, one that I wouldn't let anyone else know existed; just me, myself and I. Sometimes I did wonder if those people around me knew. Then again, I didn't really give a damn... or so I thought.

I had an interview with a food company in Jamaica. Although jet lagged, I went to it anyway. I was so tired I was hardly able to walk in the sexy black heels I had bought in Peckham; nice, sexy velvet at the back, with open toes. I wondered if they were too much; it was Jamaica not the UK! I also didn't wear the traditional suit. I opted instead for a black corduroy waistcoat, some grey trousers and a pale greyish-blue shirt. In my mind, I looked good and felt good.

The interviewer was a young girl who had an easy manner and was nice enough to talk to. We had spent hours chatting. She had a brother in Austria and she told me how she had been to Germany. We talked way into three hours after the interview had finished. I thought to myself: "Don't be fooled, I knew well I hadn't gotten the job, but the girl was pleasant to talk with." You may have wondered why I even bothered to waste my time but I knew that life had more span to it; I was just relaxing and being human. I left the interview and went back to my friends Auds and Jegs' place. We hung out for a while and then I left to go home.

I stopped at the supermarket to get a few bits and bobs. My friends had gone to Coronation Street and gotten me some fresh fruit and vegetables. With huge bravado I asked them how much I owed, knowing if they told me even $10 I would not be able to pay. Like the true people they were, they said I owed them nothing. Then again, I had done enough over time for them to warrant some fruit and vegetables; I had driven them many places for free because I had a car. I was not complaining but we seem to play what I call 'quits'... every so often.

The opening of the new school term was near and I went home that weekend and tried to rest. The days ahead would be challenging, I knew that and didn't have any clear vision of how I would overcome it. We went to church that Sunday; we had found Boulevard Baptist Church, I wore the skirt of an African outfit I had made. Monday came and I took Jasmine to school, after which I went with Auds to pay the school fees. After I gave the guy all of my $37,000, I had no money left; I felt bewildered. I took the bank slip to school and just continued like nothing had happened. After that, we went back to Auds' house to chill because that was what most days were like. Since I had moved to Havendale and found her, this had pretty much become my ritual; one of dropping Jasmine at school then running to the safe haven of Auds' home. Some days I did my other hobby of going to interviews.

Follow me on Twitter: @avabrown24

My life had been like that of late; worthless, with no job, not since April 2008. I had fallen into a painful, voluntary life of luxury. I didn't like it but sometimes I didn't mind it. I had the time when needed to do what I wanted when I wanted. Other times when I needed money for extra lessons, or the light bills, or even the food bills, I hated it. I found that my entire life was totally centred on Jasmine. From dropping her at school, to going to her quiz matches, to being her chauffeur and picking her up, to getting her supplies etc. I had no existence of my own. There were days when I just wanted to go shopping or have a cup of tea, but those were luxuries I could not afford. In London, I could get a cuppa for 50p or even go to Primark and treat myself to a pair of shoes for £3 or so. But here, I was barely able to buy mere essentials; and at times I was unable to even buy meat to go with dinner.

At least I hadn't felt as depressed as I had when I was in London. There was something about being there in Jamaica that was comforting amidst the hardship. I had the feeling that someone would catch me if I fell; in London I felt total despair. I felt as though I was totally alone always. Truth be told, I was alone. Tobore had proven he wasn't who I felt he was, my sister couldn't be relied on and my friends were typical Londoners doing their own thing.

Auds and I had met at the school; her kids were new to Quest but not new to Jamaica. She had them at the same school with Tobore's sister Collette's kids. But she had recently moved to my side of the island. She thought the school would be better. She was also running away from some other things that were not for me to talk about. But that girl did give me some insight into internally dealing with problems.

As the days in Jamaica went on the hardships heightened. When I had left for London, I left Jamaica buying burgers for $280 and just before mass the cost was up more than $300. I couldn't afford to buy them anymore.

Follow me on Twitter: @avabrown24

In my fridge were some chicken feet; it was the only meat. I simply had no means of buying anything else. Jasmine and I tried to live with what we could afford. One decision I took to heart after I came back from London was to pack her lunch instead of her buying it. Not that I didn't want the freedom of not having to worry about what to put in her lunch box each day; but I simply couldn't afford to pay the $650 per week. So, instead I sat her down and had the painful conversation that her mum really couldn't afford to pay for her lunches anymore, so from then on, she would be taking packed lunches. I promised her I would try to ensure they were healthy and tasty. In my mind, I knew how difficult that would be seeing I had limited resources of money.

That's what we have been doing ever since we got back from London. She has been so good about it. She ate whatever I provided and never once complained. There were some Saturdays when I dropped her at school and all I could afford to pack in her bag was a banana, an apple, some cheese, a tangerine and a drink, maybe some water and a crisp pack as a snack. The norm was for them to buy lunch on a Saturdays. We talked that morning and I told her it was either I pay for lunch or I could pay Mr. Good for extra lessons. I knew she would rather I was able to do both, but she said; "Mom, I will take a packed lunch." As for paying Mr. Good, I had exchanged £10 I had in my purse but it yielded only $1126, which was not enough because his fee was $1200. I needed to find a little under $100 more before Monday. I placed my trust in God that it would mature; at the same time my car's fuel tank was on empty as it had been for many days now. I had not been able to purchase more than $500 of petrol since I came back. You see the London trip was way more than $100,000 and that left me broke. Plus, my benefits from the Department of Social Services had been cut. They had wanted to see me last October for my interview because I was a no show, at least not until December, they had cut my benefits to a meagre £12 per week. Still, I would say God bless England, at least we were receiving something.

Where we lived, I had to buy tokens to do our laundry; I hadn't bought any since last October due to the lack of funds. I had been hand washing all our things and I could feel the effects on my back. I went to my friends to do my dirty linen every now and then. However, I was very uncomfortable asking them repeatedly, so I tried not to do it too often, and when I did, I took my own detergent and fabric softener. They insisted I didn't need to; but I felt that I was scrounging enough, so that was the least I could do. There were times I had laundry waiting to be done, but I didn't have the strength, literally to deal with it.

I had been tempted to go and cash in a policy I had taken out for Jasmine years ago. I needed money to pay my rent for February and I wanted to fix up the house in Montego Bay. I had to get it rented out; it couldn't continue to be locked up there doing absolutely nothing for much longer. I had it on the market for sale but the sensible thing to do was to get it painted, give it a once over and have it make some money. The real estate market was soft at the time and even though I had an offer I didn't know if the sale would go through. I had an offer of $8 million but I knew its value was much more than that and I was not going to give it way. I travelled to Mobay and got the house painted so that it could be rented out. Whether it rented for long term or short term it did not matter, we needed money coming in. I knew it was going to cost me money I didn't have. I emailed Tobore to ask for his help, but of course you could imagine what he said.

A highlight for me during this time was when Jegs and I happened to met Melanie Walker, the Beijing Olympic Champion, in the Victoria Mutual Bank. We got pictures taken with her and her autograph. She was so meek and humble. In my heart, I asked God if I could be as humble as she was. She was such a lovely person. Meeting her made our day, I still have the bank note she signed for me.

Follow me on Twitter: @avabrown24

I was going to spend some time with Keri, my friend, who I met in London the previous year, she was there studying to become a marine pilot. She lived in Port Royal. I was so impressed with what that girl had sacrificed for her career. Perhaps if I hadn't had Jasmine so young, I would have been more ambitious. I still felt tempted to complete my law degree; that had always been my passion but my motivation was so low and I felt so tired. I slept more than I did anything else; apart from eating. I hardly played with Jasmine either. For one thing, she had grown a bit more independent of me. There were times I would go into hiding in my own little world. Thankfully, she was so occupied with her end of primary school exams – her GSATS - she hardly even noticed.

I had plans to go back to London in July, but until then I was depending on an investment I had of $500,000 due to mature to help us get by. Hopefully, I would gather all of it and to be able to pay the rent for the rest of the year. I was still looking for a job; but parts of me felt like it was a waste of time. The economy was so bad and I was not motivated. It was going to take lots of intrinsic motivation to get me back on board. I was lost, so lost it was shocking.

Feelings of frustration, anger and bemusement hung over me as I reflected on where I was. I seemed to have no one to turn to. My siblings still had great expectations of my ability to help them. My brother was even looking for sheets to make his bed at a nearby construction site. His request turned into a heated conversation on the phone and I hung up. Something I reckon I was doing a lot more of lately; hanging up when I got frustrated. It was easier than arguing, or so I thought. Surely, it was easier than having long conversations I didn't want to have. It was my way of coping.

I felt hurt after that call. I had helped my mum's kids and they blew through it all and asked for more. Now that I was the one on my face, I was not asking for help, I just wanted to be left alone. I was frustrated with them all. Who was there to help me, now that I was down? I had fallen and fallen hard. The trouble with my family was they never believed I didn't have any money; even when I was starving. I was the educated one and they thought that education equalled money. They could not fathom the possibility I had none. They felt I should always have plenty to give. But at this point all my reserves had dried up and I was the one who needed help; needed reassurance that it would get better.

I wonder who could identify with me? Who could relate? Certainly my own family were too self-absorbed to realise my own fall from grace. When all is said and done, it's always going to be okay!

In the words of Lisa Nichols, my hero.

" I am my own rescue."

Follow me on Twitter: @avabrown24

Chapter Twenty Nine

THE JOURNEY OF THE UNKNOWN VISA GIRL

"You can be caught in spider webs even with your eyes wide opened - it's not being caught that matters - but its deciding this is the last web- being at your ebb!"

I haven't been involved with men for a while; in fact, I hardly went anywhere and the few times I went out, I don't think I saw anyone who peaked my interest. This could have been due to the fact that I was still going through my healing process; so, a man wasn't top on my list. In my mind, I felt that I had a man in London, Rafel, although at this stage I still feel like I was settling. I was afraid of age and the fact that I was going to be 40 in a few years, so that's why I think was settling plus there were aspects to him I liked; he was at the time, in my mind loyal and his seeming attitude to love me was welcome, needed and refreshing, or at least so it appeared at the start. Later I became aware this did not mean love but instead lust and in my opinion his visa. Yet he had so many uncultured ways. He didn't know how to use a knife and fork, he was always walking like a mountain climber, his dress sense turned me off and I can't remember smelling perfume on him ever. He had never been to the dentist and that turned me off big time. I didn't need anything else. The guy was truly not what I had imaged or anyone I had ever dated before. I had gone passed my Jamaican idea of what an educated woman like me should be going for in a man. He didn't even have a car and I also feared that he was after a visa and I didn't trust him one bit. However, sometimes I felt like I loved him, but I fear this was just pity or my own fears playing up. We kept in touch but the trouble was his entire family in Nigeria seemed to think we will going to wed and I was uncertain. The trouble was that he was my age and had no kids of his own, or any previous wife. But for all I knew, he had nothing, not even a hut, and I was probably being shallow, but that played heavily on my mind; why should I regress and pick up a man who had nothing. I was in Jamaica and he couldn't even find phone cards to call me consistently. God knows, he tried to call often, but the chats were always short and cut off quickly, or he kept telling me he had one minute remaining. I was fed up with that, and I was accustomed to men who were secure financially. Here I was, confronted with a man who not only had no western values and/or culture, he was a dead-broke man. I must say, up to that point, I struggled with that notion, and to some extent, it was his situation that prevented me from committing to him, given that he wasn't a good looker. If he had some assets or a secure job, he would have seemed much more appealing to me. Now this may sound shallow, but I was about to lose out in a divorce, and I wasn't ready to scrub up any man, not his age, anyway. You could say I was being cautious.

I know you are all thinking I am shallow; but I am this age and I have

Follow me on Twitter: @avabrown24

owned two houses in London, have a degree and an MBA and owned part
of a house in Jamaica with my ex-husband. I was his age and I have been on
my own since I was a child. I have been married and almost divorced and
had raised a child all by myself for nine years and what had he done with
his life? He kept telling me he loved me, but for God sake love can't be eaten
and he wasn't scoring any points with me here! But then my fears jumped
in and I heard myself saying; "Ava had you met this guy with a nice cash
job and nice suits you would like him wouldn't you?" And yes I would, so I
asked myself was I shallow or was I just unaccustomed to broke ass men. I
know it's a mixture of both. I wasn't used to broke-ass men and that's the
truth, probably he was also too quick to point out how broke he was. After
all, man come on, he was in his thirties, when you should have something -
it's almost half way through life - in my opinion at least.

Despite all this, I married Rafel soon after our son was born. However,
ever since we got married and even before that our relationship suffered
many issues ranging from: infidelity; abuse; and financial irresponsibility.
He promised that the birth of our son meant he would be a changed man.

We had never lived together and when we found a new home at last,
he tried to stop me from signing the papers. He pulled out because I found
out he had received his British residency visa and I was the applicant or
sponsor at my address. Yet, for more than a month I wasn't aware of this.
Many attempts to ascertain if he had got his visa resulted in him telling
me, God would take care of it. When in truth he had already received it and
was blatantly lying to me! It wasn't until I called the Home Office, who then
requested I send a letter outlining my queries; that I even heard back from
them.

To my surprise, the Home Office was able to give me the reference
number for when my husband received his visa. The relationship had been
a strange one because he has never wanted to live with us. He always had

Follow me on Twitter: @avabrown24

one excuse after another. His excuse was that he as an African man he needed to do 'this' the correct way! And even when he could contribute properly - he never took care of me as a wife - and with regards to his son there was little help given financially and otherwise.

His actions were haphazard, inconsistent and most importantly unreliable. There was one particular incident when he left the iron switched on, on the floor still hot. When I spoke to him about it and reminded him that the baby was now crawling; this ended in a very huge argument and I asked him to leave the house because I felt it wasn't the best idea the stayed there that night. He refused and became aggressive; he grabbed my right arm in an effort to take away my keys. I had to call the police, who then came and told him to leave my house and go to his own.

Another incidence was the night before my son was blessed. We had a discussion in the car a car park in Purley Way and we had a difference of opinion on what the word suburban meant. He was someone who couldn't stand not being right and as such he started shouting and swearing in front of the kids. I told him to get out of my car because I didn't appreciate anyone swearing in front of my kids. He refused to leave the car and I felt threatened, so I had to call the police again. They spoke to him on my mobile and asked him to leave. He told them I was his wife and he wouldn't leave. The police asked whose car it was and determined that if it was mine, he needed to leave. The police hung up and promised to come, soon after that, he got out of my car and I drove off, taking my kids home and left him there. Can you believe it? He didn't show up for his son's christening the next day?

Another time, we went to Elephant and Castle to eat in a Nigerian restaurant and our son was acting up. His dad got really embarrassed and started saying I wasn't raising Brad properly, because African kids didn't behave like that. A disagreement ensued and to my surprise Brad was soiled and he was acting up because he was in discomfort. We went to the car park, changed Brad's clothes and asked his dad if he could feed him while I attempted to drive home. He refused to feed his own child because he said he was disobedient and when Brad called him "dad" he didn't answer.

Tension grew - and a quarrel ensued once again about how I was allowing Brad to get away with too much - granted he was a mere two year old child. I tried to tell Rafel that we didn't live in Africa, neither should he feel embarrassed because of what people think of his child. He started shouting abuses at me and it was difficult to focus on the dual carriageway from Elephant and Castle driving towards Croydon. I pulled up on the curb and asked him to get out and he told me; "Not even the police could get him out." It became a very heated quarrel with his shouts and screamed almost shaking the car so I drove to the Brixton Police Station and it was only then that I was able to get him out.

Overall, it's been a tumultuous relationship of break up, make up based on the fear of a me being a single mum again and the underlined threat of not seeing my son. This became apparent when Rafel came to the house under the pretense to take Brad swimming. As any mother would, I went to check his bag with the simple intent of making sure he had all he needed; to my surprise, a bag was packed with all his clothes and many items Brad would need, without my knowledge. When I asked Rafel about it, he threw his regular shouting match and told me he was Brads dad too. I reminded him that the child didn't live with him so taking him without my consent did not making sense. When I asked him when he had planned to tell me; he told me he had planned to call me later and tell me. That made me somewhat uneasy and it was worsened by the fact that he left and aborted taking poor Brad swimming.

Then I had an incident, which I intend to expound more about in a later book; I was arrested by the police. Social Services got involved and

I spent a night in jail. Rafel and I were once again back together and so he was here with Brad when I was arrested. I was sent home and Social Services came round and interviewed him and asked if he had any concerns with me as the mother of his son in front of me. He told them none whatsoever, yet the court documents I received indicated that he reported me when I had made to trips abroad, one to Germany and the other to Jamaica to promote my first book. He was aware of both trips and was meant to help. This discussion had happened before he tried to take Brad without my consent. I expressed to a few friends that I felt uncomfortable leaving Brad with him after that incident. They both agreed and so I left Brad with a friend who kept him from time to time and I likewise cared for her kids in exchange.

On the second leg of my book promotion in Jamaica, I took Brad with me because I needed to feel he was safe and it was a week-long visit. Whereas the trip to Germany was only three days and taking Brad to Jamaica meant he would get to see my home and some of my family. Rafel knew I was taking Brad because this was discussed before the trip. You can imagine my shock when I learnt of his issues and in the court documents where he had called Social Services because he didn't know where Brad was. I had emails that were sent to him from Jamaica informing him that my flight had been cancelled. This proved the deceptive person he was because he knew I had not been in my house and I would be none the wiser that he had called Social Services to report me for abduction.

A few months later, I went to Ireland to promote my book and was honoured that the former Justice Minister launched my book. I had an au pair who made me uncomfortable and Rafel offered to stay in conjunction with the au pair to look after Brad. I didn't feel totally uncomfortable as he was by this time asking that we worked out our relationship and he was working on himself or so I thought. As a matter of fact, while I was in

Ireland, he had attended a counseling appointment I made for him and also paid for. In my mind and thought process I was tired of the abuse from him, the financial, verbal and emotional abuse, it was too much. I was the one dropping off Brad at nursery daily, picking him up daily and also paying the bills. When he approached me saying he was going to work on himself because he wanted to be with us, I believed him. We discussed moving into a new house and he seemed genuine. I once again believed him. Yes, this belief was based on love and I felt it was just a matter of culture clashes, coupled with the fact that I was a Western woman and not subservient as he would have liked me to be.

There were many incidents that showed his lack of care, but he had an excuse for everything. I came back from Ireland and we were very civil with each other; even made love on my return. But I couldn't go to work because I now had no childcare. I had no one to look after Brad and I asked Rafel to collect him from the nursery. By now, it was a fact that we were trying to work on the marriage and he was going to see a therapist. However, we had an argument because I came in and he felt I hadn't said hello. I tried to talk to him about childcare so that I could go to work and he flew off the handle and started shouting, screaming and did what I described to my friends as him getting so angry he couldn't calm himself down. He threatened to finish me off and that I was treating him like a dog, that I hadn't said hello and I was ungrateful because he had picked up his son from the nursery for me. I had to point out to him that picking up and dropping off Brad was my daily routine, so he wasn't doing me any favours. He shouted and told me he would deal with me. He would teach me a lesson because I was disrespectful and didn't understand that he was the man. He said he would destroy me repeatedly, as though he needed to get my attention. He said I seemed to feel that because the papers and radio stations were showing me some attention, I was all that was important. I told him to leave my home because he was shouting and our son was covering his ears. He told me to call the police and I told him I wasn't afraid to do so. He told me as he left reluctantly, that he would ensure I paid for this and that he would not stop until he destroyed me.

I sent him several text messages saying that had he been a more responsible father, I wouldn't be suffering like this; had he taken his responsibility seriously as a husband, I wouldn't be in such a bind and be so stressed. Also, I sent him an email outlining how I felt. I avoided him and that was that. It wasn't unusual for him to shout and scream and argue over every little thing; everything was a threat to his manhood. I was once again saddened but knew his pattern. This was a normal pattern, or so I thought until at my desk at work one day, I received a call from the police to attend the station. I called a lawyer and we went together, only to be told that I was reported for harassment.

Everyone around me was shocked. There was something that Rafel was up to because it wasn't the first time he had argued with me, as the instigator of the argument. But the difference was, he didn't text it, he said it. I told myself that was it; the end. He had fully shown who he was. I needed to now pay attention. When I thought it couldn't get any worst, I received the court order for molestation and other orders including: residency; and non-removal; etc. enclosed in the documents. What was shocking was that he had copies of documents from my house he had never lived in. For example, my daughter's (not his child) birth certificate and my son's passport, which had never been in his possession. It was evident to me that he has been searching through my documents and house and scheming this for a while.

I really was most alarmed to see the number of times he had allegedly reported me to the police station over the years - even while staying in my bed - yet here we were trying to work on our marriage. It was evident this was all planned for his visa regularisation. He never meant to be with me. He saw me as a scapegoat and now that I called his bluff, insisting on him moving in he was executing his plan B; to use his son to access and regularise his papers. He had told me many stories of how silly us European women were because "Nigerian men" knew the loopholes to jump through to achieve what they needed.

I wrote to the Home Office twice, expressing how fearful I was that this man was using me for his visa. Sadly, the actions required to carry through with this each time frightened me because Rafel told me very subtle stories of how many women who crossed Nigerian men lost their kids. He joked about how he could take Brad and I would never be able to find him. To be honest, I think he had an undiagnosed psychological problem that was not outright, but benign.

My pastor, who had been determined to try and save our marriage, was happy to testify on my behalf at least, so he said. Everyone around me said the way he had behaved was indicative of a person looking for a visa into England but I was not clued up to that behaviour, sadly. I was very sad to realise how many hundreds and thousands of women and men in this country are exploited like this, daily. How a simple sperm donation, without the responsibilities, give you the right to act irresponsibly and then claim the human rights so readily available.

Rafel had already told me that he would never need me to get his papers, because he had a son and the UK law protected him. While I had no issues with him using the law, as it's such a door opener, I had a problem with the lengths he had chosen to go to discredit me. I wanted the court to see him as a lying witness, and also as someone who was deceptive, a thief, and unsuitable to look after my son.

I wanted him to have supervised visits in a contact centre and the molestation order to be contested, as well as the allegations to be verified and proven and the bans lifted because they had no credibility. I also wanted to check if he had a Nigerian passport in my son's name and for him to tell the court the truth if he had committed bigamy.

I loved my husband and in my mind I felt we were going to work. Instead, he had dropped me a bombshell with an additional cost, when he barely contributed to his child and to me as his wife. Words cannot begin to explain the emotions that have gone through me. I have learnt to love more carefully and save a piece of me for ME!

"Exit strategies can creep upon us so unknowingly."

Follow me on Twitter: @avabrown24

Chapter Thirty

THE WOMAN MADE OF STEEL AND STONE

"The strength you possess seemingly only truly gets found

when your back is braced hard against the wall."

———————

A few years later, I was sitting in the Marriott Hotel in Warsaw, Poland waiting to have dinner with someone who was going to help shape my life and give me yet another quantum leap forward. He flew me to Warsaw to discuss translating my book into Polish, which was at the time optioned to become a feature film.

Now forgive me for thinking small for a moment because I never envisaged that my book would even be translated into Spanish, the language that I was more intimate with, having grown up next door to Cuba, let alone an Eastern European language. Never, never, never and I dare say never, meaning not even in my wildest dreams did I see that coming.

Follow me on Twitter: @avabrown24

Life has not always been this way; you see it had only been two days since I made love with my husband and a day later he report me to the police! Because in my frustration I replied to an email I emailed him telling how disappointed and frustrated I felt he was a husband and as a father, but also as a human being. He treated me like I was nothing; as if I didn't exist. He came to my house, ate the largest plate of food that he didn't provide; I was caring for his son and myself which were his responsibilities; I was at the end of my tether; my health was waning; I had high blood pressure; and I was worn out mentally, emotionally and physically. I was fed up of him having sex with me in my sleep, disgracing, cursing me and having no regard for me. I placed how I felt on paper and sent him an email, but it went to his entire department at work. The truth was I was venting to him and it wasn't my intention for it to go to his team. This happened because I had an opened email that he sent me before and copied to his team. That said, many men who loved their wife or their child would be mad, but they'd deal with it, but no, not my then husband; he went to the police! He had already had a plan in place and naïve me didn't know he was already in his game. I wasn't aware he was planning his escape agenda and I played right into his hands. He needed an escape and a woman was waiting. A woman who was not just waiting but waiting in his office. I didn't know this. We hadn't yet had our decree Nisi and he was about to be wed in his culture, with the real wedding - the traditional African wedding - the one his customs and tradition respect. She had no British residency visa, I was told, so I guess I understand the urgency; after all, she had been in waiting for so long, she needed to get the golden prize. He told the police I was harassing him and I was a bad mother.

Understandably, my whole world started spinning. The world that was not long ago filled with me being featured in The Financial Times, The Guardian, on TV interviews to a raving fan-base and my bad childhood was now looking like it was about to turn a corner.

Let me take you back a bit. When I met my ex, I had never felt any such intent love. I was at low ebb and my advice to you is, never to do what I now call a rebound. I believe every experience is necessary, however. He was from West Africa and he pursued me so hard that eventually, I gave in. When I met him, he possessed nothing that I'd generally go for in a man. I took time to warm up to him but he was dedicated, persistent and he took a cultured interest in my daughter. The relationship was a different one, he claimed that his mother died and he was raped by his aunt at 12 and the stories were so close to mine that I soon feel like I had found my soul mate. Before I knew it, I was in love, even though I didn't know where he lived because he made it his duty to visit me always. I kept asking to visit him, but he wouldn't let me. He said as a teacher I couldn't visit him because he lived with drug dealers and he didn't want me to lose my job. Oh, I was gullible and I believed each word. You see this medicine - his awesome love making, was a pacifier each time. Regardless of what wrongs he did me, he would show up at my home and stay a few days and the medicine fixed me. I started wanting more and he kept saying he needed time. We were now in role reversal. I was starting to feel I was losing control because he started monitoring my friends and in his view, every man wanted to sleep with me. I was his drug and before I realised it I was pregnant and he was living with another woman. I soon realised that was the reason I couldn't visit him at his home. I was about to lose my mind because not only did I feel the fool, I was played by him and his so called family. They all knew, but led me on to believe I was his everything. I was pregnant and was feeling trapped and so I invited him to come and discuss our choices. Of course, he was reluctant at first and when he did come he told me he was unsure of what his friends and family would think when they knew I was pregnant with him. He said it with such disdain. The rest of that saga ended up with him walking away

Follow me on Twitter: @avabrown24

from me the same day he found out that I was pregnant. I ran to him down crying and begging him to stay. The next day he came back saying he was immature and made a mistake and he was sorry and wanted us to take this seriously. Of course, the fool I was, meant I made love to him there and then and felt my world was finally on the right path, until I got dressed and he told me he wanted us to do things the right way and that's why he wanted me to have an abortion. Well, the moment I said no, he vanished, for five whole months I carried that child in me and I almost literally lost my mind. I was lost, my job was on the line and I couldn't cope. I was shocked, depressed and maybe even suicidal. I didn't want to have another child and on my own. My daughter was 11 and I certainly didn't want another child, not like this. This sudden tragedy as I called it, saw me broke and abandoned. Life was so hard my friend dropped £100 every time I visited her. I was the scum of the earth begging not to live. I ended up on the dole ashamed and wanted to die. The baby was rejected yet again by me; it's own mother. Life dragged by and I was so tormented. I had dreadlocks and in the interest of passing time, I sat down and used a pin to remove every piece of my locks. What I was left with was my afro on my head, looking like the mess I was in. Days seemed like years and years a whole lifetime. I locked myself away and found myself almost among the walking dead, rejected by a man who when I'd met him, hadn't been to the dentist once in his life and was wearing and owned dirty Primark underwear. Yet, there I was, pregnant with his seed and later dumped by him. But I had to live. There was my daughter who needed me and so I had to go on. I recall feeling like I was in prison.

One day and I saw him on the bus, I was huge about five months gone and the man didn't even look at me twice. I ended up losing the baby and I must say I felt relieved. R.I.P - Matthew Josiah Brown. I loved you baby, sorry for everything. Immediately after this, he came looking for me

Follow me on Twitter: @avabrown24

apologising and saying he was having dreams that he needed to come back to me. What I now believe is that he heard I was no longer pregnant and so he came back then. At the time, I didn't see or feel that so I took him back thinking he had grown up. It's stupid but I felt that I needed him. Perhaps a medical person can explain this sick behaviour to me, but I felt he was all I needed, only weeks after I lost his child.

Once again he said he was sorry, he cried and he knelt down and asked me to forgive him and like the mug I was, I believed him. A few months later, I found out he had lied to me again. You see limited vision and fear and a lack of self-esteem can cripple you. You can easily stay in a relationship that is abusive. I couldn't see my way out so I stayed. I heard the critical voice of a single mother with two failed relationships. "It's all your fault." Fear, the most subtle and destructive of all human diseases, took me over. At my age, fear held me back from doing what I knew was right. It paralysed me and placed me in a hyponastic spell. I gave up on me and I wished I had walked away then, but that wasn't the bigger picture for my life.

What happened next was enough to have awakened me, yet, I slept in fear. I fell pregnant again by him after we went for our first scan he and I went into Primark to shop for clothing as I was getting very big really fast. He picked up every piece of maternity clothing on the racks, but as soon as we approached the cashier he stood at the entrance of the payment line and left me alone. At that moment, I was over him. It was over because I was noted that this man never had anything to give, beside his medicine but was always diplomatically ready to take. I think if I am honest in that moment I left him emotionally, but physically I was tied to him. He left that day and went to his place. Yes, he always kept a room for himself and in hindsight I should have realised that this was evident of someone who was never committed, but I didn't understand it. He used me in so many ways and I was far too naive at the time to see. Our relationship was a mixture of quarrels, fights and arguments, constantly. I couldn't understand the contentious type of relationship we were having because it was as though a spirit lived in our relationship. When my son was born he wasn't around, in fact, my mother called him that day, only to find a woman answering his phone saying he was in the shower. Need I say anymore? Did he live in one room in a shared house? Can you imagine what happened before he went in the shower on the eve of his son's birth? The week that followed my son's birth are days I can never forget. Rafel decided he was going to come and visit his son. Now, he wasn't there throughout the pregnancy, and as a matter of fact, during my pregnancy he claimed to have lost his father. But I couldn't say who he was and whether anything he told me was correct. I don't know if the lady I met was his stepmother, or, in fact, his woman's mother, nothing was for sure. It was all a blur, and now I don't give a toss what was the truth anymore.

I remember one morning when I was pregnant, I went to his house on my way to work and what I saw nearly send me into early labour. I was just in time to see him getting ready for an outing with a middle-aged woman in her car. To him I was invisible, although I was heavily pregnant. I was broken-hearted and I can't say if it was the reality of what was in front of me; or the fact that I was carrying his child, which made me so angry. I was fuming. He later told me after she left that the lady was his aunt who raped him. Yeah right! It is still unproven and even though I got married to him in London she had shown up. In the same period, he lost his father or so he said and I was fool enough to visit him to give him some money in the form of a loan to help him with his ticket and other expenses to return to his country to bury his father; remember he never had any money. Years later, I realised I was merely his ATM and he wasn't in fact as broke as he proclaimed he was.

Follow me on Twitter: @avabrown24

Back to the day of my son's visit; for the first time after my mum spoke to that lady in his room, she called my home that same night, two days after I gave birth. Now what you need to know is that when I gave birth at the hospital by C-section there was no one at home to help me. It was my young daughter who took a cab home with me. It was a lonely journey home. I cried privately on my way home. The fairytale I had was cast-off and I was left alone. Though the doctors said no driving for weeks, I had to get into my jeep to get a car seat and pushchair for the baby. It was hard, what choice did I have? On my way back my daughter called me in tears, I could feel my stitches tingling as she told me the same girl who was in his room while he was in the shower had threatened her to throw acid on us - the kids - and me. She told my daughter she knew where I lived and I was to leave her man alone. I hurriedly drove back home only to find my mother at the gate with a knife waiting for me to come home. Now get this - mum was visiting from Jamaica, it was her first visit and she was jolted with fear for me. I got home and called him but of course, he lied as always, telling me it wasn't his ex-blah blah. It was not until I told him I was calling the police that he admitted she was his ex.

I didn't believe him but what he used to capitalise on that and softened me up so he could visit my son. Believe it or not he was even late and you would think that him knowing I was pregnant would mean that for the nine months he was collecting items like diapers and such for his son? Well, he turned up with a Peacock bag with four pieces of clothing for his son they didn't fit because my son was a big baby. Of course, he couldn't know this because he was absent. Before long my mother was wooed by him too and we were at it again. It all had happened rather fast and the signs I saw then, I ignored them because I felt trapped and in so deep that I couldn't turn back.

Have you ever felt like this in any aspect of your life?

Follow me on Twitter: @avabrown24

Some of my signs were namely:

- The night before we got married he slept in his room and was on the phone with his acid-threatening ex.
- He lied that he had lost his job, but in fact he was fired.
- He wasn't providing for his infant son.
- He was extra nice and promised that he really wanted a family and was glad God blessed us not just with a child but a son. The day of the wedding if I explain how I ended up there I would be lying. I didn't want to go, I felt heavy and knew I was making a big mistake this time. My first marriage wasn't a mistake, but this had red flag written all over it.
- I have never seen him early for anything, but he was on time for the wedding and what was very interesting for me was the sign that was revealed to me in the registrar's office.
- We had to meet and go over some paper details and a part of this process meant we needed to pay for the certificates. Well, what do you know, I was thinking marriage so I had money for two licenses and brought that out but he only had had money for one. If that wasn't a sign to run, nothing else was.
- The wedding went ahead and it was a dark day.
- There was no help and care - he had done nothing - I did all the work.
- I realise now that I was the worker bee for this man.
- The day ended and life went back to normal as he went back to his room and me to my house.

I felt like I was pawned to the lowest bidder. Things start going further downhill once we got married, we had constant arguments and he started treating me as though he owned me; not in a respectful way but more of; "I have the keys now you can sit and not move until I opened the door." There was something in my heart telling me there was more to this than I was realising. My intuition was telling me to wake up and listen.

As a result, I gave him an ultimatum. I told him we needed to be living together. He agreed and so Annie, my friend and I started looking at apartments online. I was willing to move out of the home I found comfortable, with my kids who were settled into a new place to please this man. I desperately wanted my marriage to work; I felt a sense of guilt from having already had a failed marriage, two kids, being on my own and feeling the pressure that is created around having a black boy in Britain. I didn't want to be a single mother again and all those fears came over me. I know I was settling, but I didn't care. Can anyone identify with a point in your life when you have settled?

Here I was settling, I wasn't getting any help from him for the mortgage, food, bills, etc. but I was ready to move in with him. My self-worth was on the floor. I got an au pair from Spain and she turned out far too intense for me, but it was his behaviour towards me that had me wondering what was going on. Anyway, I wasn't paying that any attention as we were all going to be moving in together i.e. my kids and husband and getting support from him would mean I wouldn't need the au pair. Wow, that was such wishful thinking.

In that period I was nominated for London's Leadership Peace Awards, Women for Africa Award, Diva of Colours Awards and more importantly, I was asked to be the guest speaker at Merton Young People Awards ceremony. This was my first paid speaking gig and I was totally excited. I would be addressing 300 people including parents and dignitaries. I was over the moon. I invited my friends Sher and Annie, as well as my husband. To my surprise, he failed to turn up saying he had work. A part of me couldn't believe it. I spoke at the awards ceremony and got a brilliant reception. I ran into former colleagues from my supply teaching days who were attending. I can't forget one girl called Dee, a teacher with whom I worked, asking me what I was doing there. I told her I was one of the guests. I didn't say guest speaker to be honest as she was one of the white teachers that made me feel unworthy back in my teaching days. As I walked off from her, I went to sit in the reserved seat left for me right in the second row. Wow, my friends and I were sat right behind the dignitaries. I had a little tear in my eye and I pinched myself privately.

Now be mindful, I had never heard of this school before the day the email came into my inbox. But they wanted me to be their guest speaker so I needed to deliver. I recall sending various emails back and forth asking questions like how many people would be there and what ages group etc. I needed to be great because this was what I wanted to do for the rest of my life.

Soon after that, I was invited to speak in Ireland at the Africa Black History month where my book was to be launched as well. I was delighted and jumped at this opportunity that my beloved Norma Jean had arranged for me. Norma Jean - though my first ex's cousin - loved me with a love so pure and so divine and I loved her back even more. I was so happy to be getting international exposure and I jumped at the opportunity. My then husband was meant to pay for all of us to attend and to be honest this wasn't going to cost more than £700 but he wasn't able to find it. Wow, later on, I will show you where his money was going. It was decided that I go alone so, I asked my very good friend Voneta to accompany me.

I was all packed for Ireland and he offered to stay at my house with the au pair to help ensure Brad was okay. I had no issue and thought it was great. He was, if for no other reason, almost forced by default to look after his child, and so I was happy. To my surprise, he took the opportunity to stay in my house and scour through my documents, stealing all he needed, regarding my private papers, to make his next move. I had just bought him his first car and he was chuffed. Just before I went to Ireland, he kept telling me that his office was giving him issues over his visa and he was inadvertently loading more pressure on my shoulders, worrying about his visa application. While in Ireland, I sent him pictures of the event, trying to encourage him to be a part of my world, yet he was very distant. Something wasn't right.

Now don't get me wrong, he was never a very mushy person; at least not to me and the kids. Yet, I had a need for some more warmth and though I was travelling promoting my first book, I thought at least he would be happy for me. There was flat coke, no fizz; he wasn't even responding. I recall something in my spirit telling me something wasn't right back home with him and the au pair and I as sat on the hotel bed, I called home. I recall Voneta asking me why I felt that and I told her I wasn't sure I was just feeling that way. I called home and though it was not even eight in the evening, no one answered. The au pair's mobile went unanswered. His mobile and the house phone rang out. My heart and head were uneasy and to date not that it matters anymore, I knew something about that night wasn't right. I got the au pair after many attempts. She came on the phone and the first thing she said in a sleepy voice was that he was sleeping. I will leave the rest for you to make of it what you desire.

Another episode that showed the strain I was under - once the court order was in place was that it crippled my ability to work effectively - when I was excited about my workshop at Canada Water Library. For some reason I knew I needed to check the court order once more and as I stood in my bedroom the paper fell from my hand when I stared at the time. I needed to have my son at McDonalds at 12 pm and he was to be picked up at 6pm. "Wow" was all I could think. Luckily, I had actually checked it because, not only would I be stuck with my son at McDonalds but I would also not be able to make my workshop! All those people who had paid to come to the workshop would have been let down; my brand's reputation was now on the line. Unfortunately, my daughter Jasmine who would normally help me in times such as these, had booked her driving test and couldn't help me. I started crying. I felt overwhelmed and frustrated. I was frustrated because Rafel wasn't the one who was feeding, clothing him or paying the costs his son's childcare was incurring. I was busy trying to make a livelihood and there were shackles on my feet. I needed to be free. I was crying when my son came in and he asked me why I was crying but more so who was making me cry. Of course, I dared not tell him. I hugged him and told him mummy was having a sad moment. Jasmine tried to cancel her driving test but couldn't and truth be told I wouldn't want her to either. I insisted that she went. I called my friend Annie and couldn't express myself well enough to her. I was crying and she was asking what was wrong and if the kids were okay. I couldn't speak because all I was doing was crying. I needed to be cleansed of all the pain I was seemingly carrying from all this man - Rafel - had done to me in the past year. The pain I thought I had let go of already was still there lingering and festering like an old wound of pure puss.

"Purging is absolutely necessary at different phases of our lives, but purgingonly becomes effective if you truly grasp why you are being purged."

Follow me on Twitter: @avabrown24

Chapter Thirty One

WHY THIS CAGED BIRD SANG

"Storms don't always kill you; they toss you about, and give you resilient muscles that make you 'rare metal'. They teach you to dig deeper for stuff you never knew you possessed."

———————

What happened next can only be outlined in telling you that I spent the next two years in court. I became totally broke with bailiffs on my door. I went without even having lunch at work and the lists goes on. I won't tell all that happened because my next book will go into this aspect of my life.

Now that was it, all over with Rafel. I want to express to you one last time, the lessons learnt and what this entire experience had done to me, my kids, our lives, our space, privacy, and our mind-set. Indeed, it was an utter shock to see the deception that was masterminded around me and unbeknown to me. I must say it sunk me into a place that saw me unwashed for five days.

Follow me on Twitter: @avabrown24

I stank, I became a zombie and my two kids saw me at a stage no child should see their parents. We went through moments of being unable to find food, as I struggled to pay the barristers' fees and it got to the point where bailiffs were on my doorstep. I had to stop paying my mortgage, which landed me in arrears and I lost my house in the process. I fell into deep debt that saw my utility bills unpaid, my inability to buy petrol in the winter and I had to wrap my son in a blanket as I dropped him off to school for days. What was most heart breaking was that what my husband did, saw me unable to pay his son's nursery fees for six months, nearly losing his place and me bending on hands and knees to the council for a payment plan. It broke me, and broke the spirit and wellbeing of my kids. I struggled between dislike, indifference and pain.

I struggled between whether I should reconcile with the man I loved, made wild passionate love to and had a child with, or not. The man I truly felt I had a future with and yes, it was rocky, but I truly felt that was it. And we were turning a corner when he said we would live together. I was so happy, I called Annie and shared the good news. I was ready to compromise to be his. The man I shared my meat, bed and even a t-shirt with.

The deception got even deeper to things I now know that I won't reveal in this book or ever. As time went on, I moved from dislike, hurt and pain to recovery because I pushed through the birth canal and bore greater purpose. I recalled one day I found something that was so - shocking - as I was sat at home just about to jump on a radio interview and the tears streamed down my face in between the interview. But believe me, I pushed through and that pain gradually became anger and the anger became desire and the desire became a relentless fight not to let him win.

Today, I have come to a place of ease, content and thankfulness. I have forgiven him and I needed to because, by not forgiving him I would be holding myself the prisoner. You see, what he meant for my bad had

Follow me on Twitter: @avabrown24

become my best good. He left me, dumped me and abandoned me, but God took me up. More importantly, since he left the sunrays came and that has been the best thing of all this ever since I released him. I understand that winners win and losers loose. I understand he had to do what he came to do, but I wished he had thought of all the good I did for him and we will always be parents to a wonderful child who one day will know all of the truth. I may never talk to him, but we share a son and for that reason and that reason alone I will say I wished him well. Of all he did, he ignited a victor in me, and I thanked him. I celebrated him and I truly wish that all the deception and hurt me had to make me endure paid off. May I make it known here and now because I have nothing to lose, I loved him so much and at times was too afraid even to make him know how much I loved him. Forgiven he is -

I really have - and wish him and his family, kids, partner and future God's blessings.

Overall, I went through hell throughout my life, but this one floored me. I was convicted of harassment by him and appealed and won. I was meant to die, this man I fell in love with wanted to see me dead.

In fact, he had a woman in waiting all this time and they had been uniting against me with one common goal. However, I have come to learn that the woman I am today has been elevated by what was meant to be my pain. This pain has helped to fashion me more into my purpose. I've shared stages with great speakers such as Eric Thomas, Nick Vujicic and Lisa Nicholas and I have a movie that is being produced about my life for a feature film.

Pain has certainly become purpose. I have learnt to be patient, more forgiving, not to settle and to wait for my real king to cherish me. Today, I walk in my God's assignment, thanking my ex for leaving me, because that resulted in me becoming a better woman and mother, who has decided

Follow me on Twitter: @avabrown24

not to be anyone's footstool but to see the signs and refuse to ignore them at the onset. I walk not knowing the man who was made to love me and is going to honour and respect me, as I too will adore and pour all of me into him. Whatever opens you up is never as important as what it opens. The field that is open is what truly matters.

The journey of this man Rafel had taken me through the criminal justice system, at one stage I was between criminal court and family court. The truth of the matter is the man didn't want me. He wanted a way out and our frequent arguments were as a result of the fact that he was always going to leave, but my pressure to insist he moved in with us because my son was now three and we were still living part. He always had a room, he would use traditional and culture to blame his reason and his argument at 2am was so he could leave to warm the bed of his then in my vie mistress, was a normal part of our marriage.

In the end, I appeared at the criminal court after I was found guilty of harassment appealed and I won. The judge was shocked and saddened that he did such a thing. He saw through the case quickly and as for the family court the man turned up with a Jamaican barrister who obviously was a tactical move, now this is from the man who didn't have money to even top up his oyster card. Here we were, he was paying a barrister, the man who could not help with the rent or nursery here we were he was saving all his money to take me to court. That explains why he was always broke, I was once again played and this is what financial abuse in a relationship looks like.

I was mortified and fainted from shock in the court bathroom. That was the man who, five weeks prior, accepted his first car, bought by me. The man, five weeks earlier, was in my bedroom making love with me. Nothing was making sense. I went through all sorts of emotions: frustration, deception and the list goes on. I was in cold sweats in the court and I had to compose myself. I was, after all, there to answer all counts. Those counts included: irresponsible mother, mentally ill mother, a probated test order and non-molestation order. The man had reported me to the police even days after he made love to me. You see, he was in the planning stages always, now don't get me wrong our marriage was tumultuous, but the truth is, there were areas that were workable and our issues were not bigger than any other couple, except that he had his hidden agenda and regardless of what I did, it would never work. It was doomed to failure before we started. I had no chance of making it work. There were always three of us, and at points, maybe even six in my marriage.

I won't lament it anymore, but to say that in the end he hardly saw his son, he didn't care enough. My son was at primary school and his father didn't know the name of his school, his teacher, when he was ill, where he played rugby or who his friends were. The bottom line was he had accepted in court to only see his son 12 times per year. It is still my hope that when he truly decides to love his son like a father really loves his child, he may decide to get involved. I am leaving the door wide open for my son's sake.

When I discovered he was getting married only two days after he was in court with me being vile as always, a case that ended after 26 months in court and many thousand dollars in debt later. It was over. My son would see his father 12 times a year in a centre. He didn't fight because this time the judge who had been saving my case for herself was ill and my own regular barrister had some personal business to attend to. As a result, I got a new judge and a new barrister. And she was not impressed! This man had not seen his son for three months and when asked when next he could be available he said in a month's time. That was a whole four weeks later and to top it off, he said he wasn't able to pay the £20 per month that it would take. Parts of me thought happy riddance and the sad part of me thought about my poor son. He deserved better, but I couldn't be his dad and mum combined, I could only be the best version of a mother I could be.

I walked away from court and thanked God this part of the journey was over and the reason he didn't fight this time was owing to the fact that the judge had said if he was to have his son, he would have to let me know where he was living. Of course, you know the rest of the story because his woman in waiting, in my view was living there and after her long wait he couldn't spoil it. Moreover, the weddings plans were on the way. I wasn't even bothered as I was too over him and far too focused now my new future to even care.

I was singing one of my favourite poems - in my head - Maya Angelo's Why the Caged Bird Sings.

"They say the truth shall vindicate you, sometimes your vindication takes more time than you think, but don't get impatient it does come."

Follow me on Twitter: @avabrown24

Chapter Thirty Two

THE SECRET WITNESS
WRITTEN BY AUDREIA JOSEPHS

"Icebergs are always only seen from the surface, thankfully s

ome people dive deeper and see the unseen -that which

the naked eyes can't see."

———————

As I write this, the first words that come to my mind are that this lady is a complete enigma. The dictionary definition of the word enigma states: mystery; paradox; a puzzling or inexplicable occurrence; or situation. I call Dr. Ava Eagle Brown an enigma because there is no better word to describe her.

I first met Ava in 2015. Even our meeting was a mystery.

I was at home in the day, one July day. I was watching the TV and there on the SKY TV were five amazing women who were doing a UK book tour called, The Phenomenal Women's Book Tour. They mentioned all the

Follow me on Twitter: @avabrown24

cities that they were going to host the book tour in. My city of Birmingham was on the list. The key speaker of the group was called Ava Brown. She mentioned that they would be coming to the DRUM event centre in Birmingham and gave the time and date, and that it was a free event. I hurriedly wrote the date on my calendar.

The date came and it was a beautiful sunny day. I ended up leaving home late. I had some running around to do before I could attend the event. I was upset with myself because I normally like to arrive at events early to get my seat, and to be relaxed.

The event was meant to start at 2pm and I was still in the city at 1.50pm. I needed to get a bus in a hurry.

I looked and saw one solitary double decker bus. I made my mind up that I was going to be on that bus. There were lots of people pushing to get on the bus. I joined the pushing and shoving to get on as well. There were two women holding up the queue to get on. They were asking for change. I thought they must be from out of town, because Birmingham people know you must already have the correct change for our buses. One of the ladies was quite tall and had on a beautiful wide brimmed hat and a beautiful light salmon coloured summer dress. The shorter lady of the two ladies came up with some change and paid the bus fare. I managed to get on the bus not far behind them and I got a seat next to a very friendly lady. It was now almost 2pm. I breathed deeply and said to myself that all is well. During the bus journey, I started wondering if the two ladies were attending the same event and if they knew where they were going? As I was sitting at the very front of the bus, I decided to ask the driver if the two women were looking for the DRUM venue. The driver said yes they are. By now I had got to the area where the event was to be held. I got off the bus and decided to wait for the ladies, to show them where it was. The two ladies also got off the bus and I asked them if they were look for the DRUM venue and if they were attending the book tour event?

They both smiled and the smaller of the two ladies put her hand out and introduced herself. "Hello, I'm Ava Brown, the organizer."

The other lady introduced herself too and "Wow!" I thought to myself these are the ladies I had seen on the TV. I had not recognized them because I had not seen their faces on the bus. We talked all the way to the venue.

The whole event was amazing. It ignited a fire inside me. A few weeks later, I had a discovery book writing session with Ava and that was the day she became my coach. After that conversation, I discovered there was a writer inside me. I knew we were going to become friends when she said she did not work on a weekend, but yet called me three weekends in a row to help me with my book writing. Ava's daughter had a major eye problem and she confided in me that her daughter was due to have major eye surgery. Her daughter also had bouts of unexplained illness at recurring times. She kept moving even when I could hear the fear in her voice. Ava did her Facebook videos every day and even started speaking about her daughter's eye surgery. Every time we spoke, I could see or hear her son in the background. Ava was and is so gentle with her son; even when he asked question after question. She gently answered them all. I told her that I had seen quite a few of her Facebook pictures and that it was wonderful how she brought him to most of her speaking events. She told me she had child care issues because she did not any family in the UK and had no choice but to bring him everywhere she went, which is not convenient in some instances. Ava's daughter was a few weeks post-surgery. Ava had booked a Caribbean trip for her and her two children. She told me she might not be able to go due to her estranged husband. She told me she had been in court with him for the past almost 18 months and he was trying to stop her from traveling. Ava was not letting him stop her from traveling and contacted her lawyer to get the matter sorted. The matter was resolved and Ava and her children went on their well overdue vacation.

While Ava was on vacation I read her first book Bamboo and Fern. I was totally amazed after reading about all she had been through, that she was so well adjusted. As soon as Ava got back to the UK from her vacation she was back in full work mode. She could not spend any longer than 10 days away, due to the fact she had to appear in court, with her estranged husband. She was told by the court that if she did not attend they would issue a warrant for her arrest. It was not long after this incident that Ava got very got very ill. I was worried, but felt better when her medical tests came back with the all clear. Ava was told she had high blood pressure and had to rest. She said there was no way she could rest because she was a single parent and the only breadwinner. She was also working to support some of her family back in Jamaica. Ava's main worry was that if something happened to her, who would be there for her children? At this point she was in the process of editing my book and several other people's books as well. Also, she was caring for her daughter; being asked to speak at events; planning her online seminars, etc. And at the same time telling me about an anthology she was planning on putting together. Plus telling me how much she missed her mum. She told me she had tried to bring her mother to the UK to help her with her children. She had tried on several occasions - and each time she had got her hopes up - only for the application to be turned down, which really disappointed her. Whenever she spoke about how much she missed her mum, my heart cried for her. As a mother and grandmother, I wished we lived closer and I always told her she was too far away from me. I presently have 13 grandchildren, so it would be no problem to add Ava's son in the mix.

It was February 2016 and Ava had supported me to complete my first book. Ava had mentioned a few days earlier that her birthday was coming up.. But that she no longer celebrated it, due to sharing the same date with her younger sister, who had passed away a few years ago. I called her to wish her a beautiful day, and she told me that of all days, she was yet again in court with her estranged husband. Everything was a mess that day. Ava was in tears. The female judge decided to retain her case and spoke in favour off the absent father. She would have to drive for more than an hour, to the other side of the city, so that her son's father could have visiting rights. Most of the time when Ava made those journeys on a early Sunday morning, she called me in tearful frustration. Telling me how unfair and one-sided the system was. I had never seen the system in this form before and even I was frustrated at how badly she was treated by it. After her tears, she dried them up and did a Facebook video. She knew there were people who depended on what she had to say. She constantly motivated and empowered other people with her words. And you could trust her to keep it real. While waiting in her car, she would also work on the product she was about to launch.

Ava told me about the empowerment TV programme she was also about to record and launch. She called me afterwards and told me about her day and how tired she was; after all the recording and changing clothing about seven times. Then she had to rush to the nursery to pick her son up. Then home to cook, then out to a speaking engagement. When I saw the pilot for this TV programme, Ava stood out.
She was very engaging, light-hearted and entertaining.

We launched my book in February. It was an overwhelming experience. Ava and her children traveled all the way from London to Birmingham to attend my book launch. She was an amazing midwife in helping me to give birth to my book. After the book launch, my family and I went to my

Follow me on Twitter: @avabrown24

younger sister's house and celebrated my book launch and Ava's birthday. I wanted her and her family to know she was now a part of my family. She said; "You are my British mum now."

It's an honour to be thought of in that way. In actual fact, I am one year younger than Ava's mum. It was also during this time that through our conversations, we discovered she shared a cousin with my husband.

When Ava started her webinar conference called Purposewalk, she worked so hard to bringing that event together. She interviewed various speakers from all around the world. It was a great successful event.

Meanwhile, Ava was still going backward and forwards to court. Ava's estranged husband kept telling the court of how afraid he was of her. She told me that he had previously told the police that she had been violent towards him, so he pressed charges against her. She received no kind of support, financial or otherwise and every Sunday driving for hours across to the other side of London for her son's visit with his father at the contact center.

During that time, the anthology a book, which I had also been invited to be involved with, was picking up speed and gaining more and more authors. It was also round about this time that Ava started speaking about bringing Eric Thomas to the UK. She said watch and see. I am going to bring him here. During the next few weeks Ava spoke to and connected with Eric's office, until one day she actually spoke to Eric himself. When she told me how much money was involved to bring a well-known speaker to the UK, I was in shock. I had only briefly heard about Eric Thomas. It was Ava that really introduced his work to me.

Ava had received some money from the company she used to work for. She had told me about her dream car. Now she had the money to put that dream on hold and buy another car of lesser value so she could invest in getting Eric Thomas and his team to the UK.

Follow me on Twitter: @avabrown24

One day, Ava called me excitedly telling me she was going to be given an honorary Doctorate. I was so happy for her. At first I thought that the graduation ceremony was going to take place in Ava's hometown of London. One day she called me to say the ceremony was taking place in my hometown of Birmingham.

I thought I would love to be there. But I also knew that it was by invitation only. She told me she would have loved it if I could be there, but that all of her allocated tickets were taken. I understood.

Ava and I video called each other. Sometimes she called me while waiting in the car for her son's nursery to end. At times, she was so busy she had to let him join the after school club. He loved it because it gave him the opportunity to play with the other children for even longer and it also gave Ava time to complete the various projects she constantly had on the go. I got to see her and her son's interaction. She was sad about the fact she had not had another child with her husband because this would have been company for her son. He was a highly intelligent and very active little boy and I have watched Ava having to switch from whatever she was doing to give him her full attention. I mentioned how I thought she was an amazing mother. She always replied by saying;" I don't have a choice." Sometimes, her son hugged her or drew pictures for her. He said;

"I drew this for you mummy." In those moments,

I felt so touched and emotional to be a witness of those tender moments. I would let her know how much of a gift he is. She also knew. Whenever Ava told me about her day, I said to her, I was exhausted just listening, let alone physically doing it. I once jokingly asked her if she was a twin, because she must have the other one hidden. Because in my mind there was no way one woman could keep up with all of the demands that were placed on her. She laughed and said; "No, it's just me, no twin." I had to ask again, do you ever sleep? She just laughed again. Yet, again I came off the call thinking, Wow this woman is ten women in one!

Ava's daughter was now accepted into University. She was 18 years old. They both had a difference of opinion, which ended up in a big disagreement. Ava said she was no longer bringing her daughter to the graduation ceremony and I could attend the event. I told Ava I would not accept the ticket on that basis. I told her that her daughter needed to be there and that years down the road, when she looked back at the pictures, it would not be right if her daughter did not attend such an important family occasion. Ava had also applied to the Home Office with a view of getting her mother to the UK to attend her graduation ceremony. They denied her mother a visa eight days before the ceremony. Yet again, she was devastated and in tears. I am not fully sure of what happened, but someone who was invited to the graduation ceremony ended up not being able to attend, so I was offered the opportunity to attend.

A few days later, Ava called to tell me she had become an ambassador for a homeless charity and she was going to be working out on the streets that very night. She told me this was a project very close to her heart because she had experience homelessness before in her life.

During our various conversations, Ava mentioned she would love to see her book become a movie. She even put it on her vision board. Ava had acted in few Nollywood movies before and the latest film she was in was due to premiere later in the year. Not long after that conversation, she made contact with someone who caused her to dream even bigger and to start seeing there was a possibility that her movie could happen.

When Ava came to Birmingham for her honorary graduation ceremony, she came with her son and daughter and her best friend Silvie. I had previously met Ava's children but I had never met her friend before and I knew we would get on very well. It was a gut feeling. It was a long and

Follow me on Twitter: @avabrown24

very hot June, but I was so truly honoured to be there. Plus it was a few days after my birthday.

By now Ava was in full flow of organizing bringing Eric Thomas to the UK and she had found a venue and started advertising the event. I saw how hard she worked to obtain the money to do this. At times I could hear the worry in her voice, because she did not have enough money. She said to me, where am I going to find the money? Every penny she earned went out faster than it came in. Whenever she got to the edge I wished I was a woman of means. I wanted to help her financially. I knew she could pull this event off. At the time, Ava was also building her mother a house in Jamaica. She is the eldest of her siblings and there was a lot of expectation placed upon her shoulders. While all of this was happening, there were people who only got in her space just so they could use her. People tried to use her to raise their own profile or so they could cheat and rip her off. In the meantime, she was working every possible hour to raise money to bring Eric Thomas to the UK, as well as paying lawyers and court fees, supporting her family in Jamaica, and her own family here. I often told her that her life was sweet and sour; meaning that when something negative happened, then the sweet was on its way. Sometimes I heard her quote me in her Facebook videos. Whenever she mentioned my name, I think, "Stop mentioning my name, people must be thinking who is Audreia Josephs?"

Ava told me she wanted to get Lisa Nichols to do an event in the UK. I said to her, are you for real on top of everything else that you are doing? She knew how much I loved Lisa. She also knew I had Lisa on my vision board. In June Ava was invited to speak in Madrid, Spain. Yet, again she had childcare issues. She asked her daughter to take her son to nursery and arranged for her close friend to pick him up. In the meantime, she had to fly out of the UK very early in the morning, do the event and leave Madrid late evening to arrive back in the UK the same day. If she was away from her son for more than a day, he cried for his mum endlessly. This was always the case. If she attempted to do an evening speaking engagement he clung to her and cried and let her know how much he would miss her and didn't want her to go. It was these moments that caused her to stop doing evening events. His tears broke her heart especially knowing that she was all he had.

During making the arrangements to bring Eric Thomas to the UK, Ava made contact with someone in Poland. They wanted her to bring him to an event that they were putting on. This was a very big event that they also wanted her to speak at. Ava was worried because this would be an overnight trip to discuss the details. This was of great concern to Ava, but she also knew it was an important trip she needed to do. She arranged childcare with her daughter She also cooked and got everything in order in her home. When she arrived in Poland, Ava was treated to first class. She video-called me to let me know she had arrived safely and the meeting was a success. They also wanted to translate her book into Polish. It was very overwhelming for her. These were the times I could see the little girl in her, excited and scared at the same time. I understood both feelings, and reassured her it was okay to feel that way because she was creating a new path for other people to follow. She never dreamt her book would get to Poland. In next breath, she was calling home to speak to her children. She had already spoken to them, but now she had to read a bedtime story to her son. As soon as she got back from Poland she had yet another court appearance. After court her estranged husband saw her in the car park and went down on his knees and apologized for all he had put her through. He said the wanted to end all of the court drama. She told him he was the one who had started all of this. She took him for coffee and they spoke. Deep down Ava did not trust him and wanted to know what he was up to.

Life kept moving for Ava. She was still caring for her sick daughter; making her regular court appearances with her estranged husband;

Follow me on Twitter: @avabrown24

winning awards; helping people to write their books; hosting online workshops and giving away so much free content; coaching; arranging events; and supporting her clients, myself included. She was working on her book to become a Hollywood movie - the anthology book – as well as driving for hours with her five year old son to the other side of the city and having to rush from wherever she was to pick her son up at nursery for 6pm. If anyone had ever seen Ava's Facebook video's they were usually done while she was sitting in her car, while waiting to pick her son up, or if she was unable to make one, then she would do it when he was in the car while parked somewhere. Those moments made me laugh because her son was in the child seat at the back trying to get his face and voice on the video. He usually had something to say. At times he quoted Eric Thomas. Ava turned around and said can you please be quiet that only stopped him for a few minutes. He had a speaker as a mother, so of course naturally he wanted to speak as well. He was very smart and entertaining. There were days when her son was not in nursery she dropped everything she was doing to have a date with her son and daughter. Ava had feelings of guilt that she was not doing enough for them. These were the times when we talked in depth. I let her know that as a mother who did not get it right with my children, she was doing an amazing job. And how proud I was of her.

Ava was also lonely, lonely for companionship and someone to share life with. They were some of the things that made me feel sad, because I saw what a beautiful and kind person she was. And it was sad to know that she had such a rough deal. I often told her if I could create the man of her dreams I would, and we laughed. But as always, I told her that everything we go through; we are either teaching or learning.

Ava was not only speaking to Lisa Nichols team, but Lisa herself. And she booked Lisa as a keynote speaker for an event she was hosting. Ava was also confident that Lisa would write the foreword to the Anthology that I was now a part of. Ava called me to tell me she was also invited to speak at an event in Washington on the same platform as Sheryl Lee Ralph. We were both so excited because Sheryl Lee Ralph is a Jamaican. Ava is a Jamaican and I was born in the UK to Jamaican parents - a British born - Jamaican!We were flying the flag. In one breath she was totally excited and in the other, she started worrying about childcare issues because she had to be away for a few days.

Yet again, Ava had to drive all the way to the other side of the city so her son could have contact with his father. The journey was made more complicated when the roads she used were closed and she was directed to drive through an area she did not know. She got to the contact centre late only to be told her son's father had not turned up. I was on the call with her trying to keep her calm. When she spoke to the person in charge they were very casual about it. She was mad about it because she and her family were in the Midlands at one of her client's events the night before, which was three hours away and they had hardly had any sleep. She also knew if she was the one who had not turned up she would have been reported to the courts.More and more she felt the system was against her.

Our conversations were never one-sided. I had some issues I did not share with anyone else except Ava. Ava reminded me so much of my best friend who had passed away. I think that was a part of the glue, which made us firm friends. Even though I am older than Ava, I never cross the line when she is coaching me. We lay the friendship to the side. I call her my kick ass coach.

As it got closer to the Eric Thomas event Ava worried that the venue might not be full. I assured her it would be an amazing event and she would not be given this mission if she was not guided to fulfill it. The day came. I got to the venue. I was shocked. Crowds and crowds of people almost going around the building were standing outside. Ava came outside and

Follow me on Twitter: @avabrown24

shock every person's hand who were in the queue waiting to get in. I could hardly believe she had taken off her shoes and did this bare foot. That's how real this woman was. This was amazing. The event was a huge success. Ava had Joseph McClendon 3rd and Lisa Nichols on live screen speaking to us. Eric Thomas was amazing. It turned out there were almost 2000 people at the event. There were people from Trinidad and Tobago; Romania; Poland; Spain; Austria; Germany; India; Africa; Croatia; and various other countries. I was so proud of her and her business partner and friend Silvie. This was a two-day event and both days were successful. What touched me was that Ava's head was not in the clouds. She even gave me a lift back to my brother's house where I was staying during the weekend. During the seminar Eric Thomas told us he and his team had not made it easy for Ava to get him to the UK. He wanted to see what she was made of; and if she had the staying power. Not only had Ava brought him to London, but Ava and Silvie had achieved in months, what other people took years to arrange. This was Eric Thomas' only UK event that year and the last time he came to the UK was eight years ago when he was only speaking to a few hundred people.

Ava had arranged to bring Eric Thomas to a local inner city schools so he could speak to the students. That was also a success, which was in the newspapers. Ava's daughter had gone to the hairdressers and had got her hair done. A few days later her daughter was taking out the hair extensions and there was a very large wound at the front of her scalp. Ava had to rush her daughter to the hospital to get the wound stitched. She was so upset because someone had recently died from a head injury like her daughters. Ava wanted to sue the woman. And when she went to see her, the woman was rude and did not ask how Ava's daughter was.

Also, Ava went to Poland with Eric Thomas. When they arrived, they had the biggest poster of all the speakers. Ava's picture was next to the Pope. Ava was able to bring her son and daughter with her. Ava did a Facebook live of the background scenes at the event. She spoke to more than 15,000 people. While she spoke, her words were translated into Polish. The Polish people were very receptive and loved her. She looked so relaxed as if she had found her groove. I was so very proud. I even saw her son on stage. Ava told me that a few years ago when she was speaking to a group of school children in Jamaica and said one day she would speak on the same stage as Nick Vujicic and Nick was one of the speakers at this event. Ava was sitting on a panel with various popular speakers including Eric Thomas and Nick Vujicic.

We spoke later and I asked her how she felt. She said she felt calm just like she was born to do this. After this event Ava was featured in a high profile Polish magazine and was also asked to write for the magazine. The day after Ava arrived back to the UK she was the keynote speaker for Back2Black in Piccadilly London. The day after that she was back in court with her estranged husband.

Amazingly, Ava managed to get Lisa Nichols to write the foreword for the anthology. Lisa had never written a foreword anyone's book before. Our anthology book was launched and became a best seller in three categories. During everything that was happening, Ava and her daughter had also written a daily inspirational book and were going to launch that book the same year.

Ava's daughter was very much like her mother. There have been times when her daughter has brought back friends with their babies in tow to stay over. They lived in a three bedroom house and at times Ava had given up her bed and slept on the floor so these young girls have a bed and a place to stay with their young babies. At times Ava came back home to an empty food cupboard. Some of these babies have now become Ava's adopted grandchildren.

Follow me on Twitter: @avabrown24

I had booked a coaching V.I.P and with Ava. I got the train to London and she picked me up at the station. I got to see her life up close. It was a hectic day for her. She drove from one place to the other. She even showed me the house where she used to live and told me she had sold it because she couldn't afford to pay the mortgage while in she was in court and paying money to barristers at the same time.

We had an amazing V.I.P day and then she was back in the car to go shopping before she picked her son up from school. We got caught up in traffic that was not moving. Ava only had 10 minutes to get to her son's school and she told me this was how it was most days. My heart went out to her as a woman and mother.

After that happy day, I received a tearful call from Ava. Someone had contacted her; a person who had a rope around her neck and was about to commit suicide. Ava spent hours on the phone talking to her. To the point where the person removed the rope and Ava prayed with her. I know that was not the only time that she was in that situation but every time it happened it shocked her. This impacted heavily on her because she had been given some bad news earlier. By now Ava's book *The Mango Girl* was picking up speed in becoming a feature movie. Ava had film producers and writers assigned. In fact, *The Mango Girl* team was heading off to Los Angeles to scout for investors. Ava was unable to go with them because she had to be at the launch of the anthology book.

Then Ava went to the USA to attend the Play seminar and she had arranged childcare with her daughter and an adult friend of hers. As usual, Ava kept us in the loop by doing her Facebook live of what was going on. Ava was also excited because her best friend and business partner Silvie was also on the trip. When Ava called me. I was having a major drama in my life and wanted to pass over it. I did not want to bring her in to it. I wanted her to enjoy her time away. I guess we had got so used to speaking to each other we could detect in each other's voice if there was a problem.

"What's wrong, Audreia?" She asked.

I said I was okay.

"No," she said, tell me what is going on?"

I briefly told her what was going on. I did not want her worrying about me. It was enough knowing she constantly had her children on her mind. I had not wanted to add to that. It upset me that I had become the source of some of her concern. I was at an event so could not speak to her for very long. I told her we would speak later. When we spoke later, she told me she had just finished reading a bedtime story to her son and he was crying and asking when she was coming back.

The whole trip was successful. She also met women that she had only ever spoken to via video call. The next day Ava was able to meet and have a picture taken with Sheryl Lee Ralph, plus she had also received a few signed copies of Sheryl's autobiography. She said it wasn't the best picture she had ever taken. I told her that she had her game face on in that picture. The funny thing was while Ava was meeting Sheryl Lee Ralph, I was watching Sheryl Lee Ralph's autobiography story on TV. Interesting timing is what I say! Then it was time for Ava and Silvie to be on the stage. I was so proud of both of them when I saw and heard them. They each held their own. She was only able to stay a few days because she had to get back to be with her family.

Ava told me she was going to launch her own Podcast, where she would interview thought leaders. She had lined up a few well-known people, who were going to be interviewed and she wanted me to be interviewed as a part of it. There were not many people who could stun me into silence, but Ava Brown has a good art of doing this to me. She overwhelms me. Amazing woman.

Yet again Ava was ill. Her blood pressure was high. She still had to drive for hours across the city so her son could have visitation with his father. Ava had been chasing her solicitors for weeks. This was meant to be the final hearing and they had messed up. They had told her days before she was due to go to court that there was no one to represent her in court, so she had to represent herself. The judge also wanted a report from her son's school about her son. This upset Ava very much because she had to inform her son's school and that meant giving the school access to her private life.

A few days later she was in court with her estranged husband. Her son's father was saying he did not have any money to visit his son during the holidays. Ava was mad about this. As soon as she stepped out of court she called me.

"Can you believe this man," she shouted? "I do everything for this child."

Ava was feeling not only the blood pressure but all kinds of pressure; having to find money out of thin air for the prepping of the movie; family abroad; and all kinds of demands. There were lots of things and people who came at her all at once. Some were trying to rip the soul out of her and because of her kind and generous nature she didn't see the attacks coming. Ava spent most of the holiday season in her bed. I told her that light shines in darkness and that is why you stand out.

A few days later, two men tried to grab Ava's daughter off the street while she had gone to the local shop. She managed to get out of their grip and ran home. The men chased her home. She was so frightened she had dropped her mobile phone. She ran in and told her mother about what had happened. She was scared because they knew where she lived. Ava instantly ran out to find them. Ava found a group of men by the cemetery. One of them was about to pick up her daughter's mobile phone. Ava confronted them and told them to give her the phone because it was her daughters.

One of the men asked for payment for the phone. Ava told them she would call the police. He then gave her the phone and denied any knowledge of knowing who had tried to grab her daughter. As soon as she got home she video called me. It was late in the night. Ava was mad about it all. We spoke for a while. The next day she did a Facebook live about people having a false sense of security and that we as women needed to be more aware and alert. She spoke about what had happened the night before to her daughter.

Then something very big happened for Ava, she had made connections with Oprah's team in the States and Ava sent copies of *The Mango Girl* book to them. Ava excitedly went to the Post Office and it was a surreal moment for her. I knew she had done this many times over in her head but this was the real thing.
We were both excited. I was screaming down the phone. I know this will change her and her family's lives.

Ava had a V.I.P meet face to face with Lisa Nichols, which she was very excited about but she had to scale it down because she had to use the money to go to Jamaica. Lisa was doing a big speaking event in Ireland. So Ava flew over to Ireland to the seminar and the long awaited one to one meet with Lisa.

Then Ava launched her podcast. The very first person to be interviewed was of course Lisa Nichols. It was a fantastic podcast. Ava's movie was moving from strength to strength. She had to go to Jamaica with *The Mango Girl* film crew so they could scout for film locations. The day arrived for her to go to Jamaica. Ava had decided weeks ago she was also going to bring her son with her. Now after much wrangling with the school it was agreed. Ava's daughter was working so could not join them on the trip. The Jamaican tourist board Jampro, did Ava proud. They were picked up from the plane and taken straight to the hotel where Ava's mother met her. I was given an opportunity to speak to Ava's mother via video before her mom took her son back home with her. Ava's mum was equally as excited to spend some time with her grandson. For the first time in a very long time Ava was able to enjoy the freedom of being and to relax. She could relax knowing her son was in good hands with her mother. Jampro had given Ava a

jam-packed schedule which included various TV and radio interviews. Ava and her team spent the next few days being driven all around Jamaica. She saw a Jamaica she had never seen before. She went back to places that stirred sad and painful memories in her. While Ava was in Jamaica she connected with an underage mother's foundation. She spoke to the young mothers and encouraged them. She also became an ambassador for this foundation. People were upset that Ava did not drop in to say hello. They did not understand she was on a scouting mission. All too soon her ten days were over and it was time to come back to the UK. Her son was enjoying himself so much he did not want to come back. He cried bitter tears when the time came for him to leave his grandmother.

Back in the UK, Ava became unwell again. Her blood pressure was sky high. She complained of not having enough energy. I sent her some juice recipes to help lower her blood pressure. Then there was yet again another court appearance with her estranged husband. This was meant to be the final hearing. This time Ava had a new barrister to represent her. The judge who had retained the case was ill so it was given to another judge to preside over. This lady judge read over the case and saw that Ava's husband had been wasting the courts time and resources. She could clearly see how Ava had been disrespected and taken advantage of. She made a clear decision and ruled in favour of Ava. After a 26 month battle it was suddenly all over.

That special day for her – 30 January 2017 - I received the call from her as soon as she stepped out of court. It was very emotional. I was shouting and jumping for joy. I heard in her voice the weight that had been lifted.

Follow me on Twitter: @avabrown24

She said to me; "No one will ever believe my story or journey. Audreia will you write an overview of my story for new version of *The Mango Girl?*" Yet again Ava Brown stunned me. We always joked and always said I would write her book with her because I was so close to her and her story. I never knew that the day would come so soon. Of course I said yes! And this is why you are reading it now.

Two days after the end of the court appearances Ava found out her estranged husband was getting married and having a full traditional African ceremony; something he had not given her. She also found out that he had been with this woman for years. Ava's son was six years old. It really hurt her knowing how much Rafel had used by her. Apparently, the woman looks exactly like Ava. He claimed to the courts that he could not provide for his son but here he was planning a wedding before their divorced was fully complete. She was so upset she started breaking things. She calmly called him to let him know she knew about his wedding and that if he wanted to get married he needed to complete the divorce. He wanted to know who had told her. He called her back later on that day. He wanted to know what the financial implications were for him. He wanted to know if he could claim money from Ava. He had heard about all of her speaking events and about her movie. Ava quickly let him know she was going to claim off him for her son. During this conversation he never once asked about his son.

Ava's son came into the room while she was having a conversation with me. He overheard his mum telling me his father was getting married and he wanted to know what it was all about. Ava's calmly explained to her son that his father was getting married to someone else. It hurt hearing her having to explain to her six year old son. That was a sad moment.

Since getting back from Jamaica Ava's health has not been good. She has suffered with constant headaches. While we were speaking, I asked Ava how she felt about her son after all the pain his father had put her through. She said after the first court appearance, she had initially resented her son. But as soon as she got back home from court that feeling had melted and she kissed his little cheeks and face and hugged him tightly against her. She explained she loved both her children, but her daughter was older and her son was still so young and if anything happened to her there would be no one there for him. He is a very astute child and he heard his mother telling me that her head was hurting. While I was on the video call, he placed his hands on his mother's forehead and started praying for her. As soon as he had finished praying for his mum, Ava said her headache had gone.

Since the start of 2017, Ava has discovered that people, who she thought had her back, were some of the very people who had tried to break her down. She has spent many days disappointed by people and it has brought many trust issues. Some people see her as an ATM machine. Some of it, is simply because they have seen her by herself. I do not write this excerpt overview for any type of self-gratification. I wanted Ava's reader to understand the many layers of Ava Eagle Brown. What some people do not see is what it takes to be her; the tears, pain and sadness behind all the smiles. I have referred to myself as the silent witness. Ava and I have the greatest mutual respect for each other. This is based on honesty and trust. I am honoured to contribute to Ava's book.

My prayer, wish and desire for Ava and her family is guidance, pure joy and protection.

"They say your friends are the family you choose and on this journey I am finding family I am so worthy of."

Follow me on Twitter: @avabrown24

Chapter Thirty Three
MY FULL CIRCLE

"There is a cleansing that only come from revisiting the things

that caused you pain and held you captive."

———————

I look over my life, and I must say, it's been tumultuous. I seem to have made some of the same mistakes far too often, and I had to come to a place of awakening.

That awakening came in 2013, despite the court, the drama and the tosses and turns. It was on that journey that I encountered five human beings in the personal development space that truly woke me up. They came in the form of Lisa Nichols (I call her my shero), Eric Thomas, Nick Vijuic, Steve Harvey and Abraham Hicks.

There have been others, but these three played a huge part in how I crawled my way out.

I first came upon the Steve Harvey's story, about how he had hit rock bottom and was sleeping in his car, and how he turned his life around; Lisa

Nichols couldn't buy diapers for her son, so she used towels to hold him together. Eric Thomas was a high school dropout who became homeless. Nick Vijujic was born without arms and legs. All four of these incredible global women and men have decided that their personal circumstances would not stop them. Instead, they have used their deficiencies and made them proficiencies. They have all refused to accept the life they have been given, and through their walk, they have been able to touch millions globally. Abraham Hicks (Esther), her teachings have totally transformed my mindset, vibration and life. Little did I know that I would get the chance to have met all but one of these five individuals in less than two years. I spoke on stage with Nick, Eric Thomas and most recently, spent a weekend with Steve Harvey in Atlanta. Lisa and I are working on a project together, and she has done the foreword for a book I was instrumental in compiling.

I had started working on *The Mango Girl* movie project which saw the team visiting American Film Market in Los Angeles. Many meetings around movies and my life was truly taking a very hectic but enjoyable journey. I was scared and excited at the same time.

I was involved with hosting Eric Thomas in London, and the event was beyond our wildest expectations; there were over two-thousand people from over thirteen different countries. Because of that event, I was invited to Poland, and I spoke in front of more than 10,000 people, sharing my story of pain, anguish, poverty, incest, lack, resilience, tenacity, courage under fire and purpose. It was an exhilarating experience as I also got to take my kids with me, they were so proud of their mother. I recall my daughter coming back stage and cried; my son standing on stage with me, singing a Polish song that we both didn't understand, but the atmosphere was so charged it didn't matter. As I stood on that stage in front of all that people, I was overwhelmed that the little old me, the girl, who although, still going through the stresses of my life, the court cases, the child care challenges,

God has truly blessed me as here, I was being treated like a queen in a foreign land. A land that if anyone had predicted to me while selling mangoes on that train in Jamaica, I would laugh at them.

Yet, here I was living it. I was picked up at the airport, dropped at a five-star hotel, my room was one of the most beautiful suites I have ever seen, and there was more than enough space for my kids who were later picked up from the airport. As I practiced my speech, I was overcome with pride to see Eric Thomas, the man whose words, "Pain is temporary" got me out of my own rut clapping and saying, I was doing a great job; I knew that I was unto something special. I knew that I was born to heal lives, I knew God was going to use me in a big way. I didn't know what the rest of the journey would look like, but all I know is that it would happen, my wings had just opened, and I was ready to fly.

After that trip to Poland, life was never the same. I now realized that my thoughts were becoming things, and the Bible verse that states, "As a man thinketh, so is he" came to mind. What I was thinking and preaching was now manifesting now in my own life.

Things moved really fast, and the next thing I know was that, I was in dialogue with The Jamaica Tourist Board and The Film Commissioner of Jamaica, with the view of visiting with the team to do a location scout for the movie. (Looking at the scenery etc. that will be involved in the film).

It all happened so fast, and before I knew it, I was on a flight with two of the team who have worked in the movie industry for years heading to Jamaica. It was a very weird feeling as I do go home often, but this trip was different, it was a very different trip.

I wasn't just going home to my hotel or my mum's home, I was going home to a hotel already paid for, and a driver waiting at the airport. Part of it felt surreal, and I shivered at the thought as my son and I sat on the flight. The flight was rather enjoyable as one of the team members, who was

Follow me on Twitter: @avabrown24

much older, treated my son like his own grandson; it was so refreshing to watch as not only was it a great experience for my son, it was for me too as I have never had that experience. In that moment, my son and I sort of had a similar experience at the same time. We landed in Jamaica in what seemed like the shortest flight I have ever taken home, and it sure felt bittersweet. You see, I was the girl who fled Jamaica almost in shame after being held at gunpoint, and nearly had a nervous breakdown. So, to be going home in this fashion and to some, it's nothing; but less you forget, I was the girl whose background says, if this is all that will ever happen, if the movie never gets made, this right here was a big deal. The plane landed as we did tale London with us, as it was the first time in 16 years that I landed in Jamaica onto wet tarmac; there was a downpour, and in my head, the gods were cleaning and washing off the past of all those demons off me and refreshing as well as renewing my path. We sat on the tarmac for over 20 minutes, though not happy but it was unavoidable. We eventually disembarked, and what happened next was something I see only as a scene in the movies.

Before we even took one step off the plane, there was a representative at the mouth of the plane sent by The Jamaica Tourist Board; we were walked down through the other passengers and whisked to the middle of that walkway where she was waiting from Jampro.

It all happened so quickly, and all I know is that within minutes, we were at the front of the queue, being rushed through immigration and outside where my mum was waiting for us.

It was a bit of where do I go first as Jampro needed to talk to me, mum needed to see me as well. So I decided to greet mum and give her my son so she could love on him while I spoke to Jampro, and settled the team in the beautiful car Jampro had sent to pick us up. We were given our itineraries at the airport, and I was reminded that this was a business trip; it wasn't a fun family home trip.

We all got in the car, mum included, and we headed for Kingston; this was late at night, and we were exhausted. The driver took us on a new highway I didn't even know about, and this dare I say halved the journey and it was night, such as it was needed. We arrived in Kingston about 11 PM, and the former Director of Tourism was waiting on us in the five* hotel that was prepped for us. After the introductions were done, we were all given gift bags with memorabilia, and ushered to our rooms.

Can I just be a bit ghetto here? I was overwhelmed by my room, the hotel suite was almost the size of my London home, and that's no joke. My bed in comparison to my London bed was a tennis court. You see, London has an issue with space for the most part, so a house could cost £300000 but it's a small home compared to a house in some parts of say Jamaica.

I have become so cultured to small beds and bedrooms. Needless to say, I have a king-size bed in the UK, but this one right here was not a bed, it was something else. I missed Jamaica for things like this and as for most people, a big bed is the norm back here.

My mother was so blown away by the entire suit, she didn't want to sit down on the sofa, she didn't want to disturb it. Mama has a sofa, granted; but this was different, she walked around the suit, almost absorbing each glance, each item, and standing in admiration in her mind where her daughter had gotten to. Though, in my mind, I was nowhere. I was shattered; so I jumped in the shower, and was ready to hit the sheets. I was feeling and hearing bed calling me so powerfully I didn't care that my son was there, after all, for the first time in over two years, I didn't need to worry about his wellbeing, alas, his Nan was there. She had taken over this shift and for that, I was at peace.

Mama and my son slept on the tennis court, and I slept in the living room, on the luxury sofa. I was out before you knew it, and the hot

Caribbean air massaged my face like the double glass doors were left open, as we were on the 5th floor. The next day, bright and early, mum took my son and disappeared to St Elizabeth where we are from; my heart was singing, worrying about the awful driving that goes on in Jamaica, worrying about accidents on the road but then, I went back into my vortex and was content that he was ok. I called them every 1 hour until he was safe in my mums' home. I could hear his aunties, cousins and family members that he has never met, hanging around him and in that moment, I knew I made the right choice to take him with me to Jamaica, albeit I had no childcare, but that he was getting a better education, seeing his family he has never met than sitting in a classroom in winter in the UK. That day, we had breakfast and started working from our itinerary; it was time to get rolling, needless to say, my entire body wanted to sleep and just glide into the sunset as I would do had I been on just holiday.

We set off and walked to Jampro head office which was a few blocks away; although, midway through the ten minutes' walk, there was a car to pick us up.

The meeting went well, and while there, we were thrown on Radio for a quick interview.

Our days were packed with location visits, eating the local fruits which I must say, some of them were new to me. The crew said they had never seen such variety of fruits. One of our location scouts took us to Spanish Town Market where we got mangoes, oh la la la, I sank my teeth in and forgot where I was or who I was. You see, once I see a mango, my name is called, I want to just grab it and start ravaging it.

I totally savoured each bite, and the juices that ran down my hands; nothing tasted as good as say, a well-ripened mango that was left in the sun to mature.

Follow me on Twitter: @avabrown24

Our scouting took us to schools, churches, homes and all that we needed for the pictures or exterior of the film. My days were packed with scouting and poolside meetings with directors, producers and in general, Jamaicans in the creative industry and all meetings were arranged by Jampro.

There were moments where I wished rather than sipping fruit punch and Red Stripe beer at the poolside in a meeting; I was sitting at a Jerk spot of Port Royal over a fish and festival.

Days went by quickly, and it was almost time to go; I had eaten so much food and felt fatter than I came. Between the patties, coconut water, jerk of all sorts and red peas soup, Jamaica was my food choice (place) and the team was truly having a ball. Often, you would hear them say that they have never been anywhere where the spirit of the people was so vibrant, and these men have travelled extensively. We visited the Coronation Market, not just because I love the place and it is a business area, but because it was potentially one of the sights to be used in the film.

The trip was a buzz I must say, and it all came crashing when the Jamaica Railway Corporation arranged for me to visit one of the actual trains I used as a child to sell mangoes on. It was all going well, and nostalgia was in the air until one of the crew members asked me while inside the actual train; if this is how it seemed when I was selling on it. Now, for the life of me, I cannot tell you why but tears started streaming down my face, and in that moment, I started seeing the little girl on the train on en-route to Cambridge St James Jamaica calling out, "mangoes, mangoes, anyone wants mangoes" and the faces of the people who pitied her were all insight; the ones buying to be kind, sexual encounter with her father, the gun barrel in her face, the living with someone else while Tobore stayed in his nice house, albeit he wanted to have me with him but couldn't, the migration to London, the tearing apart of my soul, all the times I was rejected, the urine smell at my fathers and all those experiences that were bad. Note, only the bad ones came crashing down, and all I know is that I was on the floor in an almost fetal position. Thankfully, I was sonly with the men, as they seemingly either didn't know what to do or how to handle it, or they felt I needed to be alone; so they walked off and left me to immerse, feel the moment, and I suppose it cleansed my soul. I can't explain why it happened, it was a simple question that just sent the floodgates open. What I do know, however, is that this was necessary. I needed it as for the first time I felt free.

Can you identify a time when you needed to be free and that moment happens?

The trip ended and I had one stop left to make; that was to visit where I actually sold mangoes, and the team wanted to see my actual community where this warrior was born. We also needed to pick-up an important person; my son. Can you believe it? My son who I have never been away from without worrying, and here I was; he was gone, and I had not spoken to him for days as each time I called, he was too busy to talk to me, he was having fun roaming in the community. When I am in London, I am never given breather with my son, I have no one also to help me and just to have had this respite, I relished it, and my soul was able to relax for a week. He was safe, and in the best hands apart from mine as I know my mum wouldn't allow a fly to land on him.

Our driver picked us up early to make the meandering drive to Mile Gully; my heart was pumping rapidly as I haven't been back there since I sold mangoes on the train. The journey was a mixed emotion one; there was anxiety, excitement, flashbacks and just wanting to get there and see the place one more time.

We got there after a 2-hour drive, and on the way there, for the first-time, I realized that Jamaica had pockets of rainforest; yes, I did geography, but it wasn't my focus at the time. It was a beautiful country with some interesting inland attractions to be seen. Balaclava looks so different, in fact, as an adult now, it didn't seem like the places that I saw as a child. You see all buildings seemed amplified through my child's eyes, as the plazas I sold mangoes on were all still there, but they were so small. It didn't seem to make sense. The platforms were almost gone as the trains were no longer working but still there. I ran into an old man who remembered me funny enough, and as I stood there, I was proud of the skills I honed at that spot I was standing in; survival, tenacity and resilience. We drove to my community, and after saying hello to a few people, we arrived at my first place I can recall being home. I saw some regular faces, and they were all excited to see me, pondered why I had two white (Caucasian men with me) but albeit, excited. I told them why I was there, and they all became excited. I took the team to my old home, and it all looked the same. Nothing had changed, I hadn't been to this particular house in many years, but there, I was standing on the very spot I ate, showered, slept and got some good old beats from mama. The team was shocked at what they saw as this one room shack to them, represented so much more of who I BE in the world, and yes, I said BE for emphasis, though grammatically incorrect. They finally got the entire movie just by being there in that moment. They were ready to leave and they got it; you see, like a book, you sometimes read 300 pages to get one lesson, and that one lesson could write a new book. That was what happened at that moment to the team. They saw my place of existence into the world, and that wrote or tweaked the entire script.

We were headed to picking up my son when one of the team members laid his hand on my shoulder in the jeep driven by our driver, and told me that he now got me, he got my assertiveness, my resilience, my courage; he got who I became and why. He saw where the fire in my belly came from; it

Follow me on Twitter: @avabrown24

came from the fight to escape that childhood. I know he meant it in a good way, and at that moment, he told me he had all he needed to tweak the script because he saw far more than the book had in it. He said, "we need to go darker with the script Ava." I was happy that he saw it and realized that the trip was so worth it as sometimes, we need to be at the moment to create amazingness. We got to my mums' home, and I said, my mum, as she was now living in her own home for the first time. I had finally placed her under her own roof. Most of my siblings were away, and I saw very few family members. Parts of me were torn, others were not as just before that trip, I was cursed out by some of them. That said, it would have been nice to see them. I had no choice in the matter, we were on schedule, and the driver had strict instructions.

Mum had all things you could think of ready for me, cereasse (a leaf tea), yam, breadfruit you name it; she didn't even have a mango. I realized my son was out of sight, and when I questioned this, I was told he was hiding in the back, and he didn't want to come with me. He loved the outdoors and wanted to stay more in Jamaica, especially with his Nana and all the many friends he had made, and cousins to play with. You see, back in London, he has very little friends, none is on our street for example, and my juggle makes it hard to answer all his play needs; though I try very hard. I had to tear him out of his grandmas' hand to get him to come with us, and he cried awfully. My heart broke as I was reminded how far apart we all were, how many family members I had in Jamaica, and how non-existent that was for me in the UK. I was heartbroken by the fact that the home office refuses my mum a visa so often, though she has been here before with no violation; at least then, my mum would get to see us, and we could feel a sense of support, and my kids could get some of their nana. We drove off, with mama and I embracing in a close embrace, one like we have never had before; you see, mama isn't the mushy type, so I had to steal this one.

Follow me on Twitter: @avabrown24

We drove to Anchovy to revisit the house where I got held up at gunpoint, and this was easier than I thought it would be. I no longer felt the emotions, I blocked it out; the house was looking good, and I felt I would be upset that I lost it, but I absolutely did not. I felt relieved not to be associated with it. The team took pictures of what they needed, and we left to settle into our hotel to sleep for our flight the next day.

We were on a plane back to London, and I felt sad, sad I was leaving Jamaica. I fell in love with the place all over again. It felt as though all the disasters that forced me out had dissipated, and I was set free from this trip. My demons no longer existed. There was so much to why I fell in love; there were gorgeous men who weren't afraid to tell you they were keen to get to know you. Now don't be fooled, they may not all qualify, but it was better than what happened in London. While I was there, I tell you, I literally had to pray because I was tempted, I had to remind myself of what I promised myself and my new partner; that I was saving myself for someone who truly deserved me.

I also valued my body and respected my kids, and didn't want another disastrous relationship. I also knew it was the temptation because of how long I have been alone; thank God, he held me close as I came back to London the way I went.

I also fell in love with how free life is. The people just smiled all day regardless, and I missed that, I missed the food, sunshine and more so, my family; regardless of our relationship, all families have ups and downs.

As I sat on the tarmac, I felt torn between my new place that I live in London and my home, the land of my birth Jamaica. My DNA fill stretched between two worlds and in that moment, I wished I was on the plane; but I had to snap back into reality as my teenager was in the UK, missing like crazy. I put on my big girl pants, wiped the teardrop from my face, and started thinking of the life back here in the UK. The flight took off, and

Follow me on Twitter: @avabrown24

whether I wanted to stay or not, I had no choice. We landed at Gatwick airport, and I was going to miss the crew, we had a great time. We said out goodbye, and the cold of 3 degrees snapped my back into reality that I hailed a cab, and headed home, wanting just to curl up and cry.

I opened my door, went to my daughter's bedroom, gave her a tight hug, and her brother crawled into her bed, and they all went to sleep. My bed was filled with one of my adopted daughters and my granddaughter; so I went downstairs to the sofa and went to sleep.

I didn't want to be sleeping in London, but here I was, we had work to do on the script, and I was not ready to focus on making *The Mango Girl* movie a reality more than ever. Wanted to help others see that where you are from doesn't determine where you end up. I don't know what God has planned for me, but it's my hope that somewhere in there, he has a Jamaican king preferably in the UK, who desires a queen and wants to live back home. I sure would like that very much.

I went through the rest of January just using that Jamaica trip to hold me together, while I planned for my event that came out of my awakening called purposewalk.

As I reflect on my journey, I am thankful you came along with me; please stay focused on appreciating the little things in life as there is abundance even in your circumstance.

Please don't forget to love daily, often forgive, and speak your truth.

Love, Ava

Everything has a way of coming full circle in our lives, I feel like I have journeyed the world, and Jamaica is where that full circle comes together for me.

Follow me on Twitter: @avabrown24

Lightning Source UK Ltd.
Milton Keynes UK
UKOW05f2154160617

303535UK00001B/96/P